WHY TAX SYSTEMS DIFFER

For Evelyn, Christina, John, Judith, Gillian, Anna, Philip and Helen

Other Books by FISCAL PUBLICATIONS

Administrative and Compliance Costs of Taxation, 1989

Practical Tax Administration, 1993

Successful Tax Reform: Lessons from an Analysis of Tax Reform in Six Countries, 1993

Key Issues in Tax Reform, 1993

Tax Compliance Costs: Measurement and Policy, 1995

More Key Issues in Tax Reform, 1995

Further Key Issues in Tax Reform, 1998

WHY TAX SYSTEMS DIFFER

A Comparative Study
of the Political Economy of Taxation

Cedric Sandford

FISCAL PUBLICATIONS
2000

British Library Cataloguing-in-Publication Data

A catalogue record for this book is available from the British Library.

ISBN 0 9515157 7 2 Hardback

ISBN 0 9515157 8 0 Paperback

Printed in Great Britain by
Lightning Source, Inc
Milton Keynes

Published by Fiscal Publications,
Old Coach House, Fersfield, Perrymead,
BATH BA2 5AR

CONTENTS

PREFACE and ACKNOWLEDGEMENTS

This book is based on a lecture series taught at the University of Bath over many years to students preparing for an M.Sc. in Fiscal Studies. The students came from many different countries and were mostly middle management in government revenue or finance departments. The expectation was that many of them would, before long, move to senior roles as policy-makers and that expectation was frequently fulfilled. The course was intended to help them in their future policy-making roles by analysing and comparing the tax systems of different countries.

It is hoped that this book will prove of value to policy-makers as well as lecturers and students in taxation (for whom it could be a course text) not least because, for obvious reasons, books on comparative taxation are rare. I have been fortunate to have had the chance to gain first-hand experience of the tax systems of a number of countries. In addition to work for the Inland Revenue and the National Audit Office in the United Kingdom, I have undertaken consultancies for the IMF, the World Bank, the United Nations Organisation and the OECD, as well as for the finance departments of the Australian, New Zealand and Canadian governments and for the Irish Tax Commission. I have also engaged in independent research in these last four countries as well as in the United States and the United Kingdom.

Despite my opportunities to study other tax systems I am conscious that I have drawn disproportionately on my own country, the United Kingdom; in particular the two case studies – on local taxation and the personal income tax unit – are both drawn from that country. For this disproportion, inevitable though it may be, I should perhaps apologise – but I believe the case studies are particularly apt to illustrate the points at issue.

I acknowledge, with gratitude, all the research grants received, of which particular mention should be made of the award under the Canadian Studies Research Programme, the Downing Fellowship at Melbourne University and an Emeritus Fellowship from the Leverhulme Trust.

My thanks are due to the students on the M.Sc. course over the years, who contributed in many ways, difficult to attribute but none the less real, to the course and hence to this book; and to the influences of colleagues both from the University of Bath and those from further afield, especially those with whom I worked on IMF technical assistance missions and OECD consultancies. Nor should I forget the accountants, politicians, civil servants and policy advisers in many countries who have generously given their time as interviewees on the range of research studies which have fed into this book.

More specifically I wish to acknowledge the following contributions: Andrew Dilnot for allowing me to reproduce figure 4.1 and table 4.2; Sijbren Cnossen likewise for table 7.2; Peter Dean, for the idea of figures 7.1 and 8.1; Mustafa Sarili for the original version of table 5.3. I am indebted to Richard Bird (as are so many economists) for the idea of the format, used in chapter 2, for comparing advanced and developing countries. An earlier version of a part of chapter 5, 'Why Have So Many Countries Adopted VAT?' was presented as a paper at a conference in Sydney organised by the Australian Tax Program at the University of New South Wales and was published in *Tax Reform and the GST An International Perspective*, ed. Binh Tran-Nam, Prospect Media Ptd Ltd., 1998; an earlier version of a part of chapter 7 appeared in *Australian Tax Forum*, Vol. 11, No. 3, 1994; and an earlier version of chapter 8 was presented at a conference in Zagreb and subsequently published in *Underground Economies in Transition*, eds. E.L. Feige and K. Ott, Ashgate, 1999. I acknowledge with thanks permission to reproduce. In the final chapter of this book I have drawn heavily on my earlier book *Successful Tax Reform: Lessons from an Analysis of Tax Reform in Six Countries*, Fiscal Publications, Bath, 1995 and my chapter on 'Tax Reform in the 'Eighties in Retrospect: What Can We Learn?', in *Further Key Issues in Tax Reform*, Fiscal Publications, Bath, 1998.

I am very grateful to Sijbren Cnossen, Cynthia Coleman, Lynne Freeman, John Hasseldine, Edward Horesh and Bill McNie for reading and commenting on one or more draft chapters and especially grateful to Chris Evans who read and commented on the whole book in draft. Their comments have much improved it. I add the usual disclaimer – any remaining errors and misjudgements are mine alone. I am very conscious of the perils of painting on such a large canvas. It is difficult enough to keep up with tax changes in one country, let alone those in a whole raft of countries; similarly new literature relevant to the whole range of topics is always being published. Some articles and books that I should have read and mentioned I will inevitably have missed. Such is the nature of the task I set myself. Yet I feel it is a task worth undertaking – and I hope the reader will agree – even if the product falls far short of perfection.

Finally my warmest thanks are due to my wife Christina for word-processing the whole and to Julia Howard for turning it into camera ready copy.

Cedric Sandford
April 2000

CHAPTER 1

INTRODUCTION – OBJECTIVES, STATISTICS AND DEFINITIONS

This book analyses and compares taxation in different countries. It looks at what tax systems have in common, how they differ and tries to explain both the similarities and the differences. The book seeks to answer questions such as the following. 'Why do developing countries rely for revenue more on indirect taxes and advanced countries more on direct taxes?' 'Why are the tax systems of developing and developed countries converging?' 'Why is the property tax the most widely used tax for local government?' 'Why do some countries have more tax expenditures than others?' 'Why have so many countries adopted VAT as their general sales tax?' 'Why do only one third of OECD countries have an annual wealth tax and the remainder do not?' And so on.

Mainly the approach is to look at what countries do and then try to find an explanation. But sometimes an alternative or opposite approach is adopted. Thus, with local taxation, we start from first principles and ask what particular requirements are needed in a local tax? Which taxes best fit the criteria? We then see how far our conclusions match the reality of country practices.

The book is not an essay in tax theory. Theory is introduced, but only in so far as it explains similarities and differences. Nor is the book intended to be comprehensive, but rather the intention is to look at some of the main issues where comparisons may be useful.

No attempt is made to confine the analysis on each topic to the same specified group of countries and reference is made to many countries around the world; but the OECD countries are drawn on most heavily because of the range of reliable and up-to-date information available about them. Where the intention is to compare developing and advanced countries or look only at advanced countries, a sub group of OECD countries is used[1]. Some OECD countries are still very much developing

[1] Australia, Austria, Belgium, Canada, Denmark, France, Germany, Italy, Japan, Netherlands, Spain, Sweden, Switzerland, United Kingdom, United States.

1

and the 15 countries which constitute the largest of the developed countries (economic indicators for which are published weekly in *The Economist* newspaper) are taken as more representative of developed countries. In other cases the full range of OECD countries as at 1994 is employed. The reason for restricting the analysis to the countries in OECD in that year is that the number of OECD countries remained stable at 24 between 1973 and 1994, but since then the number has been growing. Thus Mexico joined in 1994, the Czech Republic in 1995 and Hungary, Poland and Korea in 1996. Often in our analysis we need to look at a trend or make comparisons with earlier years. New joiners cannot provide the appropriate tax data for the earlier years. Hence it seems best to be consistent and concentrate on the 24 countries which were members in 1994.

Structure of the Book

Apart from this introductory chapter, the book falls into three parts. The first concerns tax structures. Chapter 2 compares the tax structures of developed and non-oil developing countries. Chapter 3 looks at sub-central levels of government, their taxing powers and the taxes used; obviously in these comparisons an important distinction is between unitary and federal states; the chapter concludes with a case study of the changes in local taxation in Great Britain in the 1980s.

The second part of the book looks at individual taxes or related groups of taxes. Chapter 4 examines the income tax: why the personal income tax predominates as a revenue yielder in advanced countries and some of its main features – tax base, tax expenditures, tax rates and tax units, again with a United Kingdom case study of the change in the tax unit in 1988. The chapter concludes with an analysis of corporate income taxes. Chapter 5 considers sales or consumption taxes: excises are examined and then, to explain the remarkable success of VAT, an answer to the question 'Why have so many countries adopted VAT?' is sought by examining the alternative forms of general sales tax: manufacturers', wholesalers', cumulative turnover tax and retail sales tax. Chapter 6 looks at capital or wealth taxes: the annual personal net wealth tax, death and gift taxes and capital gains taxes. Whilst capital gains are akin to income (and are included with income tax in the revenue statistics of chapter 2) because the purposes and the problems of capital gains taxes have so much in common with wealth and wealth transfer taxes, it is convenient and meaningful to consider all three together.

Finally the third section deals with some aspects of policy-making and tax administration. The two are inseparable; as Casanegra put it '...tax administration is tax policy' (Casanegra, 1990, p. 179). In chapter 7 we look at the problems of comparing tax administrative and tax compliance costs between countries; chapter 8 examines tax policy in relation to tax evasion; and chapter 9 looks at the process of tax policy-making and tax reform.

This final chapter serves as a reminder that tax differences between countries may often owe less to economic rationality than to perceived political rationality; and that historical circumstance, constitutions and legislative procedures, customs and cultures, lethargy and the costs of change, the effects of pressure groups, the influence of other countries and international groupings and agencies, all play their part; they combine with fortuitous factors, not least of which is the whim of a finance minister, to shape a country's tax system.

Definitions

Before we proceed to more detailed analyses we need to clarify our terminology – or, at least, accept that some terms are ambiguous.

'Taxation' itself is a far from clear-cut term. Should social security contributions count as taxes? Some countries prefer not to so count them. The view of the author is that, in so far as they are compulsory contributions, which is generally the case, they should so count and they have been included in comparisons of tax levels in this book. This view is given additional credence by the fact that, even where there is a separate social security fund, governments have often supplemented it from general taxation or, alternatively, placed a surcharge on social security contributions to boost general tax revenue.

Apart from the question of social security contributions, a revenue source not specifically designated taxation is sometimes of the nature of a tax. Fiscal monopolies are such a case; a state may claim the monopoly in the distribution and sale of a product, be it salt, as in colonial India, or alcoholic drinks as in various countries; it sells the product at a price above what it would fetch in a competitive market and applies the profits to state funds. Other, less clear examples of surrogate taxes are where a state agency or nationalised industry, such as a utility, with a monopoly position, is required to make a profit on its activities for the benefit of the state revenue; more confusing still is where a privatised utility, operating under regulation, is required to give a concessionary price to certain customers the government wishes to favour. Thus, in the United Kingdom, under the Water Industry Act, 1999, the regulated water industry is obliged to offer a concessionary tariff to 'vulnerable' customers – either because they are poor or because of medical needs. In effect, the remaining water customers are paying a surrogate tax to implement the government's social policies. Such measures are very difficult to identify in international comparisons, but the reader should at least be aware of their possible existence.

There is similarly a fine line between taxation measures and expenditure measures. For example, there are alternative ways of giving benefits – by a tax relief or by direct expenditure. Thus assistance for children may be by means of a tax allowance or tax credit under the income tax, or by a payment of child benefit. The first leaves government expenditure unchanged but reduces tax revenue; the second requires higher expenditure and higher tax revenue. Because the first method is the equivalent of higher expenditure, such tax reliefs have been described as 'tax expenditures', about which we have more to say in chapter 4. Another variant, employed by the New Labour Government in the United Kingdom in 1999, is to refer to a new working families tax credit (WFTC) as a 'negative tax' to be deducted in calculating the overall level of taxation. Such games with statistics justify the old adage that often 'Politicians use statistics as a drunken man uses a lamppost - for support and not illumination'!

It is well to remember that the level of taxation is a less than perfect guide to the degree of government intervention in an economy, even leaving aside command economies. The level of taxation depends primarily on the level of government expenditure. A government may pursue its policies by means of provision, transfer or regulation, or any combination of these three. If a government itself provides, eg by having state schools, government expenditure increases. If the government grants social benefits such as child benefits, unemployment benefits or pensions, government expenditure likewise increases but there is a difference from state provision in that the beneficiaries can choose how the money is spent if the transfer is monetary, or where the benefit is spent if the transfer is in the form of vouchers (eg for food or education). With regulation, the government requires certain people to do certain things; expenditure only increases to the extent of the cost of policing the regulation. Thus the government may require that children go to school up to a certain age but leave the private sector to supply the education and parents to pay for it; or it may require car owners to take out insurance or employers to provide various facilities for their employees. The more a government requires employers or its citizens to do certain things, the more it is intervening in the economy at minimum public spending and hence taxation.

The terms 'direct' and 'indirect' taxation are frequently used and can create confusion. Strictly the direct/indirect distinction is an administrative one, indicating whether the taxpayer is directly assessed for tax or through some third party. A more significant economic distinction is whether the tax base is income, expenditure/consumption or capital/wealth.

Mainly the direct/indirect distinction corresponds with the distinction between income and capital taxation (usually direct) on the one hand and taxes on expenditure (usually indirect) on the other. Thus a personal income tax is a direct tax because the taxpayer is directly assessed (even though the tax may be collected through a third party, such as an employer) whilst an excise duty such as a tobacco tax, is collected indirectly without the revenue authorities having any link with the intended taxpayer, the smoker. However, the direct/indirect distinction does not invariably equate with the income/capital and expenditure distinction. Thus property taxes on domestic property (as with the United Kingdom council tax and former 'rate') is really a tax on the consumption of house room levied on the occupier and hence is a form of direct expenditure tax; and, as we shall see in chapter 4, there have been proposals for a more general direct expenditure tax to replace, or partially replace, income tax; under this tax the taxpayer is, in essence, required to calculate expenditure by recording income, then deducting saving and adding spending out of capital.

There are particular problems of definition in comparing measures of tax burdens. The usual way is to express total taxation as a percentage of community output and this is probably the best single measure, but the definitions of numerator and denominator raise problems. We have already looked at the difficulties of defining taxation and at the differences in the totals which arise from pursuing government objectives by explicit expenditures or by tax expenditures. The definitional problems with the denominator are no less. Choices have to be made about three main measures of community output; should one use national product or domestic product; net or gross product; product measured at factor cost or market price?

National product is the value of the total output or income of the inhabitants of a country including output generated (income earned) from overseas investment and minus income due to foreigners on their investments. Domestic product is the value of what is produced within a country. The difference between gross and net product is depreciation – the allowance for capital used up in the annual process of production. Factor cost is the price paid to the factors of production, labour and capital, in generating the output and differs from market price in so far as there are sales taxes (which raise market price above factor cost) or subsidies on goods or services (which lower market price below factor cost).

It is general to use domestic product rather than national product in any comparisons between countries or in a time series analysis of the same country. It is also usual to use gross product rather than net product. In principle the case for net product would appear to be stronger, but measurements of capital depreciation are very imperfect, hence net product is an unreliable figure and therefore gross product tends to be chosen.

Again, it is probably expediency which leads to the use of market price rather than factor cost as the way of valuing output – but it is an inferior measure because it is affected by the form taxation takes. Thus, for example, if, over time, a country moved away from income tax to sales taxes (as has taken place in some countries since the introduction of VAT) even though total tax revenue and GDP at factor cost remained unchanged, there would be a fall in the percentage of taxation to GDP because the denominator in the equation would have risen. Comparisons between countries can likewise be affected by differences in their relative reliance on sales taxes. We need to recognise this possible source of discrepancy when using the figures published by international agencies which, like the OECD, generally use GDP at market prices as the basis for comparisons.

In short, whilst statistics are indispensable in international comparisons, we need to recognise that the comment of the wag can sometimes be true: 'Statistics are like a bikini; what they reveal is interesting, but what they conceal is vital!'

CHAPTER 2

TAX STRUCTURES

Introduction

In this chapter we begin by looking at some broad differences between 'industrial' countries and non-oil developing countries and give reasons for the differences. Next we examine evidence that the two groups are moving closer together in structure. Thereafter we concentrate on developed countries indicating differences in the overall levels of taxation, divergencies between countries in their degree of reliance on the various taxes and also the differences that arise within any one particular form of tax.

Taxes on Income

Table 2.1 sets out the contribution of personal and corporate income tax, capital gains tax and social security contributions to central government revenue of 23 'industrial' countries and 86 developing countries from Africa, Asia, Europe, the Western Hemisphere and the non-oil countries of the Middle East.

The statistics are taken from *Government Finance Statistics Yearbook, 1999*, (IMF, 1999). Twenty-four countries are designated 'industrial'; with the exception of San Marino in place of Turkey, these are the 24 countries which were members of OECD in 1994; but the tax detail for Germany was not recorded, so the totals relate to 23 countries. In addition a separate calculation has been made by the author for the largest industrial countries referred to in the introductory chapter (less Germany) as being a more reliable indication of the situation in developed countries; the 23 listed in the IMF publication include countries for which the classification 'industrial' is dubious, such as Iceland and Greece. The figures are the latest available to the IMF; they are frequently designated 'provisional' or 'forecast' and they do not relate to one particular year. The majority refer to 1997 or 1998, but a few relate to 1999 and some go back as far as 1992 and 1993. The IMF has had to rely on material sent in to it and there are a number of minor discrepancies. All countries listed by the IMF have been included in the analysis except for Algeria, where the discrepancies are major.

It should be stressed that the figures relate to central government only. This obviously biases the analysis for countries such as Canada and the United States where all or a large part of the indirect or consumption taxes are at state/provincial level. Conversely, they may give a somewhat misleading impression where, as with the Scandinavian countries, the predominant tax at lower tiers of government is income tax. It should also be noted that the figures refer to percentages of total revenue, not total tax revenue. This can be particularly significant for developing countries with a big income from aid.

Table 2.1 Taxes on Profits, Income, Capital Gains and Social Security Contributions as Percentages of Total Revenue

	No. of Countries	Personal and Corporate Income Tax and CGT (a) %	Social Security Contributions (b) %	Total (a) + (b) %
Industrial Countries	23	33.6	23.2	56.8
Largest Industrial Countries	14	34.3	29.1	63.4
Developing Countries				
Africa	24	21.5	2.3	23.8
Asia	18	24.4	2.0	26.4
Europe	20	17.5	23.1	40.6
Middle East	6	20.8	2.3	23.1
W Hemisphere	24	19.5	8.4	27.9
Overall (Developing)	92	20.6	8.4	29.0

Source: IMF, 1999.

When we come to look at trends over a period of years an additional complication is that the number of developing countries changes over time – partly because some do not consistently submit data, partly because of the change in the number of European countries following the breakdown of the Soviet Union.

In short, the figures are useful – indeed, the best available, for very broad brush comparisons which take in large numbers of developing countries – but they need to be used with some care if they are not to mislead.

The picture which emerges is perhaps unsurprising. The 23 countries designated industrial obtain some 57 per cent of central government revenue from income tax, CGT and social security contributions combined, whilst for the largest industrial countries the figure is over 63 per cent. For the developing countries as a whole the average is less than half that figure. Again, unsurprisingly, of the developing countries, the lowest proportion from these sources is to be found in the non-oil Middle East and the African groups of countries, with Asia next, then the Western Hemisphere (Central and South America) with the European countries obtaining the largest proportion from these sources.

In none of the 14 largest industrial countries is the proportion of total revenue from income tax and social security contributions less than 40 per cent and in only one (Denmark) is it below 50 per cent (and, in Denmark, as table 3.3 shows, almost all local revenue is derived from income tax). Conversely, in only two countries in Africa (South Africa and Zimbabwe) does the proportion from these sources exceed 40 per cent, two in Asia (Indonesia and Papua New Guinea) and five in the Western Hemisphere (Argentina, Ecuador, Mexico, Panama and Trinidad and Tobago). With Papua New Guinea, Ecuador and Trinidad and Tobago the bigger share of income tax revenue comes from corporations.

All the industrial countries and all but two of the non-oil developing countries (the Bahamas and the Netherlands Antilles) have income taxes, but the developing countries derive much less revenue from income tax. Amongst the industrial countries only Norway derives more central government revenue from income tax on corporations than on individuals; whereas a majority of the developing countries outside Europe derive more income tax revenue from corporations than individuals.

All the industrial countries with the exception of Australia and New Zealand have social security contributions, but a majority of developing countries outside Europe do not. However, it does not necessarily follow that if a country has no social security contributions it offers no social security provision. Countries choose whether to finance social security measures out of general taxation, out of social security contributions, or some combination of the two. It is for that reason we have concentrated our comparisons in table 2.1 on the combined revenue of income tax, CGT and social security contributions.

Sales and Transactions Taxes

Obviously, the other side of the coin is that the developing countries rely for revenue much more heavily on indirect taxes than the industrial countries; the more interesting feature is the difference in the forms of indirect taxation between the industrial and developing countries.

Table 2.2 Indirect Taxes as Percentage of Central Government Revenue – Industrial Countries

Number of Countries in Each Category

Percentage of Total Revenue	Domestic Taxes on Goods & Services	General Sales Taxes (Part of (b))	Taxes on International Trade & Transactions	All Indirect Taxes
(a)	(b)	(c)	(d)	(b) + (d)
Industrial Countries (23)				
0-10	1	4	23	1
10-20	2	12	0	2
20-30	11	5	0	11
30-40	6	2	0	6
40-50	2	0	0	1
50-60	1	0	0	2
over 60	0	0	0	0
Largest Industrial Countries (14)				
0-10	1	3	14	1
10-20	2	10	0	2
20-30	9	1	0	9
30-40	2	0	0	2
over 40	0	0	0	0

Source: IMF, 1999.

Table 2.2 shows that of the 23 industrial countries all but 2 (Greece and Iceland) obtain less than half of central government revenue from indirect taxes; almost half are in the 20-30 per cent bracket. Amongst these countries there is a considerable reliance on general sales taxes (usually VAT) and an insignificant amount of revenue from international trade taxes (and in all cases under 3 per cent). None of the largest industrial countries obtains as much as 40 per cent of central government revenue from indirect taxes; for the large majority the proportion is 20-30 per cent; and general sales taxes figure prominently within that total.

The position with the developing countries is very different, as shown in table 2.3. Almost two-thirds of them receive between 30 and 60 per cent of central government revenue from indirect taxes; general sales taxes are a less important source of indirect taxation than for developed countries; and many developing countries obtain a significant revenue from trade taxes.

Table 2.3 Indirect Taxes as Percentage of Central Government Revenue – Non-Oil Developing Countries

Number of Countries in Each Category

Percentage of Total Revenue	Domestic Taxes on Goods & Services	General Sales Taxes (Part of (b))	Taxes on International Trade & Transactions	All Indirect Taxes
(a)	(b)	(c)	(d)	(b) + (d)
Non-oil Developing Countries (92)				
0-10	8	29	41	2
10-20	11	18	19	4
20-30	20	29	15	4
30-40	33	12	8	20
40-50	14	3	5	20
50-60	4	1	3	19
60-70	1	0	0	17
70-80	1	0	1	6
over 80	0	0	0	0

Source: IMF, 1999.

The differences in tax structure between the industrial countries and the non-oil developing countries can be summarised as follows:

Direct Taxes
* Industrial countries obtain the majority of tax revenue from direct taxes, principally income tax and social security contributions; developing countries obtain only a minority of revenue from this source.
* Within the category of income tax, the proportion of revenue from personal tax predominates in industrial countries; corporate income tax contributes much more, proportionately, in developing countries.

Indirect Taxes
* Industrial countries obtain negligible revenue from international trade taxes; the developing countries obtain significant revenue from that source.
* Industrial countries obtain a larger proportion of revenue from general sales taxes than developing countries, which obtain proportionately more from taxes on specific goods and services (excises).

Table 2.4 puts some figures on these generalisations by presenting the figures from tables 2.2 and 2.3 in a more comparative and digestible form.

Table 2.4 Comparison of Indirect Taxes in Industrial and Non-Oil Developing Countries - Central Government

	Percentage of Countries		
	Industrial	Largest Industrial	Developing
Indirect taxes over 50% of total revenue	9	0	46
Indirect taxes over 40% of total revenue	13	0	67
International trade taxes over 30% of total revenue	0	0	10
International trade taxes over 10% of total revenue	0	0	55
Domestic taxes on goods and services over 30% of total revenue	39	14	58
General sales taxes over 10% of total revenue	96	93	68

Source: IMF, 1999

Table 2.5 Comparison of Indirect Taxes in Non-Oil Developing Countries by Region – Central Government

Percentage of Countries

	Africa	Asia	Europe	Middle East	Western Hemisphere	All
	(24)	(18)	(20)	(6)	(24)	(92)
Indirect taxes over 50% of total revenue	63	33	25	33	58	46
Indirect taxes over 40% of total revenue	83	50	55	33	83	67
International trade taxes over 30% of total revenue	42	6	0	17	21	10
International trade taxes over 10% of total revenue	88	56	10	83	54	55
Domestic taxes on goods and services over 30% of total revenue	38	44	85	50	67	58
General sales taxes over 10% of total revenue	54	67	100	17	71	68

Source: IMF, 1999.

Table 2.5 analyses the same categories as the previous table for the different geographical regions of the developing countries.

The developing countries of Africa have the highest reliance on indirect taxes, with the Western Hemisphere not far behind. Africa also has the highest reliance on international trade taxes with the Western Hemisphere similarly in second place. Europe has the mix of indirect taxes nearest to that of the industrial countries with very little revenue coming from international trade taxes and with general sales taxes contributing heavily to the revenue from domestic taxes on goods and services.

Reasons for the Differences between Industrial and Developing Countries

An income tax requires a greater degree of sophistication in its administration than indirect taxes. Many developing countries lack a reliable data base to operate an extensive income tax; more important, income tax cannot be a widespread tax in many developing countries, partly because of widespread illiteracy, but, even more, because of poverty. It would not be cost effective to try to include most of the working population within the income tax net in many developing countries. Thus, in these countries, personal income tax is confined to a small proportion of the population and large corporations often contribute the major share of income tax revenue. Much the same arguments hold true for social security contributions as for personal income tax. Broadly speaking, the poorer the country the less reliance on income tax and social security contributions and the more likely it is that the bulk of such income tax revenue as there is, comes from corporations.

It is easier to administer excise duties and trade taxes than income taxes primarily because there are far fewer collection points. Moreover, excises often have a physical base rather than an accounting base which makes them easier for an unsophisticated tax administration to cope with and promotes certainty in taxation (see chapter 5, p. 69).

These considerations also explain the much smaller proportion of revenue coming from general sales taxes in the developing countries; where the poorer developing countries have adopted a VAT it often has a more restricted base than in industrial countries.

In addition to the limited number of collection points, a further reason for taxes on international trade in developing countries may be their use as a device to protect local industry (although the more successful the protection the less the revenue). Also the multiplicity of excises in some developing countries may result from an attempt to acquire revenue from any conceivable source without a full appreciation of the distorting effects on the economy.

Convergence between Industrial and Developing Countries

Table 2.6, which examines the change in indirect taxation in developing countries between 1983 and 1999 suggests that the pattern of indirect taxation in developing countries has moved closer to that of the industrial countries.

Table 2.6 Changes in Indirect Taxation in Non-Oil Developing Countries – Central Government, 1983 and 1999

Percentages of Countries

	No. of countries		Indirect taxes over 50% of total revenue		Trade taxes over 30% of total revenue		Domestic taxes on goods and services over 30% of total revenue		General sales taxes over 10% of total revenue	
	1983	1999	1983	1999	1983	1999	1983	1999	1983	1999
Africa	33	24	72	63	51	42	23	38	41	54
Asia	20	18	60	33	27	6	53	44	47	67
Europe	6	20	17	25	17	0	33	85	50	100
Middle East	6	6	17	33	33	17	0	50	17	17
Western. Hemisphere	28	24	59	58	31	21	38	67	45	71
All	**93**	**92**	**59**	**46**	**38**	**10**	**32**	**58**	**42**	**51**

Sources: IMF, 1983 and 1999; Bird, 1987.

The figures must be used with caution. The dates refer to the publication of the *Government Finance Statistics Yearbook* and, as mentioned above, relate to the latest date for which figures were available at the time of publication. Also the differences in the numbers of countries comprising the regions, especially the very large differences in Africa and Europe, between the two years mean that we are not exactly comparing like with like. The biggest proportional difference on this score is the number of European countries which increases from 6 to 20. Probably the most reliable comparisons are obtained by omitting Europe and the Middle East (where there are only 6 countries, the majority of which derive a high proportion of central government revenue from non-tax sources) and concentrating on the changes in the other three regions.

The most dramatic change is the decline in the importance of international trade taxes, a decline visible in all regions. Africa, Asia and the Western Hemisphere also witnessed a decline in the percentage of countries with more than 50 per cent of revenue from indirect taxes; the reduction is marginal for the Western Hemisphere, but very marked for Asia. Africa and the Western Hemisphere show an increase in domestic taxes on goods and services compensating, in part, for the loss of trade taxes. All regions, except the Middle East, show a significant rise in dependence on general sales taxes. All these changes bring the developing countries closer to the pattern of the industrial countries, where, over this period, the proportion of revenue from indirect taxes remained much the same, but with a somewhat larger share coming from general sales taxes.

Why have the developing countries become more like the industrial countries? In so far as the developing countries have developed, their circumstances, such as reduced poverty levels and increased literacy, make them more like the industrial countries, and we should expect the tax systems to begin to converge. It is no coincidence that the biggest changes are to be seen in the Asian group of countries which have been most notable for economic growth and where the reliance both on indirect taxation generally and on international trade taxes has fallen most. More generally the decline in international trade taxes owes much to international agreement and pressure. The rounds of the General Agreement on Tariff and Trade (GATT) have promoted free trade and the World Trade Organisation (WTO) continues to do so, as do the International Monetary Fund (IMF) and the World Bank, so the developing countries have come under pressure to remove or reduce taxes on international trade. The increase in the proportion of indirect taxation coming from a general sales tax reflects the way in which VAT (if often in an attenuated form) has been conquering the world (see chapter 5).

OECD Countries

In the remainder of the chapter we concentrate on the 15 OECD members in 1994 which are the largest of the advanced countries, using

OECD statistics which are generally more up-to-date, more reliable and more comprehensive than those of the *Government Finance Statistics Yearbook*. Our object is to show that, within the group of advanced countries, there are considerable differences. Table 2.7 examines the differences in overall levels of taxation, expressing total taxation (including social security contributions) as a percentage of GDP at market prices and listing the countries in descending order of tax level.

Table 2.7 Total Tax Revenue as Percentage of GDP at Market Prices, 1997 – Fifteen OECD Countries

Sweden	51.9
Denmark	49.5
Belgium	46.0
France	45.1
Italy	44.4
Austria	44.3
Netherlands	41.9
Germany	37.2
Canada	36.8
United Kingdom	35.4
Switzerland	33.8
Spain	33.7
Australia	29.8
United States	29.7
Japan	28.8
Unweighted average	**39.2**

Source: OECD, 1999.

The table shows a variation in overall tax level from over 50 per cent of GDP (Sweden) to under 30 per cent (Australia, United States and Japan). Table 2.8 looks at the main groups of taxes expressed as a percentage of total taxation (this time with countries in alphabetical order).

Here again, very considerable divergence is apparent. We have already mentioned the divergencies between countries in the relative weight they put on income tax as against social security contributions: thus Australia imposes no social security contributions and Denmark obtains only 3 per cent of revenue from that source, whilst France,

Germany and the Netherlands obtain over 40 per cent of revenue from social security contributions. Correspondingly, Australia and Denmark are the two countries with the heaviest reliance on income tax (over 50 per cent) whilst France, Germany and the Netherlands are the three countries with the lowest percentage of tax revenue from this source.

Table 2.8 Tax Revenue of Main Tax Groups as Percentage of Total Taxation, 1997

	Income, Profits and Capital Gains	Social Security Contributions	Goods & Services	Property, Net Wealth, Death and Gift	Other
Australia	56.6	–	27.5	9.2	6.7
Austria	28.9	34.2	28.2	1.3	7.4
Belgium	38.6	31.8	26.7	2.9	–
Canada	49.0	13.4	24.4	10.0	3.2
Denmark	59.9	3.2	33.0	3.4	0.6
France	19.9	40.6	27.8	5.4	6.2
Germany	27.9	41.6	27.7	2.7	0
Italy	35.4	33.5	25.9	5.1	0.1
Japan	35.5	36.9	16.5	10.8	0.2
Netherlands	26.0	40.9	28.0	4.6	0.4
Spain	29.9	35.0	28.9	5.8	0.3
Sweden	41.2	29.2	22.3	3.9	3.3
Switzerland	37.1	36.9	18.3	7.7	–
United Kingdom	36.9	17.2	35.0	10.8	–
United States	48.4	24.4	16.7	10.7	–
Unweighted average	**38.1**	**27.9**	**25.8**	**6.3**	**1.9**

Source: OECD, 1999.

The divergencies regarding goods and services taxes are less extreme but still marked, with Japan, Switzerland and the United States obtaining under 20 per cent of tax revenue from goods and services taxes, whilst Denmark and the United Kingdom obtain over 30 per cent.

Although the totals are much smaller, there is also a very wide dispersion in the reliance on taxes in the group of property, net wealth taxes and death and gift taxes, from the extremes of just over one per cent for Austria to 10 per cent or over for Canada, the United Kingdom and the United States.

These broad categories hide other major differences. Thus, with income tax there are varying contributions from personal income tax (PIT) and corporate income tax (CIT) and manifold differences in the structures of each of these forms of tax. Capital gains is probably the tax where the divergencies are most extreme, with significant variations in both what is taxed as capital gains and the manner in which the gains are taxed. Countries vary in the relative contributions of excises and general sales taxes and the form of general sales tax. Similarly many, but not all, countries rely heavily on property taxation as a source of revenue for lower tiers of government; only just over one-third have annual net wealth taxes; most, but not all, countries have death and gift taxes, though there are many differences in detail as well as the important distinction between inheritance and estate taxes.

It is these differences, and differences in the policy-making process, that we explore in subsequent chapters.

CHAPTER 3

TAXES AT LOWER TIERS OF GOVERNMENT

Introduction

In chapter 2 we examined types of taxation initially in central government, then, for OECD countries, in the total tax structure of a country. In this chapter we look at how taxing powers and taxes are shared between central government and lower tiers of government, and, in particular, we consider the question, 'What taxes are most suitable for lower tiers of government?'

Unitary and Federal States

In nearly all states there is some division of taxing powers, broadly reflecting a division of functions; but we need to distinguish between unitary and federal states.

In unitary states any lower tier authorities are created by the central government and can be abolished by it, often by the ordinary process of legislation. Similarly the taxing power of lower levels of government and the form they take are determined by the central government and can be changed by it. Thus the changes since 1989 in the form of local taxation in the United Kingdom (which we shall examine later in a case study) from local property tax, to community charge, to council tax, were all enacted by the central government by the normal legislative process. Similarly, in 1978, in the Republic of Ireland, the domestic property tax was abolished and replaced by central government grant simply by the normal legislative process.

Typically in unitary states there are two tiers of government with taxing powers, central and local, but there may also be substantial regional governments with taxing powers in some unitary states, notably the Scandinavian countries. In some countries a further tier of local authority can 'precept' on a taxing tier, ie require the taxing local unit to raise additional funds for the use of the precepting authority. There may also be other arrangements: thus, in the United Kingdom, although it remains a unitary state, separate assemblies were set up in 1999 in Scotland and Wales, with the Scottish Assembly having the right to increase income tax in Scotland to a limited extent to finance additional Scottish expenditure. By local governments are meant units of government exercising local powers in part of the territory of the country, eg municipalities, districts.

In federal countries there are states (called 'provinces' in Canada and 'lander' in Germany) which have taxing powers laid down in the constitution. Such states have had a separate existence at one time but have then come together voluntarily to form a federal state (as in the case of Canada, Australia and the United States) or been coerced into one, as when Prussia brought about German unification. Typically in federal countries there are three tiers of government: the central or federal, state and local.

Under a federal government some taxing powers are specifically assigned to the federal government (invariably including customs duties) and some taxes may be specifically reserved to the states; but frequently a number of forms of tax may constitutionally be imposed by either or both. Thus, in the United States and Canada both the federal government and the state/provincial governments impose income taxes; in the United States, both federal and state governments levy death and gift taxes and this was formerly true of Canada and Australia, where both federal and provincial/state governments retain the constitutional right to impose death and gift taxes, but no longer do so (see below p. 98).

Even where the constitution allows both federal and state governments to levy the same form of tax, if one has been levying that type of tax for some time, there is strong reluctance to give up the monopoly. Thus, in Canada, where the provinces have long enjoyed the monopoly of a general consumption tax in the form of a retail sales tax, the proposal of the federal government to introduce a value-added tax (called a goods and services tax (GST)) in place of a manufacturers' sales tax, met considerable provincial opposition. It was eventually introduced in January 1991, after a gestation period prolonged by unsuccessful attempts by the federal government to reach agreement with the provinces on a national sales tax.

General Principles of Taxation

The principal question we must try to answer is, 'What are the criteria for taxes levied at sub-central government level?'

Of course, the criteria for taxes in general are relevant, ie equity, efficiency and minimum operating costs. Equity covers horizontal equity,

the equal treatment of those of similar taxable capacity; and vertical
equity, the different treatment of those of different taxable capacity,
usually interpreted as progressive taxation: that those with higher taxable
capacity should pay proportionately more than those with less. Efficiency
is concerned with the allocation of resources in the economy and implies
that taxes should distort prices, and hence economic choices, as little as
possible. Operating costs refer to the collection costs incurred by the
revenue departments (administrative costs) and also the compliance costs
incurred by taxpayers – the costs individual taxpayers and third parties,
notably businesses, incur, over and above the tax itself, in meeting the
requirements laid on them by the tax laws.

In practice these so-called principles of taxation conflict. In particular,
vertical equity may conflict with efficiency and equity in either form may
conflict with low operating costs. Further, while it is appropriate that each
form of tax be scrutinised according to these criteria, more important is
their application to the tax system as a whole, indeed, to the tax and
expenditure system. Thus, for example, each individual tax need not be
progressive if the tax and expenditure system as a whole is progressive.

These general criteria have their application to local and state taxes as
to central government taxes, but particular criteria apply to taxes levied by
lower tiers of government. Whilst broadly similar criteria apply to both
state and local taxes, their application to local taxes is often much more
important because the local government area is likely to be much smaller
than the typical state and the number of taxes allowed to local government
much fewer. Of the following criteria some are desirable but not essential,
whilst others are fundamental.

Criteria for Local and State Taxes

(1) Fundamental for a tax intended to bring in a substantial share of local
authority revenue is the requirement that the tax base should be fairly
evenly distributed across the country. Thus a manufacturers' sales tax
would be unsuitable because manufacturing industry is likely to be
concentrated in certain areas; with such a tax some local authorities would
do very well, others very badly. Similarly, a tax on hotel users would be
unsuitable as it would be much more favourable to tourist areas than areas
with little tourist attraction. These considerations are less important for the
states in federal countries or regions in unitary countries where the states
or regions are large and have a range of taxing powers; but they are vital
to local authorities.

(2) A local tax should meet certain administrative criteria. It should be economical to operate on a *small scale* and be difficult to evade. With a populous state the principle of being economical to administer on a small scale may not be important; but for a local tax in a municipality or district it is very important.

(3) Related to the problem of evasion is the requirement that the tax base needs to be localised within the jurisdiction of the taxing authority; in other words the tax base must not relate to something that is easily transferred across local authority boundaries. Thus, on the face of it a motor vehicle tax which requires car purchasers to register in the local authority where they live, or, in the case of business cars, where the business is situated, might seem a useful local authority tax; but businesses with national fleets of cars could establish a premise for registration purposes where the tax was lowest. Similarly a whisky tax would be unsuitable for local government; because of its comparatively low bulk and high value, it would invite cross boundary shopping. General sales taxes can satisfactorily be employed by states or large regional governments but it is important that the tax rates in adjacent authorities do not get too much out of line if cross boundary shopping is not to be a serious problem.

(4) A local tax should generate a high and reliable yield because a local authority is likely to have only one or two substantial sources of revenue. Again, this criterion is obviously of less importance with state governments which have a range of tax options open to them.

(5) A local tax should not exaggerate local disparities of wealth – it should not offer undue encouragement for the rich in poor areas to move to rich areas, or the rich areas will get richer and the poor areas will get poorer. This is a powerful argument against a progressive (as distinct from a proportional) local income tax, applying to states as well as local authorities. A similar argument applies to death duties which, as we show in chapter 6, have not proved very satisfactory at state level. In both Canada (1972) and Australia (1979) the federal governments vacated the death duty field in favour of the provinces/states. But in both countries there followed a competitive undercutting by states/provinces to attract rich retirees, with the ultimate result that death duties, as such, disappeared entirely.

(6) It is desirable, but not essential, for a local tax to be reserved for local use, that is, not also imposed by central government; this avoids friction

between the two levels of government and clarifies responsibility. However, it is probably inevitable that both central governments and states in a federation and central governments and large regional governments in a unitary state, should levy income taxes. Where this happens, to minimise operating costs, both should use the same tax base provided it is compatible with the criterion we consider next.

(7) It is important that a tax at local or state level should be perceptible – ie that people should know when they are paying a state or local tax; and this criterion links closely with our eighth criterion.

(8) A local tax should promote local accountability and therefore responsibility in decision-making by local or state authorities.

State and Local Taxes in Practice

Bearing these criteria in mind, let us look at what taxes are employed by sub-levels of government. For purposes of comparison we take our 15 OECD countries representing the largest developed countries.

Table 3.1 Tax Revenue of Tiers of Government as Percentage of Total Tax Revenue, 1997

	Central Government[a]	State	Local
Federal Countries			
Australia	77.7	19.0	3.3
Austria	80.2	9.3	10.6
Belgium	71.8	23.2	5.1
Canada	55.1	36.0	8.9
Germany	71.2	21.5	7.3
Switzerland	64.8	19.9	15.3
United States	68.3	19.3	12.3
Unweighted average	**69.9**	**21.2**	**9.0**
Unitary Countries			
Denmark	68.9		31.2
France	89.4		10.5
Italy	94.2		5.8
Japan	75.1		24.9
Netherlands	97.1		3.0
Spain	83.8		16.1
Sweden	69.5		30.5
United Kingdom	96.1		3.9
Unweighted average	**84.3**		**15.7**

Notes: [a] Including social security contributions and EU contributions where applicable.

Source: OECD, 1999, table 129.

The OECD statistics which have been drawn on for table 3.1 have two major limitations. For unitary countries they do not show any breakdown which distinguishes regional government taxes; regional governments are included under local government. Secondly, the table gives no idea of the degree of autonomy over taxes possessed by the sub-central tiers of government. For the majority of countries the sub-central governments can themselves determine the tax rates of between 90 and 100 per cent of their tax sources. The main exceptions are Austria, Belgium, Germany and Spain, where a substantial proportion of sub-central revenue comes from a tax sharing arrangement, but the revenue-split can only be changed with the consent of the sub-central layers of government. The principal other exception is that the Japanese government sets the tax base and the tax rate for around a quarter of the sub-central taxes. In addition some countries, for example the United Kingdom, retain some tax capping powers.

Table 3.1 shows, as we should expect, that overall the share of total taxation taken by lower tiers of government in federal states is significantly larger than the average for unitary states, with the states in a federation usually having a substantially larger share of tax revenue than local governments. However, the contrast is not so big as we might have expected. Amongst the unitary states there are two very distinct groups, with Denmark, Sweden and, to a less extent, Japan, showing a division of revenue to lower tier government comparable to that of federal states, whilst local government in the remaining unitary states has a very much lower proportion. As a general rule, the tax-raising powers of a tier of government reflects the range of its functions and the degree of its autonomy. Scandinavia has historically been characterised by a dispersion of power to regional governments with major tax-raising powers. The Scandinavian countries of Finland and Norway, though not included in the table, show characteristics similar to Denmark and Sweden.

Tables 3.2 and 3.3 reveal the distribution of tax revenue at lower tiers of government by type of tax for federal and unitary states respectively.

In the federal countries taken as a whole, the biggest single source of revenue at state level is the income tax and this is true of each country individually except for Australia which has no income tax at state level but where the states levy payroll taxes. Second in overall importance is taxes on goods and services, with the states in four of the federal countries obtaining over 30 per cent of revenue from a general consumption tax. Again, Australia is the odd one out. All the other federal countries obtain major revenue from either income tax or general sales tax or both. Why should Australia be different? The answer stems partly from its constitution and the legal interpretation put upon it and partly from historical accident. In the constitution exclusive power to levy customs and excise duties was given to the central government (known as the Commonwealth). The allocation of customs duties to the Commonwealth was to prevent the imposition of inter-state tariffs and excises were presumably considered a necessary adjunct. The constitution allowed all other taxes to be levied by either or both the states and the Commonwealth; but the states became excluded from levying taxes on goods by the interpretation the High Court put on excises. As to income tax, before the Second World War the states levied their own income taxes, but during the war they agreed to hand over their income tax collecting to the Commonwealth in return for grants. There is no constitutional bar to the states re-imposing their own income taxes, but the received wisdom is that it would be politically impossible for one state to do so save in concert with the other states and with the Commonwealth providing 'tax room'. As a result, although Commonwealth and states each account for about half of public expenditure, the Commonwealth collects more than 80 per cent of the tax revenue. The states collect their tax revenue from a miscellany of narrow based taxes and are much more dependent on central government grants than the states/provinces of the United States and Canada.

At local level in federal states the biggest contributor is the property tax, which all local governments impose except in Belgium, with income tax a very close second. The yield of other taxes is very small.

Amongst the unitary states the picture at local level is somewhat similar with the property tax predominating in popularity (all countries except Sweden imposing it) but with income and profits tax in this case bringing in the largest share of the revenue. Income tax predominates amongst the heavy spenders at local government level – ie Denmark, Sweden and Japan, but also in France (a recent development). At this level of government, only in Spain was any significant amount of revenue derived from a general consumption tax, though miscellaneous taxes on goods and services, including use taxes, provided a modest supplement to the local revenue of most countries.

Table 3.2 Revenues of Main State and Local Taxes as Percentage of Total Tax Revenues of these Levels of Government, 1997

Federal Countries

		Income & Profits[a]	Property	General Consumption	Specific Goods & Services[b]	Other
Australia	State	25.2	30.9	0	43.9	0
	Local	0	100	0	0	0
Austria	State	53.5	0.8	30.7	10.6	4.6
	Local	54.2	9.4	19.2	10.6	6.7
Belgium	State	51.6	5.4	38.7	4.3	0
	Local	82.4	0	1.5	14.4	1.8
Canada	State	55.9	6.4	19.4	18.2	0
	Local	0	86.0	0.1	1.3	12.5
Germany	State	47.4	5.2	40.6	6.7	0
	Local	77.1	21.7	0	0.9	0.2
Switzerland	State	75.5	16.9	0	7.6	0
	Local	84.4	15.0	0	0.5	0
United States	State	39.5	4.3	33.1	23.1	0
	Local	6.0	73.3	11.1	9.5	0
Unweighted Average	**State**	**49.8**	**10.0**	**23.2**	**16.3**	**0.7**
	Local	**43.4**	**43.6**	**4.6**	**5.3**	**3.0**

Notes: [a] Includes payroll taxes for Australia at state level (25.2), Austria at local level (18.7).
   [b] Includes taxes on use etc.
   '0' indicates either no tax in this category or revenue under 0.05 per cent.

Source: OECD, 1999, table 133.

**Table 3.3 Revenues from the Main Local Taxes as Percentage of
Total Tax Revenues of Local Governments, 1997**

Unitary States

	Income & Profits	Property	General Consumption	Specific Goods & Services[a]	Other
Denmark	93.4	6.5	0	0.1	0
France	95.8	4.0	0	0	0.1
Italy	18.1	34.4	0	17.7	29.8
Japan	52.6	30.4	2.2	13.8	1.0
Netherlands	0	62.2	0	37.8	0
Spain	26.4	34.9	10.9	24.6	3.2
Sweden	99.7	0	0	0.3	0
United Kingdom	0	99.1	0	0	0.9
Unweighted Average	**48.3**	**34.0**	**1.6**	**11.8**	**4.4**

Notes: [a] Includes taxes on use etc.
      '0' indicates either no tax in this category or revenue under 0.05 per cent.

Source: OECD, 1999, table 135.

The property tax owes its popularity at local level to the fact that it matches up very well to the criteria set out above for a local tax: the tax base is fairly widely and evenly dispersed; it is economical to operate on a small scale and difficult to evade; it is localised within the jurisdiction of the taxing authority; it generates a reliable yield and does not exaggerate local disparities of wealth; it is frequently possible to reserve it for local use and it can be made perceptible and promote local accountability. Its main disadvantage is that its regressiveness sets a limit to how much revenue may be raised by it, so that big spenders, whether states or local government units, need to rely on income tax. A general consumption tax is a feasible proposition for large states, but, because of the dangers of cross border shopping, it is unsuitable for small local government units, and practice, as indicated by the statistics, bears this out.

An interesting feature of the tables is that few local authorities rely exclusively (or almost exclusively) on a single source of revenue.

As we have seen, property tax (ie a tax on 'real' or 'immovable' property) is the form of local tax which is most widespread amongst the countries in our table (and this would have been true had we taken a much larger sample of countries); but there are variations in its form and its legal incidence. It may be levied on the capital value of property or on the annual value. The value on which it is levied may be actual (ie what the property could expect to fetch in the market) or assessed (ie according to some formula which probably reflects its value at an earlier date). Its legal incidence may be on the owner or the occupier. In a unitary country the same tax base will usually apply throughout; in a federal country it may differ between states. A property tax may be levied on domestic property or non-domestic property or both. (For details of these practices and theories of incidence, see OECD, 1983.)

In a number of English-speaking countries, eg Ireland, Australia, New Zealand and formerly the United Kingdom itself, the property tax is referred to as 'the local rates' or just 'the rates'.

Case Study – Recent Changes to Local Taxation in the United Kingdom

Over the past decade a series of changes in local taxation in the United Kingdom throws a revealing light on the characteristics required of local taxes.

Until 1989 in Scotland and 1990 in England and Wales, virtually the sole local tax was the 'local rate', a property tax levied on an assessed annual value of both domestic and non-domestic property, with the legal incidence on the occupier. It worked in the following way. Periodic valuations were carried out by the Inland Revenue. Then each local council with taxing powers determined the rate in the £ it should levy to raise the revenue it required. For example, if a particular house had an assessed annual value of £500 and the 'rate' was fixed at 50 pence in the £, then that householder would pay an annual local tax of £250 p.a. (There was no bar to the rate exceeding £1 in the £.)

In 1989 in Scotland and 1990 in England and Wales, the domestic rate was replaced by a poll tax or so-called community charge, which, with some minor exemptions, was a flat rate tax on every adult. The non-domestic rate remained but was 'nationalised', ie it became a national instead of a local tax with the government setting the rate in the £ for the whole country and distributing the proceeds to local government by way of grant. The following account concentrates on the changes in the domestic property scene.

The arguments against the domestic rates were essentially arguments against any local property tax. It was argued that rates were regressive between households (taxing poor households proportionately more than rich) and between areas. They were a tax on the use of house room (a necessity) and because they were a heavy tax on a particular item of expenditure, they distorted consumers' choice and generated an 'excess burden'. Furthermore, it was maintained, they were not paid by all local residents, only householders, thus omitting about half the adult population, who nonetheless benefited from local services. In addition, the infrequent valuations meant not only that valuations were out of date for much of the time, but that when there was a revaluation it led to disturbingly large variations in relative values. Local authorities themselves criticised rates for lack of 'buoyancy' – the yield did not rise as fast as costs and incomes.

In reply to these criticisms it could be responded that the regressiveness of rates between households could be mitigated – and was so in the United Kingdom – by rate rebates for the poorest households; and regressiveness between areas by equalisation grants to local authorities. Some grants of this kind are necessary under any local tax if it is to avoid exaggerating local disparities of wealth (see above, criterion 5, for local taxes). The argument that rates taxed a necessity, house room, could be countered by pointing out that, as in many other countries, house room consumption in the United Kingdom is unduly favoured, leading to investment distortion. House room was zero-rated for VAT and owner-occupiers had concessions under the income tax and capital gains tax. The view that many adults used local services but did not contribute to the rates is misleading. Most such adults were the spouses of householders; and where adult children lived with their parents, it is reasonable to assume that they contributed to the household budget and thus indirectly contributed to the rates.

The criticism that valuations have been infrequent, thereby causing big changes in relative values, is certainly true. The stated intention was quinquennial valuations, but since 1950 revaluations had taken place only in 1956, 1963 and 1973. But the fault, and therefore the remedy, lay with governments and not the rating system.

As for the objection put by local authorities that rates lacked buoyancy, whilst valid and whilst this feature created particular difficulties in times of inflation, there is a contrary argument that, on the whole, it is an advantage if revenue from rates does not automatically rise with incomes; the yield from an increase in the rate in the £ is reliable and the need to raise the rate promotes perceptibility and local responsibility.

The case for the rates is that they match up very well with the criteria for a local tax that we listed above.

The unpopularity of rates was due at least as much to their increasing burden (particularly for some householders following delayed revaluations), as to objections in principle. For a variety of reasons, including inflationary and other increases in local authority expenditure, substantial changes in grant distribution and organisational changes, rate increases were particularly heavy in the years 1974-75 and 1975-76. In 1974-75, for example, the average rate increase in England and Wales was of the order of 30 per cent; but the average conceals big differences between authorities, and some domestic ratepayers faced increases of over 160 per cent. (See *Report of the Committee of Inquiry into Local Government Finance* (Layfield), HMSO, 1976, especially chapter 1 and annex 7). It was not surprising that such increases generated an outcry and the Conservative Party's response was to promise to abolish rates without, at that time, having any clear idea of what to put in their place.

The most comprehensive report into the system of local government finance in the United Kingdom in the past half century has been the *Report of the Committee of Inquiry into Local Government Finance* (The Layfield Report, HMSO, 1976). The Committee's view was that, if local expenditure was to stay at something like its then current level, with a similar proportion financed from local sources, the rates should remain as a local tax, but with some of the strain taken off them by the introduction of a local income tax to be levied by the larger authorities. This view appealed to neither of the major political parties. After fruitlessly searching for more attractive alternatives, the best the Conservative Government could come up with was the community charge, or poll tax (HMSO, 1977 and HMSO, 1986).

The Community Charge

The following were the main arguments used in favour of replacing rates by the community charge:

(1) It related payment more closely to service use because, unlike the local rate, it was paid by all adults.

(2) It increased local responsibility and accountability because it was paid by virtually all adults, not merely householders, and because rebates to the poorest were limited to 80 per cent (not 100 per cent as under the rates).

(3) It was a 'neutral tax'; because it was a single lump sum payment, unrelated to the amount earned or consumed, it did not distort economic choices.

In response to the first of these arguments, it could be pointed out that, in the provision of local services there is very little relationship between payment and service use. For example, the main expenditure of local authorities is on schools, and adults with no children pay just as much as those with children. Indeed, much of local government expenditure is intended to be redistributive.

Moreover, as we have already argued above (p. 30), under the rates a spouse and adult children can generally be regarded as contributing their share indirectly.

This same point is a counter to the first part of the second argument. As for the second part, the restriction on the size of rebate could have equally well been applied under the rating system.

Whilst the third point, the neutrality of the poll tax, is valid, the tax carried with it a very severe downside. Because the community charge was in no way related to ability to pay, it was particularly regressive. The duke in his castle and the peasant in his cottage paid the same. Wealthy people gained very substantially from the switch from rates to community charge.

The community charge matches up well with most of the criteria for local taxes listed above (pp. 22-24) but it fell down on criteria 2 and 3. It proved very expensive to administer and there was much evasion, especially where there was a mobile population.

The community charge met with widespread opposition. It was regarded as a grossly unfair tax. The opposition was accentuated because of the level at which it was brought in; local authorities thought its introduction a good opportunity to increase their expenditure and blame the higher local tax on the central government.

As a result of this opposition, having first got rid of Mrs Thatcher as Prime Minister, for whom the community charge had become a 'flagship', (Gibson, 1990) the Conservative Government abolished it and replaced it by the council tax (Department of the Environment, 1991).

The Council Tax

The council tax was introduced on 1 April 1993. Under its provisions all domestic properties are placed in bands on the basis of an estimated capital value (strictly speaking, on the estimated amount they would have fetched in the market if sold on 1 April 1991).

Table 3.4 sets out the banding arrangements for England. (The bands for Scotland and Wales were somewhat different.)

Table 3.4 Council Tax Banding System in England

Band	Range of Property Values £	Tax Bills (as a ratio of the bill for a property in band D)
A	Up to 40,000	0.67
B	40,001-52,000	0.78
C	52,001-68,000	0.89
D	68,001-88,000	1.00
E	88,001-120,000	1.22
F	120,001-160,000	1.44
G	160,001-320,000	1.67
H	over 320,000	2.00

An average house is deemed to fall within band D and a figure is set by each local council for band D properties. The tax for properties in the other bands is then determined in fixed proportions (which local councils cannot change) by reference to band D properties. Thus, for example, properties in band A pay two-thirds of band D properties whilst those in band H pay twice band D properties. Thus the maximum difference between properties is 1:3 (band H three times band A).

The banding serves several functions. It is held to make valuations easier and revaluations less necessary. It is also intended to limit the range of bills. This is fairer to the occupier of a modest house which is high valued because it is in a high value area, but it also means that the really wealthy, say in houses valued at £1m and upwards, pay the same as someone in a home valued at £321,000 and only three times as much as someone in a home valued at £20,000.

If the local council spends at the level the government says it should (the Standard Spending Assessment (SSA)) a band D value property will attract the average national bill.

Where there is only one adult in a household a 25 per cent discount is given. There is a 50 per cent discount for any one-adult household where the adult is in a special category – chiefly people mentally impaired or members of visiting forces. There are certain other discounts including complete exemption for students. (Thus a student household with one adult who is not a student is eligible for the 25 per cent discount.) Poor households are eligible for up to 100 per cent rebate on their council tax bill.

Currently (1999), council tax pays for about a quarter of discretionary local spending.[1] Thus, if a typical local authority wishes to increase its expenditure by 25 per cent (above the estimated SSA), it will have to increase its council tax by around 100 per cent. The exact figure will vary from area to area. A local authority with high needs, low property values and many discounted properties, with a consequent heavy dependence on grants, might need to raise council tax by nearer 200 per cent to increase its expenditure by 25 per cent. Such gearing means that a small underestimation of the SSA either implies lower than standard services or a wholly disproportionate increase in the council tax. It also puts an effective brake on local authority expenditure, quite apart from central government 'capping', which was a characteristic of the Conservative Governments (1979-1997).

Lessons from the United Kingdom Experience

(1) After experimenting with poll tax, the United Kingdom has returned to what is essentially a property tax. The council tax differs from the rates in important respects: it is based on capital values (as recommended for local rates in the Layfield Report) and not annual values; on banded values rather than specific values; and it has a discount for single adult families. It could be said to be a combination of property tax, poll tax (by virtue of the single adult discount) and income tax (by virtue of the rebate to poor families). But, essentially, it is a return to a property tax base.

[1]Local authorities face non-discretionary spending in administering council tax benefit, housing benefit, and mandatory student awards which they undertake on behalf of central government.

(2) If, as in the United Kingdom, a local income tax is rejected by central government, there appears to be no suitable major alternative to, or supplement for, a local property tax. At the time of the Layfield Report (1976) about two-thirds of local expenditure was financed by grants and one-third by local domestic rates. The Committee took the view that, with growing local expenditure, this situation was unstable and the country faced a choice between localist or centralist solutions. If there was to be genuine and responsible local government then an additional source of local revenue had to be found to supplement the rates and that should be a local income tax. The alternative was the centralist solution in which local government became essentially an agency of central government with grants providing a larger proportion of local finance. The government of the day rejected the idea of a choice between these extremes; but, in fact, the centralist solution has virtually come about, with local taxation now financing 25 per cent of local discretionary expenditure and still less of total expenditure. It is instructive to look back at tables 3.1 and 3.3. Of the unitary countries listed in table 3.1, local taxes in the United Kingdom constitute under 4 per cent of total tax revenue, less than one-quarter of the average for the countries listed. Only one country, the Netherlands, shows a smaller proportion. As table 3.3 shows, these are the two unitary countries that fail to raise any local revenue from income and profits taxes.

CHAPTER 4

INCOME TAXES

Introduction

We move, now, from comparing tax structures to comparing individual taxes or groups of taxes. We saw from our survey in chapter 2 (table 2.1) that advanced countries rely heavily for revenue on direct taxes; amongst direct taxes the biggest revenue yielder is the income tax. Although developing countries place much less reliance on direct taxes nearly all of them levy incomes taxes. Amongst the advanced countries, the personal income tax predominates in revenue yield over the corporate income tax, though this is often not so with the developing countries.

We begin this chapter, therefore, by addressing the question, 'Why does the personal income tax hold this dominant position in advanced countries?' A number of official and unofficial reports have argued that a direct expenditure tax would be preferable to the personal income tax; we need therefore to consider the pros and cons of the expenditure tax and why the income tax has withstood this challenge and retained its pride of place. We next consider some major features of the income tax and the differing practices of countries – the tax base, leading on to the issue of tax expenditures; income tax schedules and the problems of international comparisons; the tax unit and the differing treatments by countries, with a case study of the changes in the United Kingdom tax unit, which well illustrates the way that policy is made in practice and the difficulty, if not impossibility, of devising a wholly satisfactory tax unit.

We then move on to corporate income tax, examining the rationale for having a corporate income tax at all. The different interpretations of the case for a corporate income tax and conflicting equity and efficiency considerations do much to account for the enormous diversity in the forms of corporate income tax amongst the advanced countries.

The Predominance of the Personal Income Tax

Broadly speaking, there are three possible bases for taxation: income, expenditure and capital or wealth. Whilst most countries utilise all three bases, in advanced countries income tax has taken precedence. The main reason is that income has generally been regarded as the best single criterion of ability to pay and a tax on it offers a high degree of flexibility. The rates of tax can be adjusted to accord with almost any interpretation of vertical equity, whilst allowances and reliefs of various kinds can recognise differing individual circumstances and so attain an approach to horizontal equity.

If the personal income tax has these virtues, why don't advanced countries raise **all** their revenue from it? To attempt to do so, especially if the rate structure was progressive, might require rates of tax which would be seriously harmful to incentives to work, save and take risks; also such tax rates would encourage evasion and avoidance; (one advantage of a range of taxes is that, whilst evasion may not be less, at least the gains are more evenly spread); also the disadvantages of income tax (such as its unfairness to those on fluctuating incomes, which we consider below) would be more serious if income tax was the only tax. Moreover, if income tax is the best **single** measure of taxable capacity it is not a comprehensive measure. For example, part of the case for taxing wealth, whether by annual wealth taxes or death duties, is as a complement to income tax, by taking account of the additional taxable capacity conferred by wealth, especially wealth which yields no money income (see chapter 6). Similar arguments could be advanced about taxes on expenditure.

There has been some trend in recent years for some advanced countries to move away from income tax towards a broad-based consumption tax, notably VAT. However, the strongest challenge to the supremacy of personal income tax has been from advocates of a direct expenditure tax, perhaps more accurately called a consumption tax. Whilst there are earlier exponents, in the 20th century, the idea that expenditure on consumption was a preferable tax base to income was first put forward by Irving Fisher (Fisher, 1906). Fifty years later Nicholas Kaldor argued for a direct expenditure tax (Kaldor, 1955). More recently the case for it has been put in a variety of official and unofficial reports from a number of different countries – including the United Kingdom, the United States, Sweden, Ireland and Canada (Meade, 1978, and C.B.I., 1985; U.S. Treasury, 1977; Lodin, 1978; the Irish Commission on Taxation, 1982; Boadway, Bruce and Beach for the Economic Council of Canada, 1987). On a more popular level, it has been advocated by Kay and King (1978 and subsequent editions) and *The Economist* newspaper (20-27 Jan., 1995). With such support it cannot be dismissed as the eccentric view of a small minority and in view of the international flavour of its advocacy, it seems appropriate to consider, briefly, the arguments for and against it. (A fuller consideration is available in the sources listed in the bibliography, for example, Meade, 1977).

The Tax Base: Income or Expenditure

A direct expenditure or consumption tax differs from a tax on individual goods and services. It is assessed on each individual on the basis of the total of his or her consumption expenditure arrived at by calculating income minus saving plus spending out of capital. Saving is exempt from tax and would only incur liability if and when the savings were spent on consumption. As a direct tax the expenditure tax would have the same potential as the income tax for progressive rates to approach whatever was deemed appropriate to attain vertical equity whilst, as with income tax, allowances and other reliefs could be employed in the interests of horizontal equity.

Arguments for an Expenditure Tax in Place of Income Tax

(1) Equity. It is argued that it is fairer to tax people on what they take out of the economic system ie their consumption, than on what they put in, ie their income – the return on the factors of production they put into the system, like the return on their labour and on their lending. The disadvantage of so doing is that, because the rich do most of the saving, taxing consumption instead of income, ie exempting saving, would accentuate inequalities of wealth. To this the advocates of expenditure tax respond that whenever the wealthy consumed their wealth they would be taxed; and their wealth could be taxed at death either by treating death as a deemed consumption under the expenditure tax or by imposing heavy transfer taxes at death. If this treatment is considered insufficient, an annual wealth tax could also be imposed on the wealthy.

A second equity argument revolves around the issue that income tax invariably relates to an annual period, which is unfair to persons whose income flow is uneven; with progressive taxation they pay more tax than those with the same total income more evenly spread. Whilst allowing tax payers with uneven income flows to average over a period of years helps in the more extreme instances, averaging is necessarily both limited in its use and imperfect in its application. Advocates of the expenditure tax argue that, because expenditure is more under the control of the individual than income, an expenditure tax is more equitable on this count.

(2) Efficiency. By 'efficiency' is meant the efficient use of the factors of production, of economic resources. It is argued that the expenditure tax promotes saving, which is tax exempt, and hence, given investment opportunities, promotes economic growth. This cannot be taken as axiomatic; given the change in the tax regime, the rate of return on saving could fall, reducing the incentive to save. Additionally, much saving is currently undertaken in order to provide a particular level of income in the future; if taxpayers continue to think in this way they may save less, for the tax exemption will mean that a given level of future income can be attained from lower current saving.

More significant as an efficiency argument is that an expenditure tax would reduce investment distortion, because it would abolish the 'tax wedge' between the return on the physical asset and the rate of return the saver receives. This distortion, moreover, is not uniform. For example, with a progressive tax it depends on the marginal tax rate of the taxpayer and varies with any tax reliefs or partial reliefs which may be accorded to particular forms of saving, like home ownership or pension contributions.

(3) Inflation. An expenditure tax deals more easily than income tax with the problems which inflation creates for a tax system. To offset the effects of inflation indexing thresholds and brackets would be required, both under an income tax and an expenditure tax. But, with an income tax, there is the additional problem of dealing with capital income. An illustration may help. A taxpayer at the beginning of a tax year has £100 in a savings bank at 5 per cent. He neither adds to nor withdraws from this sum during the year and at the end of the tax year £105 stands to his credit, of which £100 is treated as capital and £5 is treated as income subject to income tax. Fine, if there is no inflation. However, suppose that year witnessed 5 per cent unanticipated inflation. In the absence of special measures the £5 interest is still treated as income, even though the full £105 was necessary to maintain the value of the taxpayer's capital. In effect the taxpayer's real income from saving has been zero and the tax is being levied on and paid from his or her capital. Under the income tax it is very difficult to cope with the effect of inflation on capital income. In our simple example it would not be difficult; the £100 at the beginning of the year could be uprated by the rise in the retail price index and only any excess above that treated as taxable income. But matters are rarely as simple as this. Bank balances are normally added to, and drawn on, during the year and governments have fought shy of the complications of trying to remedy the injustice which inflation creates for the receivers of capital income.

The beauty of the expenditure tax is that this problem is side-stepped; it simply does not arise; consumption is taxed, irrespective of the source of the funds to pay for the consumption. No distinction is made between capital and income.

(4) Simplification.   It is this lack of distinction between capital and income which advocates of expenditure tax claim would make for a fundamental simplification of the tax system. It is the existence of this distinction which generates tax avoidance (dressing up taxed income as untaxed or more lightly taxed capital) with the consequent anti-avoidance legislation complicating the tax system. Indeed, the replacement of income tax by an expenditure tax would remove the necessity for one of the most complicated of taxes, full of inequitable compromises (see below chapter 6) and with high administrative and compliance costs, ie the capital gains tax.

Arguments Against an Expenditure Tax

What of the arguments against?

(1) An expenditure tax accentuates inequality. We have already mentioned this point; the rich are those most able to save. The expenditure tax advocates had two counter arguments: (1) that the expenditure tax penalises the consumption of the rich when they spend from capital – hence conspicuous consumption pays a heavier penalty than under the income tax; (2) the distributional effects can be offset by heavy taxation at death and, if necessary, an annual wealth tax. Such arguments are not wholly convincing. Wealth brings its possessor advantages, over and above the consumption that it makes possible, such as security, independence and, possibly, power. An income tax, like an expenditure tax, cannot take into account the taxable capacity which these features produce, but they are accentuated with an expenditure tax and taxing at death does not prevent the individual from enjoying them throughout his life. As for the option of an annual wealth tax, this would be an extra tax in the system (for most countries) with high administrative and compliance costs; moreover, its existence might gainsay the claimed advantage of an expenditure tax – its encouragement to saving.

(2) Complications.   Whilst its advocates rightly claim that a direct expenditure tax would simplify the tax structure in important respects, in

other ways complications would increase. The taxpayers' returns would be more complicated. As well as recording income, as at present, they would have to record their saving and spending from capital. Whereas, for example, in the United Kingdom at present most wage earners paying standard rate income tax do not have to complete tax returns, because tax is deducted from their earned income by their employers and from interest and dividends at source, under an expenditure tax their savings and any spending from capital would have to be recorded. This must surely mean a universal system of self assessment for such countries. For countries like Australia, Canada and the United States, which already have such a system, the change would be less dramatic. Also, as we have already noted, if an annual wealth tax on the rich was employed to offset inequality, this would mean for most countries a new tax with high administrative and compliance costs.

(3) Transitional problems. The replacement of an income tax by an expenditure tax, it is argued, would be unfair to those who have done their saving under an income tax regime and then retired (when they would be likely to draw down their savings) under an expenditure tax regime. However, it is easy to exaggerate the importance of this (valid) argument. Governments undertake partial switches from income tax to VAT without seeming to be concerned about this effect. More significantly, under an income tax, preferential tax treatment is often given for pension contributions and some other forms of saving. Moreover, arrangements are also possible to minimise this consequence (see Meade, 1978, pp. 187-94 and chapter 21).

(4) International problems. The adoption of an expenditure tax in place of income tax by one country would raise some difficult international issues. One concerns the movement of people. To minimise lifetime tax some people might wish to spend their working life (whilst they were building up their savings) in a country with an expenditure tax and then retire (when they were drawing down their savings) to a country with an income tax. The other international problem relates to double taxation treaties, which have been negotiated between countries with income tax, and would have to be re-negotiated on what might prove to be a much more complicated basis if one country had an expenditure tax whilst the other had an income tax.

These difficulties are not insuperable, but are not easy to deal with and must discourage politicians from embarking on a reform as radical as replacing income tax by an expenditure tax. One way to limit these problems is to adopt the approach of the Swedish Report (Lodin, 1978) and of the Irish Commission on Taxation (1982) which proposed the retention of income tax but at a single rate, with an expenditure tax surcharge on the better off.

However, neither the Irish nor the Swedish governments adopted the proposals, nor does any country currently employ a direct expenditure tax although, in the 1950s, there were short-lived experiments with direct expenditure taxes in India and Sri Lanka.

One merit of the recent reports advocating an expenditure tax has been to reveal, more clearly than ever before, the investment distortions under existing income tax systems. Indeed, so-called income taxes are really hybrids – part income tax, part expenditure tax, with saving **in some forms**, such as pension contributions, or mortgage payments on owner-occupied houses, being partially or wholly tax exempt.

With exceptions, the direction most advanced countries have taken in recent years is to move away from the expenditure tax features in their income tax and move towards a more comprehensive income tax base (see chapter 9).

Income Tax Base – How Comprehensive?

What should be included as income? Haig (1921) and Simons (1938) argued for a comprehensive income tax and this theme was taken up in Canada in the *Report of the   Royal Commission on Taxation* (Carter, 1966). Income was defined as 'additions to spending power over a period of time' and, it was proposed that all such additions should be taxed to income tax regardless of source – a principle famously summarised in the Carter Commission as 'a buck is a buck is a buck'. Thus income was taken to include wages, salaries, interest, profit, rent; receipts in kind; capital gains; gifts and legacies; minus depreciation.

The Carter Commission proposed that capital gains, for practical reasons, were to be taxed on a realisation rather than an accruals basis but capital losses could be set off against other income. Gifts and legacies within the family (defined as husband and wife and children under twenty-one) were to be exempt; for gifts and legacies outside the family annual and lifetime exemptions were proposed and also averaging provisions, so that a large gift or legacy in one year would not be subject to the full severity of progressive taxation. Thus the severity of the comprehensive income tax was somewhat tempered in practice. The pay-off for the comprehensive base was much lower rates of income tax than currently prevailed in Canada (the maximum rate being cut from 80 to 50 per cent).

The full Carter Commission recommendations were never adopted in Canada or elsewhere, but they undoubtedly influenced international thinking and action (Sandford, 1987). The Irish Tax Commission favoured a comprehensive income tax but at a single rate with an expenditure surtax, and proposed to include gifts, legacies and windfall gains as income (with a possible accessions surtax to tax large gifts and legacies more heavily); but likewise these proposals were never accepted by Irish governments. No country has gone as far as to include gifts and legacies as part of income, but recent decades have seen considerable moves in the direction of widening the income tax base. Capital gains taxes[1] have been introduced widely during the past 30 years or so and the tax reform of the '80s saw fringe benefits taxed or, where previously taxed, taxed more severely, either as income of the employee or, in the case of Australia and New Zealand, as a tax on the employer. (See chapters 6 and 9). This consideration of the breadth of the income tax base brings us naturally to the question of tax expenditures.

Income Tax Base – Tax Expenditures

The term 'tax expenditure' was coined by the late Stanley Surrey (Surrey, 1973) in his capacity as Assistant Secretary for Tax Policy in the United States Treasury Department. He was concerned to emphasise the point that any government measures which reduced the tax paid by individuals, or relieved specified economic activities of tax, were the equivalent, in terms of revenue forgone, to direct expenditures by government, and should be judged as such.

Willis and Hardwick, (1978) define a tax expenditure as 'an exemption or relief which is not part of the essential structure of the tax in question but has been introduced into the tax code for some extraneous reason – eg to ease the burden on a particular class of taxpayers, to provide an incentive to apply income in a particular way, or perhaps to simplify administration' (Willis and Hardwick, 1978, p. 1). Thus, for example, reliefs for particular classes of taxpayer, such as blind persons, savings incentives and *de minimus* administrative provisions would all count as tax expenditures.

---

[1] Although the author accepts the view that capital gains should be regarded as a form of income, in this book they are considered under capital taxes. The justification for this treatment is that the objectives of capital gains taxes, and the problems associated with them, are closely akin to those of other capital taxes.

The OECD (1996) identifies and defines the following five categories of tax expenditure:

(1) *Exemptions* – income excluded from the tax base (including gaps in the charge as well as specific exemptions).

(2) *Allowances* – amounts deducted from gross income to arrive at taxable income.

(3) *Credits* – amounts deducted from tax liability. If not allowed to exceed the tax liability they are termed 'wastable'; if any excess of credit over tax is paid to the taxpayer they are termed 'non-wastable'.

(4) *Rate reliefs* – where a reduced rate of tax is applied to a class of taxpayer or activity.

(5) *Tax deferrals* – where relief takes the form of an allowed delay in paying tax. The cost to the Exchequer is the equivalent of the interest which has to be paid (or forgone) on the amount deferred for the period of the deferral.

The term 'tax expenditure' is generally confined to direct taxes, but can be applied to indirect, eg zero rating, exemptions and reduced rates under VAT constitute tax expenditures. A higher than standard rate of VAT can be thought of as a tax penalty.

We shall here concentrate on personal income tax (although some of the considerations apply equally to corporate income tax). The questions we seek to answer are: why do some countries have many more tax expenditures than others? Why do some formally and publicly record and seek to quantify tax expenditures whilst others do not? Why do countries differ in what they regard as tax expenditures? Why do those countries which formally and publicly record tax expenditures differ in the way they do so?

The answers to these questions will become clearer if we first summarise the case for and against tax expenditures as an alternative to direct expenditures and consider some of the problems of measuring tax expenditures.

Arguments for Using Tax Expenditures rather than Direct Expenditures

(1) The use of tax expenditures enables an existing administrative framework (ie the tax system) to be used without the need or cost of creating a new or additional framework.

(2) By using the tax structure, the take-up of a benefit may be higher than if a separate new basis were used requiring applicants to make a separate claim. With a social security type benefit some eligible citizens might also

feel that less social stigma was attached to a tax relief than to a direct expenditure which they had to take the initiative to claim.

(3) The intended benefit may be related to certain criteria in respect of which a tax relief may be especially appropriate. For example, a government may wish to offer an investment incentive, but only wish it to go to profitable firms (which they feel can utilise it more effectively); if it is offered by way of a tax relief, only profitable businesses will be able to take advantage of it. As a different example: a government may wish to encourage charities, which meet a wide range of needs; governments themselves can hardly make the choices (or, at least, not all of them) amongst the thousands of useful charities which exist. A tax relief encourages individuals to give to charities and make the selections and a tax allowance has the advantage that it particularly encourages the rich (who can best afford it) to give, as they get the most tax advantage and the charity gets most revenue.

(4) There may sometimes be constitutional reasons for using tax expenditures rather than direct expenditures. In a federal state the federal government may control relevant taxes but direct expenditures on a particular activity may be constitutionally (or traditionally) reserved for the states. In that case, federal encouragement for this activity cannot be done via direct expenditures but has to be done by tax expenditures.

Arguments Against Tax Expenditures

In considering the relative merits of tax and direct expenditures it is important to distinguish between those which apply to tax expenditures only and those which apply equally to both tax and direct expenditures. Thus, it is (correctly) said that tax expenditures narrow the tax base and therefore require higher tax rates. But if the same benefit were given via direct expenditures the tax rate would also need to be higher. Similarly, it is argued that tax expenditures often fail to achieve the intended objective; but this is equally true of subsidies.

Disadvantages of Tax Expenditures Compared with Direct Expenditures

(1) Unless the tax expenditure takes the form of a non-wastable credit its full benefit only goes to those who are taxable. (Those who are not taxable may get a part-benefit if, but for the relief, they would have been taxable.)

(2) The first point is really a special case of this second one. Where the benefit takes the form of a tax allowance rather than a tax credit, with a

progressive income tax the value of the benefit is determined by the taxpayer's marginal rate of tax. Consequently, in absolute terms, those with the highest income get the most benefit.

(3) Tax expenditures are generally less transparent than direct expenditures; they tend to be less regularly evaluated and therefore less subject to control.

(4) Because tax expenditures are less transparent, they are more subject to political pressures than direct expenditures; and politicians can more easily give way to pressure groups by granting a tax expenditure than by giving a subsidy.

(5) A government which finds it hard to meet a commitment to reduce government expenditure may be tempted to resort to tax expenditures as a way of reducing public (direct) expenditure as a percentage of GDP. This way expenditure is effectively increased but covertly.

(6) The extensive use of tax expenditures makes it more difficult to form a judgment and obtain a consensus on the fairness of any particular tax system.

(7) Tax expenditures generate possibilities for tax avoidance.

(8) Tax expenditures complicate the tax system.

Problems with Tax Expenditures

Particular problems are associated with tax expenditures. We have defined tax expenditures as tax benefits 'which are not part of the essential structure of the tax'. But what is the essential structure? To mention just one or two of the main problems.[1] Funded pension plans may be taxed when money is paid in, when income accrues to the pension fund and when the pension is paid out. In most countries, but not all, the treatment is to exempt payments in and the investment income of the fund, but to tax when the pension is drawn. This arrangement can be regarded as a deferral of tax; if the revenues forgone as a result of payments in are treated as a tax expenditure, then the taxation of payments out should be treated as an offset. In fact none of the OECD countries currently does that and the procedure followed by the countries recording tax expenditures differs considerably. Again, take the case of the imputed income from the owner-occupation of homes. Countries differ in their treatment. Belgium computes a figure but the authorities are undecided whether it constitutes a tax expenditure or not; Finland calculates a figure based on a 3 per cent return on the capital value of the house. None of the other countries

---

[1] For further and fuller details of these problems, see OECD, 1996.

surveyed by OECD calculates tax expenditures related to imputed income from owner occupation, 'citing a combination of theoretical and practical difficulties' (OECD, 1996). Even in respect of basic personal allowances (or personal tax credits) which are invariably regarded as 'part of the essential structure', we still need to answer the question 'what level of personal allowances?' Governments change the real value of these allowances from year to year. Is the whole personal allowance or credit essential to the structure of just a part of it? And if the latter, what part?

Again there is a major problem of costing tax expenditures and still more of aggregating the costs. Each tax expenditure is costed (in terms of revenue forgone) on the assumption of a given tax rate schedule and the continued existence of all the other tax expenditures in the same degree. But if one were abolished, taxpayers' behaviour might change affecting the others. Moreover they are costed, as it were, on a marginal basis. Abolish one and the cost (in terms of revenue foregone) of the others might rise even if the take-up was the same, because if tax rates and thresholds remained unchanged some taxpayers might move into higher tax brackets. Aggregating tax expenditures gives a meaningless total and understates their cumulative effect on the revenue.

To add further to the problems, the reliability of the estimates of tax expenditures, even on the basis of these restrictive assumptions, is often suspect; calculating tax expenditures is almost invariably more difficult than calculating direct expenditures.

The idea that tax expenditures should be measured and reported is comparatively recent and studies which examine tax expenditures across more than one country are rare. The most recent of these is the OECD study of 1996. This records tax expenditure reports in 14 Member countries (out of 26 at that time) but adds the footnote that, in addition, Japan and Luxembourg have some form of accounting for tax expenditures. By inference the other OECD countries have not. Table 4.1 records for the fourteen countries when tax expenditure reporting began; the frequency of reports; whether they are required by statute and whether they are explicitly linked to the Budget. In addition it summarises the authority's view in each country of the use of the tax expenditure report. The OECD publication also lists out tax expenditures for each country individually and gives the estimated costs of them for one or more recent years. However, the definitions and treatment are so different between countries that the OECD does not attempt cross country comparisons.

Table 4.1 Tax Expenditure (TE) Reporting in OECD Countries

	Date TE Reporting Began	Frequency of Report	Statutory Obligation?	Explicit Link with Budget?	Use of TE Report	Comments
Australia	1986 (1980)	Annual	No	No	Low political profile; used by govt. advisers	TE Statement first published 1986. 1980-84 major items listed & costed in Budget
Austria	1978	Annual	Yes from 1986	No	Discussed in parlt.	TE report part of 'subsidies' report
Belgium	1985	Annual	Yes	Yes	V. useful; cited often in parly. debates	
Canada	1979	Annual	No	No	Used by parliamentarians & officials in pre-budget discussions. Moderate media interest	
Finland	1988	Annual	No	Yes	V. useful re tax reforms	
France	1980	Annual	Yes	Yes		The French authorities offered no comment on the use of the TE reports
Germany	1967	Biennial	Yes	No	Intensive use; debated in plenary session in Bundestag & Bundesrat	As Austria
Ireland	1982	Annual	No	No	Difficult to assess	
Italy	1991	Sporadically	No	No	Limited	Reports not published
Netherlands	1987	Sporadically	No	No	Recent development: maximum revenue to be forgone specified w r t 3 recent tax expenditures	
Portugal	1991 (1986)	Annual	Yes	Yes	Often used in political debate; valuable re tax reforms	Before 1991 some tax expenditures reported
Spain	1979	Annual	Yes	Yes	Not widely used in tax policy debates	
UK	1979	Annual	No	No	Limited	
USA	1968	Annual	Yes from 1994	Yes	Used in political debate in shaping tax reforms	Part of Budget but not integrated into budgetary process

Source: OECD 1996.

Answering the Questions

We are now in a much better position to answer the questions on p. 46. *Why do some countries have more tax expenditures than others?* As only a minority of countries in the world publish tax expenditure reports (and as some of those with the most tax expenditures may be the least willing to publish) we are forced to rely on inference and anecdotal evidence for some of our answers.

(1) It seems likely that, because of the lower transparency of tax expenditures compared with direct expenditures and because tax expenditures are less subject to control, that they will be most plentiful in countries where government is marked by nepotism, cronyism and corruption. These features are particularly associated with some developing countries. Whilst recognising that tax expenditures are applicable to other taxes, we have been looking at them primarily in the context of income tax. But a characteristic of less developed countries is that they rely much less on income tax than developed countries; for that reason there is less scope for tax expenditures under the income tax in less developed countries and in these countries tax expenditures may mainly occur with respect to customs duties, excise duties and trade taxes.

(2) An argument easier to document is that tax expenditures are more numerous in constitutions marked by a separation of powers. The outstanding case is the United States. It is no accident that the impetus to report tax expenditures, and the very name itself, came from an Assistant Secretary (Tax Policy) of the United States Treasury. In the United States, whilst the President may propose tax changes it is Congress that has the taxing powers. The party system in the United States is relatively weak. Both chambers, the House of Representatives and the Senate, are very powerful. Congress members are heavily dependent for re-election on their standing in their constituencies and on the funds which they need to raise locally for expensive electoral campaigns; as a result local interest groups are exceptionally powerful. Thus, to get tax legislation through Congress necessitates a complex bargaining process in which the Executive may only achieve its main objectives by making concessions, often in the form of tax expenditures, to special interests in exchange for support. (See, for example, chapter 9 below, Pechman, 1987, chap. 3; Sandford, 1993, chap. 6; Steinmo, 1993). In the 1996 OECD Report, the United States records far more tax expenditures with respect to income tax than any other country; and the figures, which relate to 1995, are less than

a decade after the much acclaimed Tax Reform Act of 1986 had made heavy inroads into tax expenditures (see below p. 187).

The United States is an extreme case; but in constitutions more akin to the Westminster system, where the second chamber is powerful and the party which controls the lower house does not invariably control the upper, as in Australia, concessions, sometimes taking the form of tax expenditures, may need to be made to secure the passage of tax legislation. As second chambers are invariably relatively strong in federal states (where they generally represent the states as such) it may well be that tax expenditures tend to be more numerous in federal than in unitary states.

Why do countries differ in their treatment of tax expenditures? The remaining questions listed on p. 46 above can be dealt with together. That some countries formally record tax expenditures whilst others do not may be partly accounted for by the relative newness of the concept; as the table indicates, additional countries keep coming aboard. Some countries may not have introduced tax expenditure reports for the simple reason that their governments wish to keep tax expenditures from the public eye for reasons we have already indicated. Other countries, noting the confusions over definitions, the differences of treatment and the difficulties of calculation, may have decided to leave well alone – at least until more uniformity of view has emerged amongst countries publishing such reports.

It is these problems of definition and the different treatments of difficult questions that largely explain why the countries with reports should have produced them in such varied forms. To add just one example to those mentioned earlier, which aptly illustrates the problems of definition and measurement; when the United Kingdom first began to publish TE lists, the authorities were so unhappy with the term tax expenditures that they refused to use it; they simply listed **all** tax reliefs, concessions and exemptions with no attempt to distinguish structural from non-structural. Estimates of the cost, in terms of revenue forgone, were only included where they felt these estimates were reasonably reliable. Since 1993 the United Kingdom's list has been divided into three categories: 'tax expenditures', 'structural reliefs' and 'reliefs with tax expenditure and structural components'. Of the cost estimates, one-third or more are marked with an asterisk as being 'particularly tentative and subject to a wide margin of error'. (OECD, 1996, p 105).

As a final comment on this subject, table 4.1 strongly suggests that tax expenditure reports have their biggest impact where they are required by law and are closely linked to the Budget or, as in the case of Austria and

Germany, are part of a 'subsidies report' which is required to be laid before Parliament.

Personal Income Tax Rates

Country comparisons of income tax rates are to be found in chapter 9 on tax policy-making and tax reform, and will not be repeated in this section. Here we examine three issues of considerable importance in international comparisons: (1) the numerous factors which may cause effective tax rates to diverge from nominal rates or may otherwise mislead in international comparisons; (2) the relationship between tax rates and the progressiveness of the tax system – to demonstrate that progression in the income tax does not depend on a plethora of tax rates; (3) tax rate differentiation between earned and investment income.

Common Pitfalls in International Comparisons of Tax Rates

It is easy to glance at two schedules of income tax rates and jump to the conclusion that one is heavier than the other, without examining the size of the thresholds and brackets. Especially is this true in looking at top rates; a comparison of top rates is largely meaningless without taking into account the level of income at which they become applicable – in one country the top rate may relate to such a high income level that hardly anyone pays it; in another it may apply to a substantial proportion of income tax payers.

Apart from this, however, nominal and effective rates may diverge because of tax expenditures in their various forms and because of tax avoidance and evasion. Further points to watch in international comparisons of income tax schedules are (1) whether there are other taxes of an income tax nature, like social security contributions, and how heavy they are; and (2) whether there are local, regional or state income taxes to take into account in addition to the federal or central government income tax; and if there are, whether they are deductible in some form in determining the federal or central government income tax liability.

Tax Rates and Tax Progression

As we shall discuss in more detail in chapter 9, one characteristic of the tax reform of the 'eighties and early 'nineties was a reduction in the **number** of rates or brackets of the personal income tax. Let us take just a few of the more outstanding examples. Canada had 13 rates in 1975; in 1988 the number had been reduced to 3. Japan, over the same period, came down from 19 to 5; New Zealand from 22 to 2; Sweden from 11 to 3; the United Kingdom from 10 to 2 (though increased to 3 in 1992); the United States from 25 to 3.

These reductions in the number of rates were intended to simplify the tax system; they were associated with large reductions in the top rates of income tax with intended beneficial effects on incentives; and, what particularly concerns us in this context, they arose in part from a realisation that a multiplicity of rates was not necessary to secure progression in the income tax.

As we have seen, advanced countries rely heavily on income tax revenue and the income tax carries with it more scope for adjustment to prevailing concepts of ability to pay than any other current form of tax. The progressivity of the personal income tax is therefore a crucial issue.

It is important to be clear about terms. A progressive income tax is one such that, the higher the income the larger the **proportion** of it taken in tax. A proportional tax is one in which tax is proportional to income at every level. A regressive tax is one in which a larger proportion of low incomes is taken in tax than of high incomes (although high income receivers may pay more in absolute terms than low income receivers). The progressivity of a tax therefore depends on what happens to **average** tax rates at different income levels. Thus an income tax with a tax free allowance (which can be thought of as a zero rate) and just one positive rate is progressive and may be more or less progressive than a multiple rate system.

An example will illustrate the point. Figure 4.1 shows two tax systems, A and B.

System A has a single rate and a larger tax free allowance; system B has multiple rates and a smaller tax free allowance. Both raise approximately the same revenue. Table 4.2 shows the average rates produced for a hypothetical population of 10 taxpayers each with different incomes.

The example makes clear that system A is more progressive than system B over the first half of the income distribution and system B over the second half. It therefore makes no sense to say that one is more progressive than the other, unless we specify more precisely to which part of the income distribution we refer. If we were to extend the income scale beyond 10,000 the less would be the progressiveness of the single rate system because the threshold becomes an ever smaller proportion of income: the average rate would move closer to the marginal rate of 25 per cent, with every increase in income, but would never quite reach it. This flattening of the average rate at higher incomes can be counteracted by one or more rates on the relatively small number of high income taxpayers, as is done, for example, in New Zealand, the United Kingdom and the United States.

Figure 4.1

Tax System A		**Tax System B**	
Tax free allowance	2,000	Tax free allowance	1100
Tax rate	25%	Tax rate on first 2,000	
		of taxable income	15%
		Tax rate on next 2,000	20%
		Tax rate on next 2,000	25%
		Tax rate on further income	30%

Table 4.2

Income	Tax System A	Tax System B	Average Tax Rate System A %	Average Tax Rate System B %
1,000	0	0	0	0
2,000	0	135	0	6.8
3,000	250	285	8.3	9.5
4,000	500	480	12.5	12.0
5,000	750	680	15.0	13.6
6,000	1,000	925	16.7	15.4
7,000	1,250	1,175	17.9	16.8
8,000	1,500	1,470	18.8	18.4
9,000	1,750	1,770	19.4	19.7
10,000	2,000	2,070	20.0	20.7
Total	**9,000**	**8,990**	**16.36**	**16.35**

It is thus easy to be misled about the progressiveness of a tax by looking simply at the structure of marginal rates.

Differentiating Between Earned and Investment Income

Some countries have in the past differentiated between the rate of tax on earned (or labour) income and on investment (or capital) income and some currently do so. This differentiation may be achieved by a surcharge on investment income (such as existed in the United Kingdom between 1973 and 1984) or by a reduced rate on earned income (such as existed in the United Kingdom before 1973 and currently in New Zealand, up to a specified limit). The arguments for differentiation are that investment income is more permanent than earned income. Earned income is more precarious, it is dependent on the individual taxpayer – restricted to his working life and subject to interruption by bad health or unemployment. Investment income also has the advantage over earned income that it can be enjoyed without loss of leisure.

The arguments for a higher rate of tax on investment income are similar (though not identical) to the case for an annual net wealth tax to improve the horizontal equity of the tax system (see chapter 6).

With the advent of sickness benefits and unemployment pay, the argument for a more favourable taxation of earned income has lost some of its force in advanced countries. Indeed, for other reasons, the differentiation seems to have gone, and increasingly be going, the other way. On the one hand is the desire of governments for macro economic reasons to increase saving in general and, for social policy objectives, to increase savings in particular directions, such as pensions (Dilnot, 1998). On the other hand is the increased mobility of capital internationally which makes for continual downward pressure on tax rates on investment income.

The Tax Unit

Countries differ in the unit they use for income tax. The differences lie primarily in the treatment of married couples. In some countries they are treated as a single unit; in others there is individual taxation and a married couple is treated the same as two single adults. However, the distinction is not always so clear cut. There may be options, ie the married couple may choose to be treated as one unit or as two single adults. Also, even under individual taxation there may be an allowance for a married couple which is transferable between them. Apart from this major distinction, there is the question of the treatment of minor children as part of a family unit and there may be special tax units besides the single adult and the married couple. Thus, in the Netherlands two people living together may be treated as a unit and in India there is the phenomenon of the 'Hindu undivided property' which is taxed as a separate entity.

Criteria for the Choice of Tax Unit

The following criteria, based on a list contained in the Meade Report (Meade, 1978, chapter 18) are all ones which, individually would receive widespread support.

(1) The decision to marry or not to marry ought not to be affected by tax considerations.

(2) Couples (ie husband and wife) with the same joint resources should be taxed the same. How income is divided between them should not affect the amount of tax paid.

(3) A person's tax rate should not be significantly affected by circumstances outside his or her control. For example, the incentive for a member of a husband and wife couple to earn, should not be blunted by tax considerations which depend on the economic position of the other.

(4) Economic and financial arrangements between husband and wife should not be dominated by sophisticated tax considerations.

(5) The tax system should be 'fair' between single and married persons; and between married couples who rely on earnings and those who enjoy investment income.

(6) Two persons living together and sharing household expenses can live more cheaply than if they were living separately; because of their greater taxable capacity, they should be taxed more than two people living separately.

(7) Any arrangement should be reasonably simple for the taxpayer to understand and for the tax authorities to administer.

(8) Each taxpayer is entitled to privacy in relation to his or her tax affairs.

(9) Finally, if a change of tax unit is contemplated, considerations of fairness and practicality dictate that on the one hand some taxpayers should not be faced with immediate heavy losses and, on the other hand, the change should not be too costly in terms of revenue.

Even a cursory examination of these criteria – all of which appear desirable, or, at least, plausible – makes it clear that they often conflict in practice. Thus to take simply the first two listed. Criterion (1): that the decision whether or not to marry should not be affected by tax considerations, is satisfied by independent taxation. But this may conflict with criterion (2): that couples with the same joint resources should be taxed the same. If there is a progressive income tax and independent taxation of husband and wife, the amount of tax paid varies with the way income is divided between them. For example, given a progressive rate schedule, if £20,000 investment income is split equally between them, they will pay less than if it is all owned by one partner; if they then equalise it by transferring the ownership of some of the assets, there is a conflict with criterion (4).

As well as a conflict of principles, some principles depend for their interpretation on subjective judgment; for example, criterion (5), on 'fairness' between single and married persons and between those with and those without investment income.

Why the Differences Between Countries?

This conflict of principles partly explains the differences between countries. In choosing the tax unit it is necessary to compromise and the form the compromise takes is very much affected by the laws, traditions and social customs of a country and by its past history. Some of these traditions may even be enshrined in the constitution. Thus, a country with a strong family and Roman Catholic tradition, like the Republic of Ireland, treated married couples as a single unit and, before 1980-81, their income was aggregated for tax purposes. However, in response to an appeal (the Murphy case, 1980) the Supreme Court decided that aggregation of a married couple's income breached the constitutional pledge by the state to guard with special care the institution of marriage and protect it against attack. Aggregation had meant that, after marriage, some couples paid more tax than they had as single individuals. The Government's response was to institute income-splitting for married couples from 1980-81, by which the tax liability of a married couple is generally equivalent to twice the amount payable by a single person with half the joint income. As a result the tax liability of married couples is at worst the same and in most cases less, than if they were charged as single persons (Commission on Taxation, 1982). The converse is, of course, that in Ireland, single persons are taxed relatively heavily.

Problems arise where customs change. The need to bring the tax system into line with the changed customs and, at the same time, ensure that the necessary measures are neither too costly, nor too unfair to particular sectors of taxpayers, results in further compromise. In line with the enhanced position of women in society the worldwide trend is for countries to move towards individual taxation. Even in Ireland, for

example, whilst the married couple remains the basic unit, married couples are offered a choice of options:
– joint assessment with either party nominated by the couple as the assessable person (instead of the husband being automatically selected, which was the position prior to 1994-95);
– separate assessment (in which case the tax payable by both spouses must be the same as would be payable under joint assessment);
– separate/single treatment (in which case each spouse is treated as a separate unit).

In the case of couples who married prior to 6 April 1993, the husband continues to be treated as the assessable person where no option is chosen. For couples who married on or after 6 April 1993, where no option is chosen, joint assessment automatically applies, with the higher earner in the previous year treated as the assessable person.

The existence of options, quotients, allowances and other special provisions makes a straight forward classification of countries difficult, if not impossible. The history of the United Kingdom tax unit over the past half century well illustrates the point.

Case Study: History of the United Kingdom Tax Unit

Prior to the Second World War, under the United Kingdom income tax, husband and wife were treated as a single unit and their incomes were aggregated in determining the rate of tax. The husband was responsible for the tax return and enjoyed a married man's allowance (MMA) which was broadly equivalent (it varied somewhat from time to time) to one and a half times a single person's allowance. This generally accorded with the social situation at the time. Wives were generally dependent on husbands; few went out to work; they looked after the household and the children.

The first major changes were brought about by the War. The need for revenue meant that income tax, which had hitherto been paid only by those in the upper end of the income distribution, was encompassing an ever widening sector of the working population and a cumulative PAYE system was introduced to cope with this extension of the taxpayer population. At the same time, the government wanted to encourage married women to go out to work. Under the then prevailing tax arrangements, any married woman who did so would immediately face income tax at the marginal rate applicable to her husband. To remove this disincentive the government introduced the married woman's earned income relief (MWEIR), by which a married woman who worked received an allowance equal to the single person's allowance to set against earned income. If the single person's allowance is designated as 1, then the allowance for a married couple with wife not working amounted to $1^1/2$ and for a married couple both earning amounted to $2^1/2$. Some single women, especially widows, who worked and who had only the single person's allowance, felt unfairly treated by this differentiation.

This system still required the aggregation of the taxable income of husband and wife, so that once the earning wife had used up the MWEIR she was taxed on subsequent income at the marginal rate applicable to her husband. For two earning couples both in highly paid employment, at a time when top income tax rates were at levels in excess of 70 per cent, this was a significant burden, a disincentive to work and an encouragement to evasion and avoidance. In response to the discontent it engendered, the government introduced the wife's earnings election (WEE) in 1972. Under this provision the wife could elect, in respect of her earned income, to be treated as a single taxpayer; but if this option was taken, her husband lost the MMA. (An election was thus worthwhile if the tax saved as a result of disaggregating earned income exceeded the loss resulting from the difference between the married and single allowances.) If the election was exercised the married couple then had allowances equivalent to 2. A husband or wife could also claim separate assessment. This made no difference to the total tax paid by the couple – the tax bill was shared between them with the available reliefs being divided in proportion to their incomes – but each had independent dealings with the revenue authorities in his or her tax affairs.

In response to growing criticism, especially from the lobby for women's rights, in December 1980 the government published a 'green paper', a discussion document (Cmnd. 8093, 1980) which outlined the prevailing system, considered criticisms of it, and looked at possible alternatives. Public comment was invited.

The 1980 green paper suggested four criteria by which any system should be judged: fairness, simplicity, sex equality and privacy. On these criteria the system did not come out well. To take just a few examples. It could be argued that the single person earning (1 allowance) was unfairly treated compared with the two earner couple ($2^1/2$); that the married couple where the wife was staying at home looking after the children ($1^1/2$) was unfairly treated compared with the two earner couple ($2^1/2$); that the options for separate taxation of husband and wife and separate assessment complicated the picture; that the principle of sex equality was violated because, whilst the options had alleviated the position somewhat, the basic principle of the husband's responsibility for the wife's tax return was unchanged and the marriage allowance, save where the wife was the sole breadwinner, was only given to married men. With respect to privacy, it was impossible for the wife to keep her income and tax affairs separate from those of her husband. In addition the tax was far from neutral in relation to social and economic arrangements; thus, there was a financial incentive for two persons, both working, to marry if their combined income was less than the threshold of higher rate tax; but to stay single if their combined income exceeded that figure, especially if they had substantial investment income (which continued to be aggregated even if they chose the WEE).

No action was taken following the 1980 green paper; a second green paper was issued in 1986 (Cmnd. 9956). Then, in 1988, Chancellor of the Exchequer Nigel Lawson introduced a reform to come into effect in 1990-91, which provided for independent taxation. As a result, a husband's and wife's incomes are no longer aggregated. Each has an allowance which can be set against income from any source – earnings or investment income. The married woman's earned income relief was abolished, but a new allowance, the married couples' allowance (MCA) was introduced equal to the difference between the married man's allowance and the single person's allowance. The MCA is transferable between husband and wife or can be divided between them.

Table 4.3 compares pre and post 1990 for single persons or married couples in various income situations. For most married couples, ie where both earn but their combined earnings keep them below the higher rates of tax and where one earns but they have little or no investment income, the tax position remained as before. The gainers were the two earner families on high incomes, who had previously exercised the WEE at the cost of losing some allowance, and who benefited from the MCA; and couples with substantial investment income which previously had to be aggregated – the wife acquired an allowance of her own to set against her investment income and, in addition, non-aggregation was likely to mean lower marginal rates.

The reform had the merit that it gave married women the same privacy and independence in tax affairs as everyone else and it removed any discrimination against marriage. Because the tax payments of most taxpayers remained unchanged the reform was effected at an acceptable cost and no-one was worse off; but virtually all the financial benefit went to the relatively wealthy.

Table 4.3
Some Effects of the Change in the Tax Unit:
Comparison of Some Situations pre and post 5 April, 1990

				Effective Allowances	
Income of Couples				Pre	Post
1	A earns}	basic	S	2	2
	B earns}	rate	M	2.5	2.5
2	A earns}	into	S	2	2
	}	higher			
	B earns}	rates	M	2	2.5*
				(WEE)	
3	A earns		S	1	1
	B doesn't earn		M	1.5	1.5
	no investment income				
4	A earns		S	1	1
	B doesn't earn		M	1.5	1.5
	A has large investment income				
5	A earns		S	2*	2
	B doesn't earn		M	1.5	2.5*
	B has large investment income				

*Also likely to benefit from lower tax rates (because of non-aggregation).
A = Andy (the man)
B = Barbara (the woman)
S = combined allowances if A and B remain single
M = married
WEE = wife's earnings election.

The system was probably simpler than its predecessor. It was not neutral as between marriage and non-marriage, nor was it neutral with respect to the financial arrangements within a marriage – how investment income was divided between husband and wife affected the tax to be paid. It left unchanged what many would regard as an unfair advantage of the two-earning married couple compared with the single woman; and that between the couple where both earned and the one earner family where the other spouse had no investment income and was looking after the children – which was likely to be the family most in need. Moreover, to have a system of 'independent taxation' but a 'married couples' allowance was an anomaly; however, to have abolished the MCA and left no-one seriously worse off would have been prohibitively expensive. Since 1990 the value of the MCA has been allowed to fall, partly because it has not always been increased in line with inflation and partly because the rate of tax which could be set against it has been reduced. Most recently, Chancellor of the Exchequer Gordon Brown, in his 1999 Budget, has announced that the MCA would be abolished, except for pensioner couples, and replaced by additional child support.

The history of the United Kingdom tax unit well illustrates the problems arising from choice of tax unit and the need to change that choice in line with changing customs. What started as a fair reflection of the social situation ceased to be so. The choice of tax unit became complicated by an emergency measure (the wartime introduction of the married women's earned income relief) which created baggage which, once introduced, was difficult to get rid of. *Ad hoc* measures helped to ease the problems created by the change of social customs, but were only palliatives. The 1988 reform still left important issues unresolved and changes continue.

Conclusion

It seems likely that neither in the United Kingdom nor elsewhere will any wholly satisfactory solution be attained. Perhaps the biggest problem is the difficulty, if not impossibility, of reconciling two widely accepted but conflicting principles: equal treatment for all individuals irrespective of sex and marital status on the one hand; and, on the other, the recognition that the overall financial circumstances of a household are relevant to the ability to pay tax.

Corporate Income Tax

Why do we need a corporate income tax – or, as it is often called, a corporation tax? A company, after all, is simply a convenient means by which a number of individuals can pool capital in order to pursue certain commercial aims in common. Why can the shareholders not simply be taxed on the profits as individuals under the personal income tax? As a matter of administrative efficiency it may be sensible for tax to be deducted at source, ie at the company stage, just as it is administratively efficient for employers to deduct income tax from the wages and salaries of their employees; but that is a different matter, not affecting the amount which individuals would pay. At first glance, to treat the profits of corporations exactly like the business profits of individuals or partnerships would seem to be not only equitable but also efficient – avoiding distortion in organisational form and as between equity and debt.

To this proposition there are objections of practicality and of principle. On the practicality side this arrangement would work satisfactorily for distributed profits, but what about undistributed profits? These are, in principle, the property of the shareholders. If all personal income were taxed at a flat rate, then that rate could be applied to undistributed profits; but where personal income is subject to more than one rate, what rate should be applied to undistributed profits? All the possible ways of trying to tax shareholders on undistributed profits have unattractive features: to attribute a share of undistributed profits to each shareholder and tax it according to their individual income tax rates would be an administrative nightmare; to tax undistributed profits at a flat rate according to some assumed average tax rate would be at best an approximation, generous to rich shareholders and hard on poor ones; to require companies to distribute all their profits would leave them without commercially necessary reserves.

Then there are the objections of principle. On the one hand it can be argued that undistributed profits, whilst nominally the property of the shareholders, should not be taxed to the full weight of the personal income tax rates because the shareholders cannot get their hands on these profits; they therefore have less value to the individual shareholder than distributed profits and should be taxed less heavily. On the other hand it can be argued that it is reasonable to tax both distributed and undistributed profits at a higher rate than other personal income because the company shareholder enjoys an advantage over the individual business proprietor or partnership in that the shareholder enjoys the privilege of limited liability.

But that, in turn, raises the question whether there would be any logic in gearing the payment for this advantage to the level of profit.

Again there are those who regard the company as a tax entity in its own right and consider that the tax on corporate income should be completely divorced from that on personal income. According to this philosophy, profits should be taxed the same whether distributed or undistributed – the so-called classical system; distributed profits are then taxed in the hands of the shareholders at their personal income tax rates. Opponents have objected to the 'unfair double taxation of dividends'. Alternatively it may be argued that undistributed profits are favourably treated. Whether that favourable treatment also applies in relation to the taxation of alternative forms of business, like partnerships, or alternative forms of capital, like debt, depends on the rate of corporation tax.

Other efficiency considerations come into play. Advocates of the classical system have argued that it increases investment: the combined corporate and personal income tax paid on dividends is much higher than the tax paid on retentions; therefore it is argued that, with the classical system, companies will retain and invest more. The opponents have replied that companies will not necessarily retain more – they may alter their pay-out ratio to maintain dividends and keep shareholders happy. Moreover, if they do retain more they may not use their retentions wisely; they will tend to reinvest in their own businesses, whereas shareholders re-investing paid-out profits would be seeking the highest return. Moreover low payouts reduce the facility of the capital markets to provide new capital for new and expanding firms, which are likely to be the innovative and efficient ones. In other words, if the classical system does increase investment, the investment lacks quality.

The position is further complicated by the presence or absence of capital gains taxes – and the terms of these taxes – which may tax increases in share values arising from retained profits; from different policies which countries may wish to pursue in relation to the taxation of foreign investment, both investment by their residents abroad and investments by foreigners in their own country; and from the fact that the tax base, corporate profits, can differ markedly between countries where there are significant divergencies from the concept of economic profit as a result of tax expenditures.

Above all, perhaps, the situation is confused because economists have failed to provide clear guidelines and answers for the politicians on the various questions raised. As Head writes, 'Company taxation has long been among the most controversial and inconclusive areas in the public finance literature.' (Head, 1997). There is no agreement on the incidence of company taxation – how far it falls on the shareholders; how far it may be passed back to suppliers or passed forward to customers. The 'traditional view' on the 'double taxation of dividends' has been challenged by a 'new view' that the effect is capitalised in a lowering of share prices and that to introduce dividend relief would simply give a bonus to existing shareholders. (For a comprehensive review of the arguments, see Head, 1997 and Cnossen, 1997.) Empirical studies have failed to provide indisputable answers.

It is hardly surprising, amid this *mélange* of factors, that politicians, affected also by ideology, pressure groups and *ad hoc* influences, have responded differently in different countries. Table 4.4 attempts to record some of the most significant features of the corporate income tax in the fifteen largest advanced countries; in particular, as well as tax rates and revenues, it classifies countries according to the extent of dividend relief. At one extreme is the classical system with no relief for dividends; at the other extreme is the situation of full relief on dividends – where the company is treated simply as a conduit – a pass-through of corporate equity income to be taxed fully at the marginal income tax rate of the shareholder – but, in practice, only in relation to distributed profits. Then there are a variety of stages in between where there is some but not full relief for shareholders of the corporation tax on distributed profits.

This relief may be given in a variety of ways. In principle it may be given at the company level by allowing dividends as a deduction from corporate profits, as in the case of interest, or by taxing distributed profits at a lower rate. Neither method applies to the fifteen countries except that Germany has a split rate as well as an imputation system. Four of the fifteen countries employ the classical system. The most common form of giving relief amongst the remainder is the imputation system, whereby all or a proportion of the corporation tax on dividends is 'imputed' to the individual shareholder and allowed as a credit against his or her personal income tax. Where relief is given by means of a flat rate income tax, the extent of dividend relief depends on the marginal tax rate of the individual shareholder (hence the designation 'various' in column 4 of the table). Under the flat tax approach all corporate profits are taxed to corporate income tax, but dividends are not accumulated with the rest of personal income tax but taxed at a flat rate below the top income tax rate. (For a full account of the various ways of giving shareholder relief, see Cnossen, 1997).

Table 4.4
Features of Corporate Income Tax in Fifteen OECD Countries

(1)	(2)	(3)	(4)	(5)	(6)	(7)
Country	Rate of Central Government CIT (excluding col(3)) 1998/1999 %	CIT at Sub-Levels of Government & Surcharges	Extent of Dividend Relief	Form of Dividend Relief	Revenue Contribution of CIT at all Levels of Government, 1997 as % of total tax	as % of GDP
Australia	36	n/a	Full	Imputation	14.6	4.4
Austria	34	n/a	Various	Separate tax	4.7	2.3
Belgium[a]	39	3% surcharge	Nil	n/a (classical)	7.5	3.4
Canada[ace]	28 (21)	Various provincial rates; 4% surcharge	Close to 100%	Modified imputation	10.3	3.8
Denmark	32	n/a	Various	Separate tax	5.2	2.6
France	33.3	Maximum surcharge of 20%	Partial	Imputation	5.8	2.6
Germany	40 undistributed 30 distributed	5.5% surcharge	Partial	Split rate and imputation	4.0	1.5
Italy	37	n/a	Full	Imputation	9.5	4.2
Japan[ab]	34.5	Various local tax rates	Partial	Special tax credit	15.0	4.3
Netherlands	35	n/a	Nil	n/a (classical)	10.5	4.4
Spain[ab]	35	Small local annual registration surcharge	Partial	Special tax credit	7.8	2.6
Sweden	28	n/a	Limited	Only for small companies	6.1	3.2
Switzerland[b]	8.5	All cantons at varying rates (av. 14%)	Nil	n/a (classical)	5.9	2.0
UK[ad]	30	n/a	Partial	Imputation	12.1	4.3
USA[ab]	35	Most states max. 12%	Nil	n/a (classical)	9.4	2.8
				Unweighted average	**8.6**	**3.2**

Notes:
[a] Lower or graduated CIT rates apply to lower amounts of profits or small businesses in Belgium, Canada, Japan, Spain, United Kingdom and United States and in some Swiss cantons.
[b] In Japan, Switzerland and the United States, the local tax is deductible in assessing profits for the central tax as is the annual local registration surcharge in Spain.
[c] The rate in brackets is for manufacturing or processing operations.
[d] Rate as from 6 April, 1999.
[e] Provincial rates are a percentage of federal rate: maximum combined rate, with surcharge is 46.12 (eg New Brunswick).

Sources: IBFD, 1999; OECD, 1999; KPMG, 1999.

Apart from the effect of surcharges, central government corporate tax rates in the fifteen countries are all below 40 per cent; rates were markedly reduced during the tax reform of the 'eighties and the tendency has been for them to creep downwards since then (see chapter 9). In a number of countries corporate income tax is levied at sub-levels of government. The contribution of corporate income tax to total tax revenue is significant, but not huge: a maximum of 15 per cent (Japan) with an unweighted average of 8.6 per cent. Too much attention should not be given to inter-country comparisons of yield because of differences in the forms of business organisation between countries. Also it should be recalled that, as profit is a residual, the yield of the corporate income tax is particularly volatile in response to changes in the business cycle.

CHAPTER 5

CONSUMPTION TAXES

Introduction

In Chapter 4 we looked at one way in which consumption could be taxed, ie the direct expenditure tax. Other ways of taxing consumption are listed below.

(1) Taxes on consumption goods and services themselves. This category covers both taxes levied at the consumption stage and those levied at an earlier stage in the production chain, but where the tax is expected and intended to be passed forward to the consumer. Taxes on goods and services are the most important category of consumption tax and we concentrate on them after a brief review of other categories.

(2) Fiscal monopolies and public utilities. As an alternative to an excise duty a government may produce or/and distribute certain goods and sell them at a higher price than they would have been sold untaxed in a competitive market. The profit becomes government revenue and could be regarded as equivalent to an excise tax. Examples of goods which are or have in the past been fiscal monopolies are tobacco products, alcoholic drinks, salt, matches, playing cards and oil products. It can also be argued that, where a public utility supplying water, electricity or gas is publicly owned and the government requires the utility to operate at a profit, which goes into general government revenues, the position is similar to a fiscal monopoly.

(3) Licences to supply, own or use certain goods or services. Governments may sell licences to allow private enterprises to supply certain goods or services (eg supply liquor or operate betting shops); or to permit people to own or use certain 'goods' (eg a dog, gun or television) or do certain things (eg fish or hunt). The revenue from many of these licences is small and often the most important purpose is control. For OECD countries the most important from a revenue view point is motor vehicle licences, which can be regarded as an alternative to higher excises on cars or motor fuel, as well as providing a mechanism of control.

(4) Other taxes or regulations which may contain an element of consumption taxation. Elements of consumption taxation can be found in taxes not obviously levied on consumption. In particular a tax which is levied on the annual value of domestic property and where the legal liability is on the occupier (like the local rate levied in England before 1990 – see above, p. 29) is, in effect, a tax on the consumption of house room. Again, in so far as a corporate income tax (or even a personal income tax or social security contribution) is passed forward into prices, it contains an element of consumption tax. This brings us into the difficult and disputed area of the effective incidence of taxation. In this book we conform to the general practice by which property taxes are treated as a form of capital tax and 'consumption taxes' are confined to the direct expenditure tax and the first three categories listed above.

Taxes on Goods and Services

Taxes levied on the sale of goods and services are the most obvious and most important way in which consumption is currently taxed, though some such taxes may also include elements of taxation of investment and intermediate goods.

Apart from customs duties and export taxes, they can be divided into two categories (1) taxes on selective goods or services, generally called excises (or excise taxes or duties) and (2) sales taxes. The borderline between them is not entirely clear cut, but with excises the goods to be taxed are normally specifically and individually enumerated, whereas general sales taxes are defined in a comprehensive manner with the exceptions enumerated.

Excises

Excises are typically 'specific', ie the tax base is related to some physical characteristic of the product (eg weight, volume, number) but they may be *ad valorem*, ie proportional to price, and occasionally (as with cigarette duty in the European Union) the tax base is a combination of the two. Specific taxes may have advantages in relation to control (eg the excise officer can measure the amount leaving the factory or warehouse) but they have the disadvantage that in inflationary times their yield falls in real terms unless the rates are continually adjusted for rises in the cost of living index.

Virtually all countries levy excises and some excises, notably on tobacco products, alcoholic beverages and on motoring (by means of registration licences and motor fuel products) are virtually universal. When he wrote his seminal work on excise systems, Cnossen estimated that some 70 per cent of excise receipts derived from these traditional excises (Cnossen, 1977). The position is unlikely to have changed much since then, but it could if the carbon tax were widely adopted (see below).

Why should excises be so popular with governments? The reasons are not hard to find. If appropriately chosen they are good revenue yielders and with low administrative and compliance costs. A study in the United Kingdom (Sandford, 1989, p. 168) estimated the costs to Customs and Excise of administering hydrocarbon oil duties, tobacco taxes and taxes on alcoholic beverages taken together, were 0.25 per cent of the tax revenue they generated and the compliance costs were 0.20 per cent – at a time, 1986-87, when the administrative costs for all taxes were estimated at 1.16 per cent and the compliance costs at 2.52 per cent. Since then the United Kingdom tax rates on both hydrocarbon oils and tobacco products have increased in real terms, so the current cost:revenue percentages would almost certainly be lower.

In developing countries excises may be particularly valuable; as Cnossen stresses, 'excise systems may contribute substantially to certainty in taxation. By focusing on single commodities and prescribing in detail control and collection procedures that are attuned to the peculiarities of each production process or the way in which a service is rendered, the policy-maker leaves no doubt who should be taxed and to what extent. No room is left for an arbitrary determination of tax liability' (Cnossen, 1977, p. 121).

From the revenue point of view the characteristics of commodities most suitable for excises are large sales volume, few producers, ready definability and inelastic demand – which implies no close substitutes. Moreover the more inelastic the demand the less the 'excess burden' of the tax in distorting consumers' choice and hence also production patterns (Sandford, 1992, pp. 193-94).[1]

The three main excises – on alcoholic drinks, tobacco, motoring – all share these production and demand characteristics; hence their popularity with governments. But if their use is near universal there are major differences of tax rates even within an excise category which are explained by domestic circumstances. Thus, it is no accident that Australia, France,

[1]For a fuller account of the incidence and 'excess burden' effects of excises, see Cnossen, 1977, pp. 56-8.

Germany, Italy, Luxembourg, Portugal and Spain, all big wine-producing countries, have nil or very light duties on table wine and tax spirits much more heavily (O'Hagan and Reilly, 1995, p. 75); and that Australia, Canada, New Zealand and the United States, all countries with a relatively low density of population to land area, are all at the lower end of the tax rates on motor vehicle fuel (OECD, 1996, pp. 19-21).

In addition to the revenue purpose of excises, there may be a particular justification for excises on particular products. A number of, often controversial, arguments have been advanced to justify particular excise taxes. We look at three main ones here. (For additional arguments, see Cnossen, 1997, especially pp. 8-9).

Special Reasons for Excise Taxes

(1) To discourage the over-consumption of products which may harm the consumer or others, such as tobacco and alcoholic drinks. Whilst these arguments can be used with some validity in respect of both these products, it should be noted that tobacco was heavily taxed in many countries before it was recognised to have harmful effects on health; and that moderate consumption of alcohol may be beneficial to health. Moreover, if the health argument for taxing alcoholic drinks were the over-riding consideration, because excess of *alcohol* is what damages health, we would expect the level of tax on different alcoholic drinks to be proportional to the alcoholic content – but this is very far from the case, see the above paragraph. (For an analysis of the various arguments regarding the taxation of alcoholic beverages, see O'Hagan and Reilly, 1995; and in relation to tobacco, see O'Hagan, 1998.)

(2) To alter the distribution of income by taxing 'luxuries' more than 'necessities'. This can be attempted either by a higher rate of general sales tax or by a separate excise. The problem here is to define, satisfactorily, what is a luxury and what a necessity. The rich may spend more than the poor on items like jewellery and cosmetics, but even the poor buy cheap versions. Consumer durables, for example electrical goods like television sets and videos, have attracted excises, but the poor may not regard such items as luxuries; and certainly the luxuries of today become the necessities of tomorrow. Cnossen concludes from his extensive analysis of excise systems that, while not an ideal index, 'In many developing countries almost certainly some progressivity can be imparted through the heavy taxation of expensive cigarettes, liquors, refined sugar, expensive

clothing ... gasoline, passenger cars, foreign travel, hotel rooms, restaurant meals, admissions and club dues... In high-income countries that have reasonably administered global progressive personal income taxes, the income distribution role of excise systems is very limited, if it exists at all' (Cnossen, 1977, pp. 54-55).

(3) To seek to allow for externalities, to ensure that, where there is a social cost over and above the private cost of production or consumption, the producer or consumer pays something nearer the full cost. This case for an excise tax was first advanced by Pigou early in the 20th century (Pigou, 1920). Economists refer to differences between private and social costs as externalities. To give some examples: on the production side, to quote a time-honoured case, a factory which belches black smoke into the atmosphere causes costs to the community in terms of higher laundry bills and increased medical expenditure, not taken account of by the factory owners. Innocent bystanders are meeting part of the costs and production is larger than if all the costs were being met by the producer. A tax on the product can counteract the effect of this misallocation of resources. Ideally the tax should be such as to equate the marginal social cost with the marginal revenue and the proceeds of the tax should be used to compensate the local victims – but this can at best be achieved only as an approximation. On the consumption side, taxes on tobacco have been justified on the grounds that smoking puts up medical bills and, where there is a national health service free (or subsidised) at the point of access, smokers create costs for the rest of the community. (There is a counter argument, however, that, because smokers on average die earlier than non-smokers, there is a saving on state retirement pensions which exceeds the additional cost to the health service.)

The externality argument has been given a major extension by the recent emphasis on 'green' or environmentally friendly policies. Taxes have advantages over 'command and control' policies in that they are flexible and not only discourage the consumption or production of the product in question but also act as incentives to substitute eco-friendly alternatives.

Specific excises to achieve environmental objectives have been levied on a number of products by various countries, for example:
*   agricultural fertilisers in Austria, Finland, Norway and Sweden;
*   shopping bags made of plastic or paper in Belgium;
*   drinks sold in disposable containers in Denmark, Finland and Sweden;

- gases used as aerosol propellants (eg CFCs) in Denmark, Finland and the United States;
- waste disposal in landfill sites in the United Kingdom, intended to encourage businesses to produce less waste and engage in more recycling.

Much of the emphasis has been on road transport because of its range of environmental externalities: noise, atmospheric pollution, the effect of road building on the natural environment, accidents, congestion and the wear and tear on publicly-owned roads. Because road transport is already subject to a number of different taxes in most countries – sales taxes on new cars, vehicle registration charges, motor fuel taxes – the pursuit of environmental objectives has mainly taken the form of increasing the rates and changing the structure. An example of rate changes is the United Kingdom policy of increasing motor fuel taxes annually by more than the rate of inflation. Tax structures have been changed in various ways. Registration charges and taxes on new vehicles have been differentiated according to their environmental attributes, eg higher charges with size of engine or/and weight of vehicle; lower charges where a catalytic converter has been fitted. Thus, for example, in Austria, the motor vehicle tax is based on engine power of passenger cars, with a differentiation between catalyst and non-catalyst cars; on loading capacity for trucks; and on net weight for buses (OECD, 1996). Lead free petrol is commonly taxed at a lower rate than leaded petrol; this practice is followed by all the European members of OECD except Greece, Iceland and Austria which, in 1993, replaced a tax discrimination against leaded petrol with an outright prohibition on its use (OECD, 1996). Some of the threats to the environment are international in their impact, most notably, global warming. Carbon dioxide emissions from the use of fossil-fuel energy are the most important man-made contribution to global warming. Coal, gas and oil contain carbon and combustion of these fuels releases this carbon into the atmosphere as carbon dioxide (CO_2). Many countries signed agreements at an international conference in Kyoto setting targets for the reduction of their carbon dioxide emissions.

This situation has generated particular interest in the idea of a carbon tax. A carbon tax is designed to tax CO_2 emissions indirectly by taxing the fuel which gives rise to them. Fortunately the proxy is a good one. In principle the tax rate on the fuel should vary with its carbon content, so that, for example, fuels with a higher carbon content per unit of energy, such as coal, bear a higher tax burden than fuels with a lower carbon content per unit of energy, like natural gas.

Taxation lends itself particularly to this issue. The use of fossil-fuel energy is so pervasive in the economy that regulation would be extremely difficult; taxing the fuel reduces the demand for the products and also encourages the use of the least carbon content fuels, as well as innovation with non fossil fuels. As the tax required to fill its eco-purpose will need to be high, it will generate revenue to permit significant tax reductions elsewhere. (For a fuller account of a carbon tax and some of the problems to which it gives rise, see Smith, 1998.)

A carbon/energy tax was proposed by the European Commission in 1991, but met with strong opposition from some member states and has not been implemented. So far, with the principal exceptions of the Scandinavian countries, governments have preferred to try to meet their target obligations by traditional measures rather than tax measures. But, if the problems of global warming become more serious, that may well change.

According to the OECD, (1996, p. 13) Norway leads the field in environmental taxes (11 per cent of total tax revenue, 5 per cent of GDP) with Denmark next (7.3 per cent and 3.7 per cent respectively). In Finland and the Netherlands environmental taxes also show a growing importance. There can surely be little doubt that excises for environmental purposes are set to increase; to quote from the OECD: 'Explicit environmental considerations tend to play a growing role in the design of tax reforms' (OECD, 1996, p. 13).

The first part of table 5.1 shows the contribution to revenue from specific goods and services (excises) in 1965, 1990 and 1997 for the fifteen largest advanced countries. The dates are chosen because 1965 was the first year in which OECD collected these statistics, 1997 is the latest year for which the statistics are available at the time of writing and 1990 can be taken to mark, very approximately, a change in trend. Between 1965 and 1990 the revenue contribution from excises fell markedly; overall as a percentage of tax revenue it dropped by almost exactly one half and this major decline affected all fifteen countries. Since 1990, overall, this decline has been stemmed, with the average remaining at much the same level (7.1 per cent in 1990, 6.8 per cent in 1997). Indeed, whilst modest decline continued in some half dozen countries, in the remainder the decline ended and, in Denmark, the Netherlands and the United Kingdom it was reversed. These three countries have been to the fore in taxing for environmental purposes.

Table 5.1 Trends in Consumption Taxation
Fifteen OECD Countries

	Taxes on Specific Goods & Services as Percentage of Tax Revenue			Taxes on General Consumption as Percentage of Tax Revenue		
	1965	1990	1997	1965	1990	1997
Australia	22.7	15.3	13.8	7.4	8.0	8.4
Austria	18.0	9.0	8.2	18.7	20.8	18.6
Belgium	13.0	8.4	8.4	21.1	16.1	15.2
Canada	16.8	10.6	8.4	17.8	14.0	13.9
Denmark	29.2	11.2	11.8	9.1	20.7	19.8
France	14.3	8.7	8.8	23.3	18.8	17.8
Germany	14.6	9.2	9.0	16.5	16.6	17.6
Italy	24.1	10.6	9.7	12.9	14.7	12.6
Japan	25.0	7.3	7.6	–	4.3	7.0
Netherlands	14.7	7.5	9.5	12.4	16.5	16.0
Spain	18.4	10.5	10.2	22.2	16.0	16.4
Sweden	19.2	9.2	8.0	10.4	14.9	13.6
Switzerland	19.0	7.1	7.0	9.4	10.1	10.0
UK	25.2	12.7	13.9	5.9	17.0	19.5
USA	15.1	7.1	6.8	4.8	8.0	7.8
Unweighted average	**19.3**	**9.6**	**9.4**	**12.8**	**14.4**	**14.3**

Source: OECD, 1999.

The first part of table 5.2 shows that, as a percentage of GDP, the decline in tax yield between 1965 and 1990 was much less – at under 30 per cent – than for tax revenue. Two main factors appear to have been responsible. On the one hand, the rates of the excises were not increased in line with the rise in prices in what was a very inflationary period, because of the unwillingness of governments to increase prices when they were seeking to combat inflation with prices and incomes policies. On the other hand, as a percentage of GDP, government expenditure and taxes increased by something like 40 per cent over the period 1965-1990, but the extra tax came from other sources than specific goods and services. The main contributors were personal income tax and social security contributions, but also, to some extent, as the second part of tables 5.1 and 5.2 show, taxes on general consumption. As a percentage of tax revenue these rose by 12 per cent between 1965 and 1990; as a percentage of GDP by over 60 per cent.

The averages for table 5.2 reveal that, as a percentage of GDP, the combined revenue from excises and general sales taxes was not very different in 1997 (9.5 per cent) than in 1965 (8.8 per cent); but the ratio between the excises and general sales taxes had been almost completely reversed. As a percentage of tax revenue the combined sales taxes were significantly less in 1997 (23.7) than in 1965 (32.1). To a further analysis of general sales taxes we now turn.

General Sales Taxes

General sales taxes can take a variety of forms and they may be either single or multi-rate. We can distinguish, in particular, between single stage and multi-stage taxes. Figure 5.1 illustrates the main forms.

Figure 5.1 Forms of General Sales Taxes

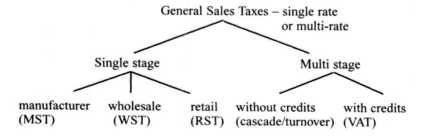

General Sales Taxes – single rate
or multi-rate

Single stage   Multi stage

manufacturer   wholesale   retail   without credits   with credits
(MST)   (WST)   (RST)   (cascade/turnover)   (VAT)

Table 5.2 Trends in Consumption Taxation
Fifteen OECD Countries

	Taxes on Specific Goods & Services as Percentage of GDP			Taxes on General Consumption as Percentage of GDP		
	1965	1990	1997	1965	1990	1997
Australia	5.1	4.5	4.1	1.6	2.4	2.5
Austria	6.1	3.7	3.6	6.3	8.5	8.2
Belgium	4.0	3.7	3.9	6.6	7.1	7.0
Canada	4.4	3.9	3.1	4.6	5.1	5.1
Denmark	8.7	5.3	5.8	2.7	9.8	9.8
France	4.9	3.8	4.0	8.0	8.1	8.0
Germany	4.6	3.4	3.3	5.2	6.1	6.6
Italy	6.2	4.1	4.3	3.3	5.7	5.6
Japan	4.6	2.3	2.2	–	1.3	2.0
Netherlands	4.8	3.3	4.0	4.1	7.3	6.7
Spain	2.7	3.6	3.4	3.3	5.5	5.5
Sweden	6.7	5.1	4.2	3.6	8.3	7.1
Switzerland	3.7	2.2	2.4	1.9	3.1	3.4
UK	7.7	4.6	4.9	1.8	6.2	6.9
USA	3.8	2.0	2.0	1.2	2.2	2.3
Unweighted average	**5.2**	**3.7**	**3.7**	**3.6**	**5.8**	**5.8**

Source: OECD, 1999.

Let us illustrate from the 24 member countries of OECD in 1994. None of them currently has a manufacturers' sales tax (MST) but the federal government of Canada did until the end of 1990. Australia currently (1999) has a wholesale sales tax (WST) but is due to replace it by a VAT (called a Goods and Services Tax – GST – to be operative from 1 July 2000). Apart from Australia, the OECD country to levy a WST most recently was New Zealand, which replaced it by a VAT (called a GST) in 1986. Both Canada and the United States have retail sales taxes (RST) but at provincial/state level. No OECD country currently has a turnover (cascade) tax but in the 1960s and early 1970s, this form of tax predominated amongst the countries which originally formed the EEC. As for VAT, all 24 OECD countries except the United States have now adopted it or are about to do so. Table 5.3 indicates the changes in these countries. Value added tax is probably unique in world fiscal history. A generation ago it was virtually unknown. Now it is approaching the universal.

In a book published in 1988, Alan Tait of the IMF cited over 50 countries which had adopted VAT and another 9 which had a modified form of VAT. Since then VAT adoption has proceeded apace and the number is now over 100. As well as OECD countries a majority of the countries which composed the former USSR and former Yugoslavia have adopted VAT or are in the process of doing so. VAT is also continuing to be adopted amongst the developing countries; most recently, a number of the sub-Saharan African countries have adopted VAT, are about to, or are seriously considering it. The obvious question is: Why have so many countries adopted VAT?

Influence of International Groupings or Agencies

Undoubtedly the spread of VAT has been hastened by the requirements of international groupings and the advocacy of international agencies. Indeed, there may even have been a 'bandwagon effect' – of keeping up with the Joneses; but it would be wrong to stress the bandwagon effect, for the experience of introducing VAT in both advanced and developing countries has not been invariably happy. For example, in Canada where the opposition was intense, there was something of a constitutional crisis and the government introducing it suffered a catastrophic defeat in the subsequent general election; in Ghana a VAT was introduced but had to be withdrawn because of the opposition.

Table 5.3
General Sales Tax Systems in the OECD Countries in 1967 and 1999

Countries	1st January 1967	1st January 1999	Date VAT introduced
Australia	W	W	Due July 2000
Austria	T	VAT	January 1973
Belgium	T	VAT	January 1971
Canada	M[a] + R[b]	VAT[a] + R[b]	January 1991
Denmark	W	VAT	July 1967
Finland	VAT[c]	VAT	October 1990
France	VAT[d]	VAT	January 1968
Germany	T	VAT	January 1968
Greece	M	VAT	January 1987
Iceland	R	VAT	January 1990
Ireland	W + R	VAT	November 1972
Italy	T	VAT	January 1973
Japan	None	VAT	April 1989
Luxembourg	T	VAT	January 1970
Netherlands	T	VAT	January 1969
New Zealand	W	VAT	May 1986
Norway	R	VAT	January 1970
Portugal	W	VAT	January 1986
Spain	T	VAT	January 1986
Sweden	R	VAT	January 1969
Switzerland	R[e]	VAT	January 1995
Turkey	None	VAT	January 1985
United Kingdom	W	VAT	April 1973
United States	R[f]	R	No VAT

Single-stage Taxes		Number of Countries[g] 1967	Number of Countries[h] 1999
M	Manufacture	2	0
W	Wholesale	6	1
R	Retail	7	2
Multi-stage taxes			
T	Turnover	7	0
VAT		2	22
No general consumption tax		2	0

Notes: [a] At federal level only   [e] Wholesale tax in certain cases
[b] At provincial level only   [f] At state and local level only
[c] Partial only. Full VAT in 1990   [g] Canada and Ireland counted twice
[d] Partial only. Full VAT in 1968.   [h] Canada counted twice.

Sources: Various.

The decision of the original six members of the European Economic Community to adopt VAT as the Community's general sales tax meant that other countries wishing to join the Community had perforce to follow suit. The European Union now comprises 15 states with others knocking at the door. But again it would be misleading to stress this compulsion unduly. Some governments, of which that of the United Kingdom was one, indicated that they would have introduced a VAT irrespective of their application to join the EEC, whilst others, such as Sweden, had introduced a VAT before there was any serious intention to seek membership.

It is true also that the IMF and possibly the World Bank have encouraged countries to think in terms of introducing a VAT as a broad-based consumption tax and this encouragement – and often technical assistance in introducing it – promoted the spread of VAT.

But many other countries, not influenced by the desire to be members of EEC and not subject to IMF influence, decided to adopt VAT. Moreover, we have to ask why the original EEC members favoured VAT and why the IMF has encouraged its adoption. The short answer is that, subject to one or two reservations which we shall consider later, it was believed to be a form of broad-based consumption tax superior to any others on offer.

What Need for a Broad-Based Consumption Tax?

Perhaps we need to examine why a broad-based consumption tax has been considered necessary. Amongst developed countries the need for a high revenue-raising consumption tax has become more urgent as public expenditure has risen and the pressure on existing taxes has grown. Thus, to pay for public expenditure growth, between 1965 and 1990, the (unweighted) average of tax revenue of the 24 OECD countries rose from 26 per cent of GDP at market prices to 37 per cent – a rise of some 40 per cent. In many countries this put particular pressure on the income tax, especially because revenue from excises and death duties was falling as a percentage of tax revenue and of GDP (see above and chapter 6).

At the same time, a series of studies was stressing the welfare loss from high marginal rates of tax (eg Browning, 1978; Stuart, 1984; Ballard, Shoven and Whalley, 1985) and the tax reforms of the 'eighties (discussed in more detail in chapter 9) with their emphasis on tax neutrality, were characterised by reductions in personal income tax rates, especially at the top end. The revenue was partly made good by broadening the income tax base through an attack on tax expenditures and tougher taxation of capital gains and fringe benefits; some governments, such as the USA and

Canada, also raised more from corporate income tax; but many governments also looked to broad-based consumption taxes for additional revenue (Sandford, 1993). This move was sometimes further encouraged by the belief that taxes on consumption rather than on income would encourage saving and might reduce evasion and avoidance.

As for the developing countries, most have been struggling to increase their tax take. For them personal income tax is not and cannot be a major component of tax revenue. They are countries where the vast majority are poor and illiteracy is high. Moreover, (as we saw in chapter 2) a major source of revenue, trade taxes, have declined in yield because of international pressures from GATT and the World Trade Organisation to reduce them in the interests of free trade. Thus, they too, have often sought some form of broader-based consumption tax to supplement excises.

Let us examine the various possible broad-based general sales taxes, as set out in figure 5.1 and consider their advantages and disadvantages.

Manufacturers' Sales Tax and Wholesale Sales Tax

The advantage of an MST lies in the relatively small number of businesses from which tax has to be collected. By taxing at the manufacturing stage rather than at later stages in the production and distribution process, it is easier and less costly to administer the tax, evasion can be more effectively controlled and compliance costs are lower in total, though they may not be lower for the firms which have to comply. (Some people might consider it an advantage that the tax is hidden; the final consumer is frequently unaware that he or she is paying tax. Others would regard this lack of transparency as a disadvantage.) These advantages may be decisive for a developing country.

But there are significant disadvantages, as was apparent with the Canadian federal MST which existed pre-1991.

(1) The tax has a relatively narrow base. All personal services, which form a growing proportion of expenditure in advanced countries, are necessarily excluded from the tax base. Consequently, for any given revenue, tax rates have to be substantially higher than with an RST or a VAT.

(2) The tax rate relates to the point of manufacture and not the point of consumption. Because mark-ups differ between products at the retail stage (eg higher mark-ups for valuable durable items like jewellery and lower for

mass produced items of regular and widespread consumption, like bread) a single rate at the manufacturing stage means varying rates as a proportion of the retail price. Any attempt to allow for this factor in the tax rate structure is inevitably imperfect and complicated. Thus consumers' choice, and hence production patterns, are distorted.

(3) Because it is levied at a single stage before the retail stage, the MST inevitably creates some distortion and manufacturers seeking to minimise the tax in various ways create further distortion.
   (a)   The MST favours goods bearing the brand of a retailer compared with goods sold under a manufacturer's trade mark, because, with the retail brand, advertising and distribution costs come after the tax point, whilst with the manufacturer's brand they come before. Consequently, manufacturers try to push as many activities as possible beyond the tax point by setting up separate companies for activities such as packaging, transportation to market, storage, insurance, market research. In the absence of the tax the manufacturer might undertake those activities himself.
   (b)   MST may distort industrial location. The cost of transporting materials to the manufacturing point is included within the tax base. The cost of transporting the finished product need not be so included. The MST may result, therefore, in location nearer to the source of raw materials rather than the market for the finished product, when, in the absence of the tax, location nearer the market might be more cost effective.

(4) There is no satisfactory way of securing neutrality in relation to international trade. Because the MST includes within the tax base some capital goods and intermediate products, some tax creeps into export prices and import substitutes. On the import side, because the effective tax rate to the consumer for home produced goods varies in an irregular way, it is not possible to know what is the proper rate to apply on imports to secure neutrality.

(5) Stocks held by wholesalers and retailers will carry MST. This raises their costs and creates windfall gains if tax rates are increased and losses if they are reduced. (In fact the traders argue that they never gain. If rates go up, some traders will sell off existing stocks at the old price and the others have to follow suit to compete. If rates go down, some traders will immediately start selling at the lower price, the rest have to follow suit and

make a loss.)

Thus, to sum up, the MST suffers from a narrow base and creates distortions, ie infringes the principle of tax neutrality in a variety of ways.

The WST has the same advantages as an MST compared with an RST or a VAT but not to the same extent. A WST may well involve more tax collecting points than an MST but far fewer than a VAT.

Likewise the WST has similar disadvantages to a MST but not quite to the same extent:
(1) The tax has a similarly narrow base because it excludes personal services.
(2) The effective tax rates to the consumer will differ because of different mark-ups.
(3) Attempts to avoid the WST by pushing activities beyond the tax point will create distortions, as with the MST, though the scope is less.
(4) It is similarly difficult to secure neutrality in respect of imports and exports.
(5) Retailers (though not wholesalers) will have to carry tax paid stock with its attendant disadvantages.

Essentially, for both the MST and the WST, these disadvantages occur from the location of the tax point at a stage in the production – distribution chain prior to the final consumer.

They do not apply to an RST or to VAT which, though it is collected multi-stage, is a tax on the domestic consumer.

The Turnover Tax

The turnover tax (cascade tax or cumulative tax) is a multi-stage tax without credits. In the late '60s and '70s such taxes existed in a number of countries, including Austria, Belgium, Germany, Italy, Luxembourg, the Netherlands and France and, until 1986, in Spain.

Under the turnover tax, tax is charged on a wide range of goods and services at all stages of production and distribution. Tax is generally chargeable, usually at low rates, whenever a sale is made by one firm to another and to the final consumer.

The advantage of the turnover tax is that it is relatively easy to administer. But it suffers from serious disadvantages.
(1) It involves tax levied on tax – the total amount of tax varying with the number of sales to the final consumption stage. Hence consumers' choice

is distorted.

(2) The tax distorts industrial organisation. Because tax is levied on every transaction, integrated businesses gain advantages over unintegrated businesses. It therefore promotes vertical integration – encouraging firms to undertake manufacturing, assembling, wholesaling and retailing operations simply to avoid the tax which would have been paid if these activities had been carried out by separate businesses. The tax therefore discourages specialisation and may conflict with competition policy. Moreover, the amount of tax on a product varies according to the degree of vertical integration; and the more the vertical integration the less the tax revenue from a given rate structure.

(3) The tax is not a tax on final consumption. It is levied not only on finished products but also on intermediate products and capital goods.

(4) It is not and cannot be, neutral in respect of foreign trade. Because similar goods bear different rates of tax according to the number of times they and their components have been bought and sold, export rebates and import charges have to be an average. Even if these averages are roughly correct, which is very difficult to check, integrated firms get an export subsidy whilst the unintegrated businesses fail to recover on their exports the full tax they have paid. International competition is thereby distorted. This was the prime reason that the EEC adopted VAT as the general consumption tax. Five of the original six members had turnover taxes, which did not permit the imposition of unambiguous border tax adjustments. It was also relatively simple to convert a turnover tax into a VAT – by allowing the deduction of input tax.

Comparison of RST and VAT

Given the big disadvantages of MST, a WST and a cumulative turnover tax, unless the administrative simplicity of these forms is the over-riding consideration, the real choice is between an RST and a VAT. Both are largely free of the disadvantages of the other forms of sales tax that we have outlined.

Both are taxes on domestic consumption. Although in one case the tax is collected single stage and in the other multi-stage, the tax charged to the consumer is the rate specified, not varying either because of the mark-up or the number of times a good changes hands. Both can include personal services within the tax base. In fact, if the rate(s) and coverage are identical, a VAT and an RST should have the same economic effects apart from any differences arising specifically from the different methods of collection. (An Appendix to this chapter gives a simplified picture of the operation of VAT and demonstrates this point.)

Comparison of RST and VAT

A VAT is collected at every stage of production and distribution. Each 'trader' (using that term to cover all those registered for VAT in any part of the system of production and distribution) in each tax period, pays tax on inputs, collects tax on output and hands over to the revenue authorities the difference between output tax and input tax. If, for any tax period, the input tax exceeds the output tax, the trader receives a refund. Exports are zero rated (ie there is no tax on them and input tax is refunded) and imports are charged the appropriate rate of VAT.

The RST is a single stage tax. Primary producers, manufacturers, wholesalers and retailers are usually required to be registered; but they only have to account for sales to non-registered persons (usually consumers) or for own personal use. Tax between registered traders is said to be 'suspended' until the final stage when goods are sold to unregistered persons. Registered persons have a licence number which has to go on the invoice when they are purchasing tax free.

Why then should one be preferred to the other? There are three main issues we need to examine in comparing VAT and RST. (1) the levels of administrative and compliance costs; (2) the vulnerability to evasion; (3) neutrality with respect to international trade.

In making these comparisons we have to rely largely on inference as there is little empirical evidence of the kind which would facilitate these comparisons.

(1) Administrative and compliance costs. On the face of things it would seem that the administrative and compliance costs of an RST are less than those of a VAT, but the difference is not as large as might have been imagined. Moreover, there is one consideration which could tip the balance the other way.

On the administrative side, it is likely that the same number of businesses need to be registered in respect of both taxes: under RST businesses which do not sell retail need to register in order to get an exemption licence. But, even if there are the same number of registered businesses, under RST there are not the same number of accounts to be checked. However, the difference is not as large as might be thought; in the United Kingdom it was estimated that 72 per cent of VAT registered traders engaged in some retail selling, including sales to their own employees (Sandford *et al*, 1981, p. 141).

Further, under RST no trader receives cash refunds, whereas under a VAT system this happens for traders in zero-rated goods, including exports. Where regular refunds have to be made, traders may, as in the United Kingdom, be allowed to make returns more frequently – which raises administrative costs; and it may also be considered that returns claiming refunds require extra careful examination.

On the compliance cost side more traders making returns means more compliance cost (though with offsets for the traders in the form of cash flow benefits). Additionally, VAT demands more extensive input records than RST (since under VAT tax payments to the revenue authorities are the difference between output tax and input tax). However, there is some offset to these costs in that these more extensive records may be used as managerial aids.

On these counts, the advantage would seem to lie clearly with the RST. However, a significant advantage of VAT over RST is that it permits a sizable small firm exemption without much loss of revenue, because tax on inputs is collected anyway. The higher the small firm exemption limit, the bigger the savings in both administrative and compliance costs.

(2) Vulnerability to evasion. It would appear that, whilst certainly not completely evasion proof, a VAT has advantages over an RST in its capacity to restrict evasion.

  (a) The VAT credit mechanism provides an audit trail. Purchases and sales under VAT require an invoice. It is on the basis of the invoice that a trader can recover input tax. In principle, up to the retail stage, purchase and sales invoices can be checked against each other. In practice a complete matching is hardly possible; but if suspicions of evasion are aroused, eg that a trader was over-stating input tax, a check can be made of the suppliers' sales invoices.

  (b) The VAT system has a self-policing element. Apart from the retail stage, where the purchaser cannot reclaim tax, the interests of buyer and seller, with respect to evasion, are opposed to each other; thus collusion is more difficult and less likely. To illustrate the point: the seller, who wishes to evade tax wishes to understate the tax he has received, so that he can retain some of it. The buyer, on the other hand, wants to overstate the tax he has paid because he can recover input tax. There is thus no way they can adjust the invoice to benefit them both.

  (c) The limitation of the two previous arguments is that they do not apply at the retail stage and this is generally the most vulnerable stage. However, with VAT, the tax authority only collects a proportion of tax at the retail stage; the essence of VAT is multi-stage collection, whereas under RST **all** the tax is collected at the retail stage.

It has been argued, that, whilst the revenue authority only gets a proportion of the VAT from the retail stage, the final consumer pays the full tax, so, in principle, the whole of the tax is at risk at the retail stage; if a retailer understated the tax collected and overstated the input tax credit, he could effect substantial evasion. In practice a retailer could not get away with this for long or to any considerable extent. The input tax is subject to the audit trail; moreover there are recognised mark-ups for different retail products – giving recognised ratios between input and output – and significant divergencies would arouse suspicion.

(d) A very significant advantage lies with VAT in respect of the considerable number of goods and services of mixed use – like a spade, which can be an input to a business or a consumption item for digging the garden; or a railway ticket, which can be for a business journey or a pleasure trip. Under VAT tax is always charged, whatever the intended use, which is no concern of the seller. If the good or service is a business input, the onus is on the purchaser to claim the tax credit. Under RST if the purchaser quotes an exemption licence number, no tax is levied. It is up to the tax authority to prove that the exemption claim was false.

False exemption claims are the vulnerable point in the RST. It is true that under VAT there is a particular potential source of evasion in false claims for tax refunds, which does not occur in an RST. But claims have to come from the purchaser of the goods, thus drawing the attention of the VAT authorities to potentially dubious cases which can be scrutinised and checked by the tax authorities. On the other hand, under RST a 'business' can make false exemption claims and then 'disappear', without its activities ever having been brought to the notice of the tax authorities.

(e) Joint audits of VAT and income tax as, for example, in Germany, or the exchange of information between VAT inspectors and income tax auditors, are probably easier and more appropriate with VAT than RST because of the closer link between value added and income.

On this issue the balance of advantage seems to lie clearly with VAT;

however, the lower administrative costs of the RST mean that more resources might be available to combat evasion; but this would then nullify the administrative cost advantage of the RST.

(3) Neutrality with respect to international trade
It is generally accepted that the credit mechanism of VAT and zero rating of exports, though not perfect, is superior to RST as a way of ensuring that tax does not creep into costs and therefore export prices and that domestic goods bear exactly the same tax as competing imports. Because of the problem of joint use, under RST some items like stationery, fuel, office furniture, computers, tend to be taxed and, when used by businesses, enter into costs.

Where VAT is a national tax, it is an advantage of VAT over RST that the tax (save in a free trade area) is collected on imports at the border. On the other hand, the fact that RST is not collected until the good is sold to an unregistered person (normally the final consumer) makes RST particularly useful as a state tax in a federal country; it is a natural destination-based tax.

Controversy on the Relative Merits of VAT and RST

In the 1980s the relative merits of VAT and RST were a matter of controversy, both in the economic literature and in the policies of countries. The conventional wisdom (as set out in Tait, 1988, p. 19) was that, at national level, the advantage might lie with an RST if rates are low; but as rates rise the advantage shifts to VAT: the administrative and compliance costs do not rise (or do not rise much) as rates increase and form a smaller proportion of the revenue; and the advantages of VAT in respect of evasion become increasingly significant.

The different views taken by the Australian and New Zealand Governments in the middle 1980s illustrate the differing attitudes to VAT and RST. The full arguments are set out in the Australian Draft White Paper on tax reform (Commonwealth of Australia, 1985, pp. 129-132) where the RST is referred to as a Broad Based Consumption Tax (BBCT) and the New Zealand Government publication *GST the Key to Lower Income Tax* (1985, pp. 11-13). However, the arguments are conveniently summarised in OECD 1988, as follows:

'The Australian Government took the view that the advantage of VAT in combating evasion had been overstated: the self-policing properties of VAT did not apply at the retail stage and if evasion, by marginally overstating purchases and understating sales, was indulged in at each stage in the chain, suspicions would not be aroused but the cumulative tax loss would be significant. Whilst the Australians accepted that exports and intermediate goods could be more readily freed from tax under VAT than under RST, they were impressed by the lower administrative and compliance costs which they expected with RST. The Australian Government, moreover, did not envisage a tax rate in excess of 12 per cent. An important consideration in the tax choice was the time needed to introduce each tax. The Commissioner of Taxation had estimated that it would take twelve months longer to introduce a VAT than an RST. Given a parliamentary term of three years and the Government's desire to see transitional problems resolved before the next election, this difference was seen as a significant factor in favour of RST.

'New Zealand, on the other hand, took the view that VAT was definitely superior to RST in combating evasion because of the smaller amount of tax collected at the retail stage, the reduced dependence on the collection of revenue from numerous small retailers, the more complete audit trail and the immediate taxation of imports.

'The relatively low level of RST elsewhere suggested that VAT had a greater potential for revenue than RST. In regard to administrative and compliance costs, the New Zealand Government took the view that these could be minimised by appropriate policy decisions, in particular exempting small taxpayers but otherwise having a comprehensive tax base with a single rate of tax.'

(OECD, 1988, pp. 107-8)

A few postscripts to this difference of opinion are appropriate.

(1) The New Zealand GST, whilst approved by only a minority of the population before the event, was approved by a majority once the full package, of which it was a part, was firmly in place; and whilst at first the New Zealand Nationalist Opposition opposed the tax and proposed major changes, they soon dropped these proposals (Douglas and Callan, 1987 and Douglas, 1989).

(2) The broad based consumption tax in the form of an RST met with

almost universal opposition at the Tax Summit organised by the Australian Government in 1986 and the proposal was dropped by Prime Minister Hawke (see chapter 9). There is at least an outside possibility that if, instead of an RST, the Australian Government proposal had been a VAT, it might have been successful as, unlike the RST, it would almost certainly have had business backing.

(3) *The Hawke Memoirs* throw an interesting light on the story, indicating that the crucial factor in the Australian Government's choice between VAT and RST was the shorter time the latter would have taken to introduce in a country where the maximum length of a parliament is three years. Hawke writes:

'Tax changes had to be considered, implemented and bedded down, all in the space of a three year Parliament. It was, for example, a timing problem that prevented the Government from opting in the White Paper prepared for the Tax Summit of 1st July for the most efficient consumption tax. The Government ended up preferring a retail sales tax and not the more efficient value-added tax.' (Hawke, 1994, p 300)

(4) It is also very significant that subsequent proposals for introducing a broad-based consumption tax in Australia have focused on a VAT (which, as in New Zealand and Canada is referred to as a GST) rather than an RST; and it is a VAT, not an RST, which is due to come into effect in Australia in July 2000.

Another recent convert to VAT from an RST is Switzerland, which changed over in 1995, after a long period of vacillating between the two (Due, 1994). Interestingly, the rate at which VAT was introduced was only 6.5 per cent.

Today there seem to be few, if any, proponents of the view that RST is superior, save as a state or provincial tax within a federal country.

The reasons for the attractiveness of VAT might be summarised as follows:

(1) It is a good revenue-yielder. Its wide base means that a small rise generates considerable revenue.

(2) It is neutral in its treatment of goods relatively to services; and, if a single rate is employed with minimum zero-rating and exemption, it achieves a practicable neutrality as between different products.

(3) It is a relatively effective mechanism for securing neutrality in

international trade.
(4) It is more evasion-proof than its principal rival, the RST.

There has emerged something of a consensus that VAT is the most efficient form of general consumption tax. Whilst it undoubtedly has disadvantages, notably high compliance costs and regressiveness, these can be minimised by appropriate policy measures.

Variations amongst Countries

Table 5.4 Comparison of VAT Rates in European Union Countries
1 August 1999

percentages

	Standard rate	Reduced rate[a]
Austria	20	10,12
Belgium	21	1,6,12
Denmark	25	
Finland	22	8,17
France	20.6	2.1,5.5
Germany	16	7
Greece	18	4,8
Ireland[b]	21	4,12.5
Italy	20	4,10
Luxembourg	15	3,6,12
Netherlands	17.5	6
Portugal	17	5,12
Spain	16	4,7
Sweden	25	12,6
United Kingdom[b]	17.5	5

Notes: [a] The Rates Directive (92/77/EEC) allows member states to have a maximum of two reduced rates, one of which may be below 5% provided that either (i) it was in force on 1 January 1991 or (ii) the standard rate was 13% or below at that time. It also allows member states to have an intermediate rate between 12% and the standard rate.
[b] Zero rate applies to a wide variety of goods and services.

If VAT has been conquering the world, nonetheless countries differ widely in the structure and rates they give their VAT. The consumption type VAT using the invoice system has become virtually universal, but within that system there is much variety. In many developing countries a modified form of VAT exists which, for example, may stop short at the wholesale or even manufacturers' stage. As between advanced countries differences are pronounced as to threshold (or registration level) coverage and rates, let alone administrative details such as filing and collection periods.

Thus, even within the European Union, where there have been repeated attempts at harmonisation, some countries eg Belgium, France and Italy have very low or non-existent registration (threshold) levels whilst in the United Kingdom the threshold is very high (£51,000 as of March 1999, or about $US82,000). The United Kingdom and Ireland have a range of zero-rated products whilst most countries restrict zero rating to exports and some use a lower rate for items like basic foodstuffs and 'merit' goods, such as books. European Union Directives currently lay down a minimum standard rate for members of 15 per cent and (subject to some exceptions) a minimum reduced rate of 5 per cent. Before this ruling a number of EU states, including Belgium, France and Italy, had higher rates of VAT. Currently (1999) some states, Denmark and Sweden, have standard VAT rates of 25 per cent, whilst others, like Germany, keep close to the prescribed minimum levels for EU members. The rates applicable to the European Union countries are set out in Table 5.4. Many of the differences owe much to historical and cultural factors and, sometimes, to the effectiveness of particular lobbies.

Annex to Chapter 5

A Simplified Model of the Working of VAT

Table 5A Simplified Example of Operation of a 10 Per Cent VAT

	Input Price	Value Added	Output Price	Paid to Revenue by	Amount
S supplies M	NIL	200	220	S	20 (20-0)
M buys from S and sells to W	220	400	660	M	40 (60-20)
W buys from M and sells to R	660	100	770	W	10 (70-60)
R buys from W and sells to C	770	300	1,100	R	30 (100-70)
C buys from R	1,100	–	–	–	–
			Total Revenue		**100**

S = Suppliers to M   R = Retailer
M = Manufacturer   C = Consumer
W = Wholesaler

The prime purpose of this Annex is to show how, apart from the method of collection including the credit mechanism, a VAT and an RST should have the same economic outcome. The model is an expository device to demonstrate this point. As an explanation of the working of VAT it is unrealistic in three ways: (1) It assumes that the initial supplier has no inputs. (2) It follows the same 'goods' through all the production and distribution stages. This, of course, is not how VAT works in practice; no goods have to be followed through, the trader is simply concerned with total inputs and total outputs in each charging period. (3) The example seems to imply that prices must necessarily rise by the amount of the tax, ie that each supplier is able to pass forward to the consumer the full amount of tax and that no burden falls on the supplier. Whilst the tax as the difference between market price and factor cost is always met by the ultimate consumer (and this is the same whether VAT or RST) the imposition of the tax may have altered factor cost, eg by reducing profitability in the short term.

Table 5A shows the multi-stage collection of the VAT. Had an RST been in place instead of a VAT at the same rate and coverage, no tax would have been paid until the good was sold to the consumer (assuming that all the other 'players' were registered). The price to the consumer would have been the same as with the VAT, the amount the Revenue received would have been the same, but all the tax (100) would have been handed over by the retailer. (Note that, in practice, businesses further back in the chain often make some retail sales, if only to their own employees, and would have to account for tax on them).

Where goods are zero rated for VAT, as with exports, no VAT is charged on output and VAT on inputs is refunded. Thus, suppose the goods are exported at the wholesale stage instead of being sold to R, W would charge no tax on the export sale (which would be at 700) and would receive a refund from the Revenue of the tax (60) paid on inputs.

Where goods are exempt for VAT no tax can be charged on outputs and there is no refund of input tax. This, of course, does not prevent the trader seeking to recover input tax in his price, but he cannot bill it as tax and does not have to account to the Revenue. Thus suppose the goods were exempt at the retail stage (eg because the retailer's turnover was below the registration level) the retailer would have paid 70 VAT on inputs and would, if he could, recover it in his price by charging his customers 1,070.

CHAPTER 6

CAPITAL OR WEALTH TAXES

Introduction

The chapter begins with a broad look at capital/wealth taxes – what the terms mean, what forms the taxes can take and their common objectives and problems. We then examine the mix of these taxes in OECD countries, consider the trends in the largest 15 advanced countries and suggest reasons for them. Thereafter we seek to answer the principal questions which the comparisons raise about each of the main types of wealth tax: the annual personal net wealth tax; death duties (with complementary gift taxes) and capital gains taxes.

Types of Capital/Wealth Tax

In fiscal terminology 'capital' and 'wealth' can be used interchangeably. Economists tend to think of capital as a stock of assets to be used for future production and wealth as a stock of assets to be drawn on for consumption – but the assets are the same. We generally talk of an 'annual wealth tax' and a 'capital gains tax' but we could equally well talk of an 'annual capital tax' and a 'wealth appreciation tax'. Similarly death and gift taxes can be called 'wealth transfer taxes' or 'capital transfer taxes'.

The characteristic of these taxes is that, in principle, they relate to the whole range or genus of assets: cash and bank balances; real property such as houses; personal property such as jewellery, pictures, furniture, cars and boats; stocks and shares; and business assets. All these assets, taken together, comprise the tax base of any of these forms of wealth tax, unless expressly excluded. Thus a real property tax, such as we discussed in chapter 3, is not, in this sense, a wealth tax as it relates to a particular category of wealth only, although that category forms part of the assets that form the base of a wealth tax. An annual personal net wealth tax is sometimes referred to as a 'net worth tax' – which conveys the impression of the tax being levied on the total net assets of an individual.

Wealth taxes fall into three broad categories: taxes on wealth stock, on wealth transfer and on wealth appreciation. Figure 6.1 indicates the possibilities.

Figure 6.1 Types of Capital/Wealth Tax

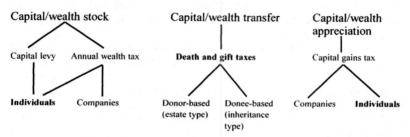

The taxes and taxpayers in bold are those on which we concentrate. No country currently imposes a capital levy, but it has been proposed and used as a once-and-for-all tax to help deal with the aftermath of a major disaster or upheaval, such as a war. An annual wealth tax is imposed by a very few countries on both companies and individuals; Luxembourg currently does so and Germany did, before 1997 – in both cases at low flat rates. To do so means that the same assets are taxed both in the hands of companies and as shares possessed by individuals and thus discriminates against the company form of business. We shall confine ourselves to the personal annual net wealth tax, which we shall henceforth refer to as annual wealth tax (AWT) for short. With capital or wealth transfer taxes (WTT) we are talking about taxes at death and on gifts. We shall say very little about gift taxes, which are primarily used in support of a death duty and bring in only a very small fraction of the revenue from death duties. An important distinction is whether a death or gift tax is levied on the donor or the donee; in the case of death, whether the tax is on the taxable value of the estate (the property left at death) or whether it is levied on the value of the shares received by the individual beneficiaries.

As mentioned in chapter 4, capital gains are generally regarded by economists as a form of income. The argument for considering them with capital taxes rather than income taxes is that they have similar objectives to the other two forms of capital tax and also similar problems; so it is convenient and helpful to look at them all together. The capital gains of companies are usually treated as the equivalent of other business income and we confine our attention to taxes on the capital gains of individuals.

Objectives and Problems

Apart from revenue yield, there are two common objectives of each of the three types of wealth tax we are examining, although, for each, the emphasis is different. These objectives are horizontal equity, the equal treatment of those with the same taxable capacity and vertical equity, the heavier taxation of those of greater taxable capacity, usually interpreted as progressive taxation.

Wealth brings its possessor advantages over and above the income, if any, derived from it: security, independence, opportunities for advantageous purchase or borrowing on favourable terms; moreover any income derived is obtained without loss of leisure. To be horizontally equitable, the tax system should take account of the taxable capacity conferred by these advantages. This can best be done, ideally, by an AWT as a supplement to income tax. (Some countries have attempted to do this by taxing investment income more heavily than earned income, but this fails to take account of the advantages conferred by assets which yield little or no money income.) Alternatively, a death duty can be regarded as a 'long stop' way of taking account of these advantages of wealth. A capital gains tax (CGT) is required for purposes of horizontal equity so that gains are treated as, or nearly as, other forms of income.

The vertical equity argument rests on the value judgment that the tax system should be used to diminish, or at least constrain the growth of, income and wealth inequalities. The most powerful taxes for this purpose would be a heavy and progressive AWT or/and a heavy and progressive death and gift tax which would limit the transmission of inter-generational inequality. However, even a modest AWT contributes to the desired objective since, by and large, it is the rich who own wealth and as a result of its threshold even an AWT at a single rate has an element of progression. Similarly a CGT would, by definition, only apply to those with capital, and, if the rates followed the lines of a progressive income tax, it would constrain inequalities.

The common problems of wealth taxes are two-fold – disclosure and valuation. High value items of low bulk are especially difficult for revenue authorities to locate. As to valuation the basic problem is that, for many of the assets which form the tax base, unlike income tax or sales tax, there is no market value arising from an economic transaction to give an objective valuation at the time it is required. Consequently, for many assets, either special valuations have to be made solely for tax purposes, or the problem is circumvented by using market valuations in relation to a different time from that which is ideally required. Both these measures create difficulties which, as we shall see later, go some way to explain different country practices.

Forms of Capital/Wealth Taxation in OECD Countries

Table 6.1 sets out the forms of wealth taxation as in 1999 of the 24 countries which were members of OECD in 1994. The table requires some explanation. W in the second column means that the country has an AWT. In the third column an E stands for an estate-type death duty (where tax is levied on the total taxable property left by the deceased) and H stands for inheritance-type tax (where tax is levied on the shares received by the beneficiaries). Denmark and Italy have an estate duty and an additional inheritance tax, but the inheritance tax does not apply to beneficiaries in the direct line or to a spouse of the deceased. Ireland has a very small probate duty (2 per cent above a modest threshold) but the main tax is a form of inheritance type known as a Capital Acquisitions Tax. The H and E for Switzerland reflects the practice of different cantons; most have an inheritance-type tax but a few have the estate type. The G for New Zealand stands for gift tax; New Zealand abolished its estate duty in 1993 but retained a gift tax. All the countries with death duties also have supplementary gift taxes, but gifts between individuals in the United Kingdom only become chargeable if the donor dies within seven years of making the gift. The United Kingdom is unique in another respect. Although the form of tax is an estate-type, it is called an 'Inheritance Tax', flouting the accepted terminology[1].

The most difficult tax to classify is the CGT, because of the enormous diversity of practice. We have attempted to distinguish those countries where only business capital gains are taxed (B); those where capital gains are taxed to income tax on a fairly comprehensive basis (I); and those where there is a separate CGT on individuals (C). It does not follow that

---

[1] From 1894 to 1974 the United Kingdom had a (donor-based) estate duty. By 1974 this tax (which applied to gifts only if made less than seven years before death) had fallen into disrepute and it had become a by-word for tax avoidance. When the Labour Government came to power in 1974, Chancellor of the Exchequer Denis Healey converted it into a (donor-based) Capital Transfer Tax by including gifts from the same donor and making the tax cumulative over a lifetime. After the Conservatives returned to office in 1979, first Sir Geoffrey Howe and then Nigel Lawson, as Chancellors of the Exchequer, proceeded to reduce the period of cumulation. Eventually, in 1986, Nigel Lawson abolished the gift tax element altogether for gifts between persons, save those made within seven years before death. This made the tax almost identical to the former estate duty (but with much lower rates on the largest estates). With the gift element largely gone, to call it a 'Capital Transfer Tax' was no longer appropriate. Presumably Nigel Lawson was reluctant to revert to the designation of the old, discredited, estate duty. In defiance of logic and accepted terminology, he therefore called it 'Inheritance Tax'.

where there is a separate tax it is necessarily less severe than where gains are taxed under the income tax code; it is rare for gains to be subject to the full income tax rates. The capital gains taxation in Italy and Portugal were particularly difficult to classify. In Italy certain gains from the disposal of real property are taxed to income tax whilst gains from the disposal of stocks and shares are taxed to a separate 'substitute' income tax. Gains in Portugal are taxed within the income tax code but in a completely separate schedule. The threefold classification for Switzerland reflects the differing practices of the various cantons.

Currently only nine (just over a third) of the 24 countries have an AWT, but five other countries have had an AWT and abolished it. Japan had an AWT for a few years just after the Second World War; Ireland introduced an AWT in 1975 but abolished it in 1978 following a change of government; more recently Austria (1994), Denmark (1997) and Germany (1997) abolished AWTs which were all of very long standing (over 75 years). The United Kingdom's Labour Government 1974-79 came close to introducing an AWT but, in the event, shelved it and the subsequent Conservative Government was opposed to an AWT and it gradually dropped out of Labour's agenda.

Of the current AWTs (1999) all are of long standing except those of France and Spain. France introduced the tax in 1982, repealed it in 1987 and then restored it in 1989. Spain introduced an AWT in 1978. These two wealth taxes differ significantly from the remainder. Most countries with AWTs maintained (in response to an OECD questionnaire) that the main objective of the tax was horizontal equity and little mention was made of reducing inequalities. France, however, stressed the argument of reducing excessive inequalities, whilst Spain indicated an objective of increasing the progressivity of the tax system (OECD, 1988). These differences are reflected in tax structure; the French and Spanish AWTs each have high thresholds (equivalent, in 1997, to over US$900,000 and over US$200,000 respectively) well above the average level and both have progressive rates with maxima above those of any of the other countries (1.8 per cent and 2.5 per cent respectively).

Before 1972 all 24 countries had WTTs. From Jan. 1, 1972, Canada abolished its estate duty at the federal level, leaving death and gift taxation to the provinces; but they engaged in a competitive reduction of rates to attract wealthy retired people, and ended up with no death and gift taxes at all. Much the same happened in Australia in 1979, where the federal estate duty was abolished and the states followed the lead of Queensland in abolishing their death and gift taxes.

Table 6.1 Forms of Capital/Wealth Taxation
in OECD Member Countries, 1999

Country	Annual Personal Net Wealth Tax	Transfer Tax at Death and on Gifts	Capital Gains Taxation
Australia	–	–	I
Austria	–	H	B
Belgium	–	H	B
Canada	–	–	I
Denmark	–	E and H	C
Finland	W	H	I
France	W	H	I
Germany	–	H	B
Greece	–	H	B
Iceland	W	H	I
Ireland	–	P and H	C
Italy	–	E and H	C/I
Japan	–	H	I
Luxembourg	W	H	I
Netherlands	W	H	B
New Zealand	–	G	–
Norway	W	H	I
Portugal	–	H	C
Spain	W	H	I
Sweden	W	H	I
Switzerland	W	H and E	C and I and B
Turkey	–	H	I
United Kingdom	–	E	C
United States	–	E	I

W   annual personal net wealth tax;
E   estate-type transfer tax;
H   inheritance-type transfer tax;
P   probate tax;
G   gift tax only;
C   separate capital gains tax;
I   comprehensive taxation of capital gains to income tax;
B   the taxation of capital gains of businesses (whether incorporate or not) but no comprehensive taxation of the capital gains of individuals.

Sources: IBDF, 1999; KPMG, 1999.

The New Zealand death duty may also owe its demise, at least in part, to what had happened in Australia, because of the free movement of nationals between New Zealand and Australia: following the abolition of the Australian death and gift taxes, New Zealand increased the threshold of its estate duty to such an extent that, in 1984, it yielded only a quarter of one per cent of tax revenue, down from 1.32 per cent in 1976 (Sandford, 1987); then, in 1993 the New Zealand government abolished the estate duty altogether, but left a modest gift tax in place.

Ireland's WTTs are of particular interest. Until 1974-5 Ireland had an estate duty (dating back to 1894). In 1974 a gift tax was introduced and in 1975 a tax on inheritances, replacing the estate duty. Initially there was lifetime integration of gifts and inheritances from the same donor in the new inheritance tax; from 1984 this was changed to any donor. Such a tax is often referred to as an accessions tax. Spain is another country where the death and gift tax combination have an additional element designed to make it more effective in curbing inequalities in wealth distribution; the tax rate takes account of the net wealth of the beneficiary (within four broad bands). On the estate duty side, the United States uses a unified estate and gift tax system that applies to the cumulative total value of all transfers made by an individual during life and at the time of death.

Typically, under the inheritance taxes, there are varying rate scales (or/and thresholds) according to the relationship of the beneficiary to the donor or deceased person. The estate duties of the United Kingdom and United States provide for tax free transfers between husbands and wives (subject, in the United States' case, to the test of citizenship).

Apart from the enormous variety of treatment for capital gains, not only by reference to the three categories indicated in the table, but also in the detail within those categories, the most interesting feature about the CGTs is their relative newness. No country had a CGT before the beginning of the twentieth century (although AWTs and death duties were common before 1900). By the time of the Second World War four of the 24 OECD countries had fairly comprehensive CGTs - Norway (1911), the United States (1913), Denmark (1920) and Sweden (1928). All the other comprehensive gains taxes date from 1945 or after; CGT is probably the next most rapidly growing tax after VAT; but comprehensive gains taxes are far from universal; and, when installed, are probably the taxes most subject to amendment.

Clearly this overall comparison throws up some major questions. Why do only a third of OECD countries have AWTs and why has the number been falling? Why are WTTs much more widely employed than

AWTs? (Until 1972 they were universal and, as we described above, have ceased to be so almost by accident); and why is there such variety in the forms of CGTs?

Before we tackle these major questions, we need first to look at the revenue derived from wealth taxes, which may offer some clues to help us answer these questions, and then sum up on the trends in wealth taxation which emerge from the overall survey.

Table 6.2 gives the yield of AWTs and WTTs for 1997, the latest year for which the figures are available at the time of writing (derived from OECD, 1999); they are expressed as percentages of tax revenue and of GDP. The yield of CGTs is not included because some of the countries which tax gains as part of income tax do not record separate figures for gains; in any case figures for capital gains taxes invariably under-estimate their contribution to revenue; one purpose of a CGT is to discourage the transfer of income to capital gains as a means of avoiding income tax. In so far as a CGT succeeds in this objective, it increases the yield of ordinary income tax.

What stands out most prominently from table 6.2 is how little revenue these taxes yield. Spread over the 24 OECD countries the average yield from AWTs is only 0.36 per cent of tax revenue; and if we confine our attention to the 9 countries which continue to have AWTs (ie excluding Austria and Germany who have abolished the tax but obtained some residual revenue in 1997) the average yield is less than one per cent of tax revenue. For only 3 countries does the yield exceed one per cent of tax revenue: Luxembourg, Norway and Switzerland, which easily tops the revenue yield table with taxes levied at the cantonal stage.

The position is somewhat similar for death and gift taxation; here too, only 3 countries, France, Japan and the United States, obtain more than one per cent of tax revenue from this source. Because WTTs are much more common than AWTs the average of the 24 countries is higher, but the 21 countries with death duties (ie omitting Australia, Canada and New Zealand) on average obtain significantly less from WTTs than the countries with AWTs obtain from that tax.

When the revenue from AWTs and WTTs is combined, they yield more than one per cent of tax revenue for 9 countries of which 7 are countries with both kinds of wealth tax.

Table 6.2 Revenue from Annual Personal Net Wealth Tax and Death and Gift Taxes in OECD Countries in 1997 as Percentages of Total Tax Revenue and GDP at Market Prices

	Annual Wealth Tax (a)		Death and Gift Taxes (b)		Total Wealth Taxes (a) + (b)	
	% of tax revenue	% of GDP	% of tax revenue	% of GDP	% of tax revenue	% of GDP
Australia	0	0	0	0	0	0
Austria	0.01	...	0.11	0.05	0.12	0.05
Belgium	0	0	0.75	0.34	0.75	0.34
Canada	0	0	...	...	...	...
Denmark	0	0	0.39	0.19	0.39	0.19
Finland	0.10	0.05	0.50	0.23	0.60	0.28
France	0.27	0.12	1.08	0.49	1.35	0.61
Germany	0.06	0.02	0.30	0.11	0.35	0.13
Greece	0	0	0.79	0.27	0.79	0.27
Iceland	0.97	0.31	0.28	0.09	1.25	0.40
Ireland	0	0	0.52	0.17	0.52	0.17
Italy	0	0	0.16	0.07	0.16	0.07
Japan	0	0	1.66	0.48	1.66	0.48
Luxembourg	1.75	0.81	0.33	0.16	2.08	0.97
Netherlands	0.55	0.23	0.67	0.28	1.22	0.51
New Zealand	0	0	0.01	...	0.01	...
Norway	1.25	0.60	0.22	0.10	1.48	0.70
Portugal	0	0	0.23	0.08	0.23	0.08
Spain	0.46	0.15	0.58	0.19	1.03	0.35
Sweden	0.57	0.30	0.19	0.10	0.76	0.39
Switzerland	2.57	0.87	0.88	0.30	3.45	1.17
Turkey	0	0	0.04	0.01	0.04	0.01
United Kingdom	0	0	0.56	0.20	0.56	0.20
United States	0	0	1.12	0.33	1.12	0.33
Unweighted average of:						
24 countries	**0.36**	**0.14**	**0.46**	**0.18**	**0.82**	**0.32**
9 AWT countries	**0.94**	**0.38**				
21 WTT countries			**0.53**	**0.20**		

Totals do not always add exactly because of rounding.
...   less than 0.005

Source: OECD, 1999.

Trends in AWTs and WTTs

A number of trends can be discerned in what we have so far examined:

(1) A decline in the number of AWTs. A decade ago exactly half of OECD countries had AWTs. Now the proportion is just over one-third.

(2) A decline in the number of death taxes; all countries had them in the 1960s; now only 21 of the 24 countries have death duties. Notably, too, all the decline has been of the estate type of death duty. In the 1960s, apart from the Swiss cantons and the countries which had a dual structure of both estate and inheritance tax, six countries, all the English-speaking ones, had estate duties. Three, Australia, Canada and New Zealand abolished them without replacement, whilst Ireland switched from an estate duty to a form of inheritance tax.

(3) The period since the Second World War has seen a big increase in the number of countries with fairly comprehensive capital gains taxes; in the 1980s there was also a movement to tighten up CGTs and make the rates more nearly akin to ordinary income tax rates, though the last few years have seen some reversal of this trend (see chapter 9).

(4) There has also been a substantial decline in the revenue contribution of AWTs and WTTs, but with a modest reversal of this trend over the past decade. This is clearly shown in table 6.3. Tables 6.3 and 6.4 show the pattern of combined yield for the 15 largest advanced countries, as a percentage of tax revenue and of GDP respectively, by looking at four years: 1965 is chosen as the first year of OECD revenue statistics; 1976 and 1985 are years for which the OECD undertook special studies on capital taxes (OECD, 1979 and OECD, 1988); and 1997 is the latest year for which the statistics are available (OECD, 1999).

As a proportion of total tax revenue the average yield of combined AWTs and WTTs over the 15 largest advanced countries almost halved, from 1.69 per cent of revenue in 1965 to 0.86 per cent in 1997. Decline in revenue contribution characterised all 15 countries with the notable exceptions of France and Japan, which both more than doubled the yield, with that of Spain being much the same in 1997 as in 1965, having fallen considerably in between.

Table 6.3 Combined Revenue from Annual Personal Net Wealth Taxes and Death and Gift Taxes as a Percentage of Total Tax Revenue for 15 OECD Countries for the Years 1965, 1976, 1985 and 1999

	1965	1976	1985	1999
Australia	2.74	1.37	0.01	0
Austria	0.85	0.73	0.51	0.12
Belgium	1.17	0.72	0.58	0.75
Canada	1.48	0.25	0.03	...
Denmark	2.09	0.81	0.92	0.39
France	0.56	0.46	0.85	1.35
Germany	1.53	0.76	0.42	0.35
Italy	0.85	0.20	0.23	0.16
Japan	0.71	0.85	1.19	1.66
Netherlands	1.86	0.85	0.94	1.22
Spain	1.09	0.65	0.49	1.03
Sweden	1.29	0.62	0.68	0.76
Switzerland	4.46	3.42	3.06	3.45
United Kingdom	2.62	0.88	0.64	0.56
United States	1.99	1.41	0.77	1.12
Unweighted average	**1.69**	**0.93**	**0.75**	**0.86**

.... less than 0.005

Source: OECD, 1979, 1988 and 1999.

Why this revenue trend? The following are suggested reasons, some of them somewhat tentative.

(1) The decline is more relative than absolute. Table 6.4 shows that the decline in tax revenue between 1965 and 1997 as a percentage of GDP was much less (29 per cent) than as a percentage of tax revenue (49 per cent) – indeed, as a percentage of GDP the average over the 15 countries has changed very little since 1976. Over the period as a whole, GDP has been growing, but, especially in the earlier years, tax revenue grew much faster. Between 1965 and 1997, for the fifteen countries as a whole, tax revenue as a percentage of GDP grew by 43 per cent (OECD, 1999, table 3); this extra revenue came not from wealth taxes but from income tax, social security contributions and, latterly, in some countries, from consumption taxes.

(2) Clearly, the decline owes much to the abolition of death duties by three countries and the abolition of three long-standing AWTs by three others more recently. As we have seen, the abolition of the death duties had an accidental element about it; we may understand more about the abolition of three AWTs in the 1990s when we have examined the pros and cons of annual wealth taxes in the next section. But these abolitions do not account for the whole of the decline; there were two new AWTs in France and Spain to offset, at least partly, those which were abolished. Moreover, with the exception of these two countries and of Japan, there was a significant decline in the proportion of tax revenue from all the remainder of the 15 countries whether or not they abolished a wealth tax.

(3) It seems likely that, over this period, incomes grew more than wealth – which would mean that, at any given tax rates, the revenue from income and consumption taxes would increase more than from wealth taxes.

(4) The growth in number, and often in severity, of CGTs over the period may have encouraged countries to ease the burden of other wealth taxes or, at any rate, not increase it. Indeed, with Canada there was a direct link between a new federal CGT, introduced in 1972, by which death was generally treated as a deemed realisation, and the federal government's relinquishing death and gift taxes to the provinces.

(5) Death duties and AWTs were a particularly fruitful field for tax avoidance by an increasingly sophisticated taxpayer population, doubtless encouraged in this direction by exceptionally high rates of death duties in some countries. For example, in 1969, in the United Kingdom, the top marginal rate of estate duty was 85 per cent, with a ceiling of 80 per cent of the total estate; the rates had remained largely unchanged between 1949 and 1969, during which period more or less continuous inflation had increased the real rates significantly by assimilating the same real value of estate into ever higher tax brackets; by the 'seventies the United Kingdom estate duty was being widely referred to as 'the voluntary tax', 'a tax paid by those who disliked their relatives more than they disliked the Inland Revenue'. Tax avoidance both reduced the tax yield and encouraged finance ministers to cut the rates; but once avoidance had taken hold, cutting the rates probably did not significantly diminish the extent of avoidance.

(6) Whilst not perhaps universal, witness the French and Spanish taxes, from the 'eighties there may well have been a decline in the desire to

reduce inequalities. Whilst this desire had characterised much tax reform in the 'sixties and 'seventies, in the 'eighties it was efficiency and economic growth that generally held sway (see chapter 9).

Table 6.4 Combined Revenue from Annual Personal Net Wealth Taxes and Death and Gift Taxes as a Percentage of GDP at Market Prices for 15 OECD Countries for the Years 1965, 1976, 1985 and 1999

	1965	1976	1985	1999
Australia	0.64	0.39	0	0
Austria	0.30	0.28	0.22	0.05
Belgium	0.36	0.30	0.27	0.34
Canada	0.38	0.08	0.01	...
Denmark	0.63	0.34	0.45	0.19
France	0.20	0.18	0.39	0.61
Germany	0.48	0.28	0.16	0.13
Italy	0.20	0.05	0.08	0.07
Japan	0.13	0.19	0.33	0.48
Netherlands	0.62	0.37	0.42	0.51
Spain	0.16	0.13	0.14	0.35
Sweden	0.46	0.30	0.34	0.39
Switzerland	0.92	1.07	0.98	1.17
United Kingdom	0.80	0.31	0.24	0.20
United States	0.51	0.40	0.23	0.33
Unweighted average	**0.45**	**0.31**	**0.28**	**0.32**

...   less than 0.005

Source: OECD, 1979, 1988 and 1999.

We turn now to the main questions thrown up by our survey of wealth taxes; the relatively small number of countries with AWTs; the much greater 'popularity' of WTTs, and the very varied treatment of CGTs.

Why so Few Countries with Annual Wealth Taxes?[1]

Why do so few countries employ an AWT? Why have five countries abandoned an AWT? Why have others dithered about it? France adopted

[1]For a fuller treatment of the issues discussed in this section, see Sandford, Willis and Ironside, 1975.

it, abolished it and then re-introduced it, while the United Kingdom Labour Government of 1974-79 promised it but then drew back. Of course there were particular reasons for most of these changes of heart; ideology played a part – governments of the Left are much more favourably inclined to AWTs than governments of the Right. Moreover, as we have seen in the tables 6.2 to 6.4, the yield from AWTs is generally trivial, which make them less attractive to introduce and easier to dispose of. For all that, the case for an AWT appears to be strong and likely to appeal to any government seeking to provide an equitable tax system. To understand the lack of popularity of AWTs amongst governments we need to explore more fully the pros and cons.

An annual personal net wealth tax, to give it its full title, taxes the value of the total assets of a person, less debts and after allowing for assets explicitly excluded or subject to favourable treatment. All AWTs contain exclusions; there is invariably a threshold, sometimes on an individual and sometimes on a family basis and also other exclusions or favourable treatment of particular assets for administrative, social or economic reasons.

Five arguments have been put forward to support an AWT of which the first two, which we have already mentioned, are the most important.

(1) Horizontal equity. An AWT is needed to supplement an income tax to take account of the additional taxable capacity conferred by wealth, irrespective of the income, if any, derived from it. The classical case for the AWT on horizontal equity grounds was put forward by Nicholas (later Lord) Kaldor in a report to the Indian government (Kaldor, 1956). He contrasted a beggar and a maharajah: the beggar has no income; the maharajah has no income, but a stock of gold and jewels. Under income tax, each would be taxed the same, zero. But the maharajah clearly has a higher taxable capacity than the beggar; hence the need for an AWT to secure horizontal equity. The same argument can be expressed in another way; an AWT is needed to tax assets like jewellery, pictures, antique furniture, which do not yield a money income but an income of satisfaction and which can, if desired, be converted into money.

The argument applies not only to nil-yielding assets. Two people may receive the same money income from assets of different value; then the person with the higher-valued asset has a bigger taxable capacity than the other, which is not taken into account by an investment income surcharge but is taken into account by an AWT.

(2) Vertical equity. An AWT can check or reduce inequalities of wealth and income. A modest AWT, such that income tax and AWT combined can be met from income, puts some constraint on inequalities; or the tax may be more radical, such that, after allowing for a reasonable level of consumption, the combined weight of income tax and AWT exceeds income – so that the tax can only be paid by encroaching on the taxpayer's wealth. In practice none of the OECD countries levies the extreme form of AWT. In the countries with the highest AWTs, France and Spain, a 'ceiling' provision restricts combined income tax and AWT to a maximum of 85 per cent, and 70 per cent, respectively, of income.

(3) Efficiency. An efficiency argument has been put forward by economists but does not figure amongst the reasons given by countries in the OECD survey (OECD, 1988). It has both a negative and a positive aspect. An AWT can be a partial substitute for income tax; then it is argued an AWT would have less disincentive effects than an equivalent tranche of income tax. The tax base of an AWT relates to past and not present effort, therefore it is not a disincentive to work if the object of the work is consumption. (The effect on saving may be a different matter, as we mention below.) The positive argument is that, because an AWT imposes a charge on wealth irrespective of the income from it, if any, the AWT acts as an encouragement to use assets more productively. Thus if a man owns land which is allowed to lie waste, he pays no income tax on it, but if there is also an AWT he will be taxed on its capital value and this will encourage him to cultivate it, or develop it, or sell it to someone who will cultivate or develop it. Similarly, an AWT may encourage people to transfer from nil-yielding assets, to income-yielding assets, or from low yielding assets to higher yielding assets (especially if the imposition of AWT has been associated with a cut in income tax). In the same way an AWT may discourage the holding of idle cash balances and encourage more efficient stockholding policies.

(4) Administrative. An AWT provides the tax administration with data that can help check evasion. Returns on wealth can be cross-checked with investment income returns and with data on inheritances and gifts.

(5) Extraneous. Where macro economic policy is imposing hardship on the poorer section of the community (as, for example, an incomes policy to combat inflation) the imposition of, or increase in, an AWT, may make the policy more generally acceptable because it is seen that the sacrifices

are not all on the poor. To take a completely different example, where, as in Spain, the government wishes to relate the rate of death or gift tax to the level of wealth of the beneficiary, AWT returns can establish the level of wealth without the need for a separate inventory and valuation.

These arguments constitute a strong theoretical case for AWTs. The case, however, is undermined mainly by a series of practical considerations stemming from the problems, already mentioned, of disclosure and valuation. In addition AWTs may have some adverse economic effects and raise some particularly difficult problems of how to treat certain important assets – though these are also fundamentally problems of valuation.

(1) Disclosure. Tax officers cannot be given the right of entry and search of people's houses. Thus for the reporting and valuation of items inside the house the tax authorities mostly have to rely on the honesty of the taxpayer. In Sweden, for example, the tax authorities accept that many valuable items inside the house go unreported and, when they are returned, it is often at a nominal rather than market value; and there is little the authorities can do about it. One outcome of this situation is inequity as between the honest and the less than honest. Under the Danish AWT (recently abolished) because of the problems of disclosure, the authorities took the view that 'the tax stops short at the door'; items inside the house were excluded from the AWT base.

But where does this leave the horizontal equity argument, when jewellery, valuable furniture, paintings are either excluded altogether or the tax on them largely evaded? The 'maharajah argument' begins to look very thin. In fact the exemption of, or substantial underpayment on, assets of high value inside the house can have the wholly perverse effect that more, rather than less, wealth goes into these kinds of assets in order to minimise the tax.

(2) Valuation. Valuations for AWT are taken on a particular date, eg January 1. Even for stocks and shares regularly quoted on the stock exchange this may work unfairly if the stock market falls thereafter. For most other assets, special valuations have to be undertaken specifically for tax purposes. With real property the common practice in well-ordered AWTs, as in the Scandinavian countries, is to undertake regular valuations every four or five years, which are then used for property tax purposes as well as AWTs. However, because the valuations are not annual, either by

custom or law valuations are set somewhat below the market level against the possibility of falling values between valuation dates. This often means that, in the year before a new valuation is due, the AWT valuation for real property is much below the market value. This discrepancy does not make for horizontal equity between the owners of real property and the owners of stocks and shares valued at market price.

Similar problems arise with the valuation of private businesses, where the task of valuation is complex and the tendency is to undervalue. Where valuations for AWT purposes are undertaken for assets such as antique furniture or pictures, the valuation is inevitably very problematic.

In the older established AWTs administrative costs are kept down by linking valuations to other taxes where possible and by using formulae valuations. If that is not done, as with the short-lived Irish AWT, the administrative costs are high and the compliance costs even higher (Sandford and Morrissey, 1985, pp. 106-23). So there is a major administrative cost to set against the administrative advantage of extra data collection.

(3) Economic effects. One economic detriment arises from the valuation problems we have just discussed. Where some assets are valued at market price and others at appreciably less, there will be investment distortion and consequent inefficiency. Moreover, it is all very well to argue that an AWT encourages the efficient use of resources by the transfer from nil or low-yielding assets to higher yielding assets; but what if the low yield is unconnected with inefficiency? A new business with good prospects will often make little or no profit in its early years: machinery and workforce have to be assembled, advertising and marketing put in place, and so on. All this takes time. During this period, whilst it is earning little or no profit, the business will pay little or no income tax; but, in the absence of special tax holidays (which create their own problems) it will be paying AWT – which is thus a deterrent to, or a drag on, a new business. Similarly, a well established and profitable business may lose its main market for reasons outside its control (such as the imposition of a tariff barrier) or suffer from the effects of a generalised recession. In these circumstances, whilst the burden of income tax is eased, the wealth tax hampers needed restructuring. (The depressed European market in the '90s almost certainly helped to account for the abolition of three European AWTs.)

If an AWT is more than very modest, with no ceiling provisions, it could also have significant detrimental effects on the growth of private businesses, on agriculture and on saving.

(4) Treatment of particular assets.   Two major forms of asset raise particular issues for an AWT. In principle there is a strong argument for including within an AWT base the capitalised value of pension rights. The case can be seen most clearly in its extreme form, if we contrast the situation of a businessman who puts all his savings into the business, planning to live on the sale proceeds on retirement, with that of a civil servant on a non-contributory, inflation-proof, occupational pension. Unless special provisions apply, if the value of pension rights is not included in the AWT base, the businessman pays AWT on the business assets during his working life and then on the assets he acquires to provide his retirement income from the sale proceeds of the business. The civil servant pays no AWT on pension rights during his working life nor on any capital sum which provides his retirement pension. But there are problems about taxing pension rights; they are not a marketable asset and cannot normally be given or bequeathed; the holder might die without realising them; and the current value of future pension rights is difficult to determine. Moreover governments have generally encouraged citizens to acquire pension rights by offering income tax reliefs and it would then seem strange to be taxing them. In practice no country includes the value of pension rights within an AWT base.

An even more disputable issue is that of the capitalised value of future earning power. Is it right in principle that this should be included? If so, how can it be done satisfactorily in practice? The argument can be seen most clearly if we contrast the position of a man with two sons, on one of whom he spends a large sum to send him to the Harvard Business School, whilst to the other he gives stocks and shares of the same value. The Harvard-educated son acquires substantial additional earning capacity on which he pays no AWT, whilst the other son pays AWT on the value of the assets he has been given by his father.

Even if the issue of principle is regarded as clear-cut (and not all would agree on that) the practical problems of including the capitalised value of future earning power within the AWT base are formidable. The value of future earning power cannot freely be exchanged for cash and is inseparable from the present owner; there is more uncertainty attached to it and it will have a shorter life than most capital assets. Added to which are the problems of measurement – such as what the future income is likely to be and what is the appropriate discount rate to arrive at the present value.

As with pension rights, no country includes the capitalised value of future earnings within the AWT base. But these exclusions raise questions about the horizontal equity of the tax.

It would be foolish to suggest that what may be regarded as esoteric arguments about capitalising future earning power, or even much less esoteric arguments about the value of pension rights, have played a significant part in influencing governments in not introducing, or in abolishing AWTs, though the arguments of economists on these issues may possibly have had some influence. Even without them the problems raised by disclosure and valuation and the possible economic detriments are enough to explain governmental hesitation. The key argument for an AWT is horizontal equity. But such horizontal inequities emerge in the process of implementing an AWT that it is a fine balance whether or not the AWT is worthwhile. Some governments have decided it is whilst others have decided it isn't. Even some, who introduced an AWT many years ago, when wealth was mainly visible and possibly easier to tax than income, have recently changed their minds.

Why are Wealth Transfer Taxes More Widespread than Annual Wealth Taxes?

We have seen that, before 1972, all OECD countries had death duties, with some provision for taxing gifts and that the abolition of death duties in three countries since then may have owed more to accident than design. Why are WTTs more popular with governments than AWTs?

A WTT is less suitable than the theoretically ideal AWT in promoting horizontal equity, but, given the imperfections of an AWT in practice, a death duty does at least, once in a generation, take account of the advantages conferred by wealth.

More positively, a death duty is the most convenient and effective way of using taxation to reduce wealth inequalities. It is levied at a time when the former owner can no longer use his or her wealth; when the property is bound to change ownership anyway; and when for beneficiaries other than the spouse of the deceased (who can be favourably treated) the inheritance is often in the nature of a windfall. Moreover inheritance is a main, if not the main, cause of the perpetuation of inequalities of wealth and of income in OECD countries, and if reducing inequalities is a prime objective, governments may well feel that there is a special moral justification for taxing wealth which has not been acquired by the hard work and enterprise of the beneficiary. A death duty is also less likely to have the detrimental economic effects of a high AWT (Sandford, 1995, pp. 60-64).

Above all, however, the bugbears which so dogged the AWT are avoided or minimised with a WTT. At death an inventory of the property of the deceased and a valuation is often required anyway, not just for tax purposes, but to carry out the will of the deceased or implement the law of intestacy. With a sizable estate a professional executor or administrator is likely to be involved with a reputation to maintain for honesty and integrity. Thus there is less likelihood of evasion through non-disclosure than with an AWT, especially as, in many cases, valuable items will be specified in a will, a public document.

As to valuation, it is often in the interests of the various beneficiaries to ensure that valuation is properly carried out; frequently property has to be sold both to pay the death duties and to meet the claims of the beneficiaries, so that a market value is available; and because in any year the number of properties on which death duty is paid is much less, and the rates are much higher, than with an AWT, the tax authorities can afford to negotiate on the more difficult valuations without the administrative cost becoming disproportionately high. Moreover, issues of the current value of the pension rights of the deceased and the value of future earning power simply do not arise with a WTT. Admittedly, gifts may often require valuations solely for tax purposes, but the number and amount in any year are relatively small.

Why is there such Variety in Forms of Capital Gains Tax?

Capital gains taxes differ not only in the ways outlined in table 6.1, but in a multiplicity of detailed provisions. Why all this diversity? Real capital gains are the equivalent of real income – being net accretions to wealth. Horizontal equity requires that they should be taxed as other forms of income. For this purpose the ideal CGT would be one in which gains were treated exactly as other forms of income, assessed and taxed annually, with losses allowed as offsets against all forms of income. Untaxed gains at death would be subject to tax as other income.

Whilst most economists would probably accept the validity of the previous paragraph, some would say that there is a conflict between horizontal equity and efficiency; capital gains are a major way in which enterprise is rewarded – and therefore it is better either not to have a CGT at all (the view of the majority of the United Kingdom Royal Commission on the *Taxation of Profits and Income*, 1955) or, if there is one, to temper its severity and treat capital gains more favourably than other forms of income. Others might reject altogether the equivalence of capital gains and income, arguing, for example, as Wallich (1965), that people make a sharp distinction between ordinary income and capital gains; they respond to an increase in capital gains not by treating the gain as income, but by being prepared to spend a higher fraction of ordinary income as a result of accrued capital gains. Still others would make a distinction between short and long term gains, taking the view that short term gains are in the nature of a windfall profit and should be treated as ordinary income for tax purposes, whilst long term gains either should not be taxed at all, or, if taxed, should be treated more favourably.

Thus, issues of principle account for major differences in the way countries treat capital gains. But the practical problems we associate with wealth taxes – in particular the valuation problem – account for other differences. The ideal horizontal equity treatment, postulated in the first paragraph of this section, assumes that accrued gains are assessed each year. To do so requires that gains are valued twice in the first year of operation – at the beginning and end – and annually thereafter, and that, as with an AWT, the valuation would be specifically for tax purposes. The problem, however, is more acute than with an AWT because, for example, valuations of real property every four or five years just would not do for assessing annual gains. Thus countries seek to get round the valuation difficulties by taxing gains when they are realised, not as they accrue. But this raises some major problems of its own.

Before we examine these problems, two other snags about taxing accrued gains annually as income might be mentioned. One is a liquidity problem: a big and possibly short term rise in the stock market might leave taxpayers facing a huge CGT bill which they could only meet by parting with assets – which might be deemed unduly harsh. Conversely, in a year of a major stock exchange fall, if losses can be offset against other income, a millionaire might be paying no income tax at all – which might be regarded as unacceptable.

To revert to the use of realisation as the solution to the valuation problem: most realisation takes the form of a sale of assets, when a market valuation is automatically available. Where a gift is made, a valuation of any gain has to be determined; but gifts requiring special valuation are a small minority of all gains. Hey presto! – the valuation problem is largely solved. The trouble, however, is that assets are realised after being held for widely differing time periods. Where a gain has accumulated over a number of years, it would seem unfair to add the whole of the gain to the income of the year of realisation, which, with a progressive income tax, would push the taxpayer into higher brackets than if the gain had been evenly spread. Hence countries ease the burden in various ways, for example, the United Kingdom by a separate threshold, the United States by lower rates, Canada by only charging a proportion of the gain to income tax. There are also other problems: where more than a year has passed before realisation, ought some allowance to be made for inflation? Some countries have thought so and have indexed the acquisition price – although latterly, as we see in chapter 9, with less inflationary times, countries such as Ireland, Australia and the United Kingdom have removed indexation. Again, with realisation rather than accrual as the method of operating the tax, how should accrued gains be treated at the taxpayer's death? The logic of the situation would seem to be either to treat death as a 'deemed realisation' and tax the gains before any calculations of death duty, or allow deferred liability, so that the inheritor of the property carries over the liability of the deceased and, when the asset is disposed of, tax is paid on the whole gain from the time it had been acquired by the deceased. One or two countries use the first method, for example, Canada (except for a surviving spouse); more commonly, the second method of deferred liability is employed (eg Sweden and Australia where the asset was acquired by the deceased after the introduction of CGT, 20 September 1985). The most frequent treatment, however, is complete exemption at death, with the inheritor taking the value at death as the acquisition price (eg United Kingdom, Ireland, United States and Australia, where the asset was acquired before the introduction of CGT).

Which treatment is followed often has some relationship to whether there is a death duty. Thus, as we mentioned above, Canada, which generally treats death as a deemed realisation, abolished its federal estate duty at the same time as it introduced its CGT. The United Kingdom and Ireland at first treated death as a deemed realisation, but, in response to complaints of double taxation (although the bases of the CGT and estate duty were really quite different) both changed to complete exemption of CGT at death (generating a significant 'lock in' effect).

Besides differences of principle, derived from varying interpretations of the nature of a capital gain, and of practice, stemming fundamentally from the valuation problem, as always in tax policy-making, other influences, such as we discuss in chapter 9, play a part. Thus for social and political reasons, the main asset of most individuals, their house or flat, is invariably given special treatment – only the extent of it varying between countries. Pressure groups generate exemptions. External developments exert their influence – like high inflation, which, associated with large speculative gains was sometimes a reason for introducing a gains tax, or low inflation, a reason for removing indexation. Moreover uncertainty and differing views on the likely economic effects explain some of the differences between countries.

All these problems and influences help to explain the differences between countries which tax the capital gains of individuals on a comprehensive basis, and why other countries have fought shy of introducing comprehensive gains taxes. (For further discussion of these issues, see Evans and Sandford, 1999.) Capital gains taxes are inherently complicated and inevitably have high compliance and administrative costs. To quote from the majority report of the Royal Commission on the Taxation of Profits and Income (1955): 'A tax on capital gains...... cannot be expected to prove a tax of simple structure or one that would be free from a number of rather arbitrary solutions of its various problems'.

CHAPTER 7

ADMINISTRATIVE AND COMPLIANCE COSTS

Introduction

In this chapter we start by examining the costs to government of collecting taxes, primarily, but not solely the costs of the revenue departments. We look at attempts to compare these administrative costs across countries and point out the hazards of these comparisons. In effect we are answering the question why administrative costs differ. This brings us to the question of tax compliance costs, the costs which taxpayers incur in order to comply with the tax law. Administrative and compliance costs together can be termed tax operating costs. We point out the problems of international comparisons of compliance costs by reference to a comparison of the VAT costs of small businesses in Canada, New Zealand and the United Kingdom. Finally we look at the varied reaction of countries to the growth of tax compliance costs.

Comparisons of Administrative Costs

The costs to a government of collecting tax are, mainly, the costs incurred by the revenue department or departments. But there are other costs: the costs of preparing legislation and the time of the legislators in enacting and amending it; the overheads associated with parliament; and similarly the costs of the courts in so far as they are concerned with tax cases. Further, there are the costs of what are, essentially, interest free loans to the private sector. These arise where there is a time gap between the economic transaction generating the tax and the date at which the tax must be remitted to the government. For instance, with a VAT, in each specified collection period a business collects tax on its outputs, pays tax on its inputs (which will normally be less than it has collected on its outputs) and then has a period of 'grace' before the balance has to be remitted. That such periods between collection and remission of tax are a cost to the government becomes clear if we postulate that the government decided to reduce the grace period. It would then get a once and for all

117

increase in revenue which could, say, be used to reduce the national debt and hence generate an annual saving to the Exchequer. Obviously some grace period must be allowed if only to give businesses time to do the accounting; and circumstances can arise in which businesses may be required to hand over tax receipts before they receive payment from their customers, in which case the government gets the benefit. But, generally, in a tax system, the advantage works very much to the benefit of the private sector. As we shall see later, this can be regarded as an offset to compliance costs which, for large firms, may be very substantial.

It is probably best and is normal practice in calculating 'administrative costs' to confine the term to the costs of the revenue department(s) in administering a given tax or tax structure. The main costs will be staff salaries and pension obligations to staff, office accommodation (including heating, lighting and cleaning), equipment and transport including the costs of maintaining and repairing buildings, office equipment and vehicles. Staff related costs are by far the most important for revenue departments and represent something like three-quarters of the total.

A measure sometimes used to compare the performance of tax administrations, either as a time series for a particular country or between countries, is the ratio of administrative cost to tax revenue – which can be used for one tax or the tax system as a whole. This ratio can be expressed as a percentage ($\frac{\text{admin. cost}}{\text{tax revenue}} \times \frac{100}{1}$) or in the form of the average cost to the revenue authorities of raising 100 units of revenue.

Recent Australian history offers an example of the use of this ratio in international comparisons. In November 1991, the main Australian opposition to the then Labor Government published *Fightback! The Liberal and National Parties' Plan to Rebuild and Reward Australia.* A chapter headed 'The Need for Income Tax Administrative Reform' refers to the enormous complexity of tax legislation, which, it says, is raising concerns about the administration of tax and the operation of the Australian Taxation Office (ATO) itself. The narrative continues:

'An illustration of the consequent administrative inefficiencies is shown [by the fact that] the cost of the revenue collection in Australia runs at $1.09 per $100 collected (1989/90) compared with the US 51 cents per $100 collected (1989). The very wide discrepancy between the two does not appear to be explicable other than by likely administrative and policy-induced inefficiencies.' (pp. 139-40)

Some little time later, the then Commissioner of Taxation, Mr Trevor Boucher, in a volume of evidence he presented to the Joint Committee of Public Accounts (Boucher, 1992) in effect replied to this accusation, as follows:

'Comparison with Overseas Tax Authorities

'3.54 Subject to some qualifications described below, Australia's cost of collection ratio compares quite favourably with that of other overseas tax authorities which administer income tax systems, such as Japan, New Zealand, United Kingdom and Canada. Figures quoted are obtained from their Annual Reports and are quoted as cost for collecting 100 currency units.

Country	1987-88	1988-89	1989-90	1990-91
United States	0.54	0.51	0.52	unavailable
New Zealand	1.43	1.50	1.63	unavailable
Japan	1.02	0.99	0.95	0.92
United Kingdom	1.67	1.62	1.61	1.70
Canada	1.08	1.17	unavailable	unavailable
Australia	1.03	1.02	1.04	1.14

'3.55 While international comparisons of this kind are frequently made, particularly by tax administrators, contemporary tax literature dealing with cost of collections ratios emphasises the limitations of such comparisons, when assessing overall efficiency and effectiveness. In brief,
* international comparisons of any statistical data are notoriously difficult to undertake because of the difficulty in getting data from different countries on a reasonably standard conceptual basis;
* demographic, political, social, economic, legal and government factors can significantly effect (sic) elements of the 'cost of collections' ratio.

'3.56 These latter factors are particularly relevant when comparing the costs of collections ratio of the Internal Revenue Service in the United States with agencies in other western countries. Putting aside sheer economies of scale, it also needs to be recognised that with the United States, income tax is also administered at a state level. The above ratios for the USA do not reflect this additional factor, one which could, in our view, have a significant bearing in arriving at a comparable cost of collection ratio.' (pp. 52-4)

In other words Mr Boucher is implying that Australia's efficiency of collection is as good, or better than, a number of overseas countries. Where it looks decidedly worse, that is, by comparison with the United States, then the broad reasons which may explain differences and have nothing to do with efficiency, come into play. These two sets of comparisons, each seeking to lead the reader to opposite conclusions, do nothing to establish the efficiency or inefficiency of the ATO. For a particular country, the ratio of administrative cost to tax revenue has some value as an input:output relationship, but in comparisons, especially international comparisons, there are many reasons for ratios to differ, which have nothing to do with the relative efficiencies of the tax administrations. Many of these reasons are widely understood and, indeed, in fairness to Mr Boucher, some were referred to by him. We will briefly review those which are generally appreciated, but then concentrate on two major causes of differences which have not been widely recognised or accorded the importance they deserve.

Reasons for Differences in Cost:Revenue Ratios

Lack of Common Definitions. The quotation from Mr Boucher mentioned the problem of getting data on a comparable basis. The definitions of administrative cost, and even of revenue from a particular tax, may differ. For example, let us suppose that tax offices are in buildings owned by the state. Then the cost of this accommodation may be omitted from the administrative cost figures entirely, or included at a nominal shadow rent, or valued at the opportunity cost – what the offices could be let for on the open market. This last figure is what an economist would consider the appropriate valuation, but not all tax authorities would adopt this valuation method.

Again, not all revenue authorities would follow what an accountant or economist would consider an appropriate policy regarding capital expenditures. For example, suppose an authority in a particular year adopted a policy of computerising its offices and thus incurred a major capital expenditure. This might all appear in the accounts as expenditure in that year, with nothing thereafter; or a proportion of the expenditure only might be recorded in the year of purchase, with the remainder of the cost allocated to subsequent years as the equipment was gradually depreciated. Such differences of treatment distort both time series and inter-country comparisons.

Let us take revenue from a particular tax. In some countries capital gains taxation is part of the income tax code (for example, the United States, Canada and Australia); in others the CGT is a separate tax (as in the United Kingdom and Denmark). Where it is part of the income tax code, the revenue from taxing capital gains may or may not be recorded separately from the rest of income tax. In yet other countries there is no CGT; and where there are gains taxes the base of the tax will differ. Comparisons of cost:revenue ratios for income tax will be distorted if one country includes the revenue from taxing capital gains as part of income tax and the other does not. One of the purposes of a CGT is to discourage attempts to avoid income tax by converting income to capital gains. The cost:revenue ratio of a separate CGT will underestimate revenue by failing to take account of the income tax receipts which are the result of taxing gains.

Again, in some countries (for example, the United Kingdom) social security contributions (called national insurance contributions in the United Kingdom) are collected by the revenue department along with income tax, for a fee which may be nominal, and at most reflects marginal costings. Whether the cost:revenue ratio relates to income tax alone or to income tax plus social security contributions makes a major difference to the figures.

Differences in Tax Structure. A complicated tax structure with many tax expenditures (which may be justified on equity grounds) is bound to be more expensive to administer than a simple structure. Particularly relevant is the threshold for an income tax or the registration limit for a VAT. In some countries (for example, New Zealand) income tax starts on the first unit of income, though there may be a rebating system or offsetting social security provisions. In other countries (for example, the United Kingdom) there are allowances, for example, personal allowances, which are tax free and may be sufficiently high to remove significant numbers of income receivers from the tax net. The point is that collecting small amounts of tax from numerous low income receivers raises the cost:revenue ratio.

The New Zealand VAT (GST) has a threshold which is only about one-third of the United Kingdom threshold for VAT. There may be good economic reasons for having a lower threshold, but to do so pushes up the cost:revenue ratio.

The Make-up of the Tax Population. Just as the structure of a tax affects the cost:revenue ratio, so does the structure of a taxed population.

Differences between countries in the proportion of self-employed persons in the taxpaying population will cause cost:revenue ratios to differ. The complications of calculating the taxable income of the self-employed mean that the administrative costs are much higher per unit of income from the self-employed than from employees; further, in the latter case, the employer does much of the collecting work for the government. This is quite apart from the fact that tax evasion (which reduces revenue and raises costs) is much more prevalent amongst the self-employed than employees.

Similarly on the side of indirect taxes. The same sales tax revenue requires much more administrative effort to collect from a large number of small firms than from a small number of large firms.

Rates of Tax.   Tax rates are a vital consideration in determining cost:revenue ratios. A country where total tax revenue is a higher proportion of GDP, *ceteris paribus*, might be expected to have a lower cost:revenue ratio than another country with a similar number of taxes where total tax revenue is a lower proportion of GDP. Similarly with individual taxes. The United Kingdom offers a good example. In 1977-78, as well as a zero rate, VAT in the United Kingdom was levied at an 8 per cent standard rate and a 12.5 per cent higher rate. In 1979 the higher rate was abolished and the standard rate raised to 15 per cent. The effect, once the change was fully implemented, was to reduce the cost:yield ratio by almost a half, from just over 2 per cent to just over 1 per cent.

Revenue Fluctuations Apart from Tax Rates.   Other factors, on the demand or on the supply side may generate revenue fluctuations without any effect, or any proportionate effect, on administrative costs. Thus, for example, changes in the level of activity of an economy affect revenue yields, particularly from profits taxes and capital gains taxes. Moreover an unanticipated inflation may have more effect on income tax and sales tax yields than on administrative costs, at least in the short run.

In the United Kingdom the cost:revenue ratio of petroleum revenue tax has fluctuated widely mainly because of fluctuations in output (whilst administrative costs remained relatively stable) but also because of fluctuations in price.

Direct Expenditures or Tax Expenditures.   The manner in which a country delivers benefits or incentives may have a significant effect on cost:benefit ratios. A benefit delivered in the form of a tax expenditure will both raise tax administrative costs and reduce tax revenues. The same benefit administered as a direct expenditure will not reduce tax revenues nor will the cost of administering it be borne by the revenue department.

Various Other Influences. There are many other reasons for cost:revenue ratios to change over time or differ between countries. A reform programme which introduces new taxes or substantially restructures existing taxes and may require transitional measures (often referred to as 'grand-fathering' provisions) may increase administrative costs and alter cost:revenue ratios, at least in the short run. Changes in methods of administration may change ratios or differences in administrative methods may affect comparisons between countries (an influence we examine in more detail below). A change in the tax unit (or differences in tax unit between countries) may affect the ratio; thus, individual taxation, requiring the separate assessment of husband and wife, may increase administrative costs because of the additional numbers to be assessed, as compared with the treatment of married couples as a single unit. Comparisons between the cost:revenue ratios of federal governments, will be distorted where one allows state taxes to be deducted from federal tax and another does not. We could go on. However, we will concentrate on two vital factors affecting cost:revenue ratios: the effectiveness of tax administration and the need to take account of compliance costs to the taxpayers.

Tax Effectiveness and Cost:Revenue Ratios

A vital consideration in international comparisons of cost:revenue ratios is how much of the maximum potential revenue the country succeeds in collecting. We can define this as the degree of tax effectiveness. By maximum potential revenue (MPR) we mean what would be collected with the current tax system if everyone paid what was legally due. The shortfall between the amount of tax actually collected and the MPR can be called the 'tax gap', or 'tax effectiveness gap'. The situation can be illustrated by figure 7.1.

Figure 7.1 shows the relationship between total tax revenue and administrative cost. The line AB indicates the maximum potential revenue (tax rate(s) x tax base) at a particular time. It should be stressed that the MPR (and the tax gap) is difficult to calculate with any degree of precision: it will, of course, rise, or fall, as a result of changes in tax rates or tax base or decisions of the courts on potential avoidance schemes. But this does not affect the basic argument.

Figure 7.1 Relationship between Total Tax Revenue and Administrative Cost

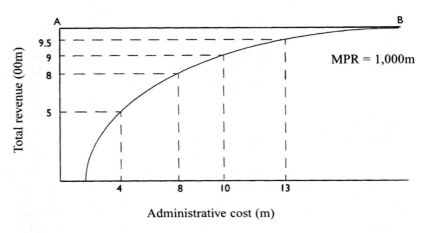

Administrative cost (m)

To collect 50 per cent MPR (500 million) admin cost = 4 million; cost:revenue ratio = 4 ÷ 500 = 0.8 per cent
To collect 80 per cent MPR (800 million) admin cost = 8 million; cost:revenue ratio = 8 ÷ 800 = 1.0 per cent
To collect 90 per cent MPR (900 million) admin cost = 10 million; cost:revenue ratio = 10 ÷ 900 = 1.1 per cent
To collect 95 per cent MPR (950 million) admin cost = 13 million; cost:revenue ratio = 13 ÷ 950 = 1.37 per cent.

The total revenue curve begins at a point to the right of the origin because some administrative costs have to be incurred before any revenue can be collected. The curve rises very steeply at first; additional units of administrative costs will generate very substantial revenue. But as total revenue begins to approach the MPR line, it flattens out. Additional increments of administrative cost generate decreasing additions to revenue and it becomes flatter and flatter the closer it gets to the MPR. The vertical distance between the total revenue curve and the MPR line at any point is the tax gap. (It should, perhaps, be pointed out that there are certain assumptions implicit in this formulation, most notably that the cost of additional units of administrative labour and capital is constant. If, for example, unit labour costs rise as more labour is employed – or, for that matter, if all administrative staff get a pay rise – the curve would move to the right and the cost:revenue ratios would rise. Similarly, the position of the curve implies a given administrative strategy or technology; for example, if there was a major change in the proportions of capital and labour, with, say, computers replacing some staff, leading to an increase in efficiency, the curve would rise.)

In our example, which is perhaps not unrealistic, half the maximum potential revenue can be collected on a very low cost:revenue ratio; the cost:revenue ratio rises thereafter. Yet, it is by no means obvious that the lowest cost:revenue ratio should be the preferred position. The lower ratio goes with lower tax effectiveness. The 95 per cent effectiveness level, with the much higher ratio, may well be preferred and, in the broader sense, represent a much more efficient administration. It is more equitable as between honest and dishonest taxpayers and offers bigger revenue potential. In other words, quite apart from the other problems, we can only meaningfully compare cost:revenue ratios between countries with similar tax effectiveness.

The information expressed in figure 7.1 can be put in another way. There is a trade-off between the level of tax rates and tax effectiveness. If we are seeking a particular total tax revenue we can obtain it by any of a number of combinations of nominal tax rates and administrative costs. An increase in administrative cost, of the kind which generates increased tax effectiveness, will enable any given revenue to be obtained with a lower structure of tax rates. But an increase in administrative costs for a given tax revenue necessarily means an increase in the administrative cost:revenue ratio. (Strictly speaking we need to allow for the effects of the additional administrative cost in reducing the revenue available for other purposes and talk of total revenue net of administrative cost; but the basic argument is unaffected.) Again, it is not axiomatic that higher (nominal) tax rates and a lower cost:revenue ratio is to be preferred to lower tax rates and a higher cost:revenue ratio!

Tax Compliance Costs and Cost Revenue Ratios

The other major limitation in comparing cost:revenue ratios between countries, or in the same country over time, is that administrative costs in isolation are only a part of the story. They take no account of tax compliance costs – the costs which taxpayers incur in meeting the requirements of a tax or tax system.

Compliance costs are the costs over and above actual tax payments and over and above any distortion costs inherent in the tax or tax system.

For personal taxpayers they include the time taken to complete tax returns and store and retrieve the necessary tax data; payments to a tax adviser or tax preparer; and miscellaneous costs such as transport to visit a tax adviser or the tax office.

For businesses they may arise from taxes on the product, the profits or the employees and include the costs of learning legal obligations, and of collecting, recording and remitting tax to the authorities.

Together the administrative and compliance costs may be called tax 'operating costs'. It is the operating costs – the total real resources taken up in running the tax system – which is the important concept from the standpoint of the economy as a whole. Moreover, all the estimates of the total compliance costs of the major central government taxes – personal income tax, corporate income tax and VAT – have shown compliance costs to be a multiple of administrative costs. To compare administrative costs without mentioning compliance costs is thus to omit the major component of operating costs. When we include them, the comparisons can look very different.

Of course, seeking to include tax compliance costs raises problems about the availability and reliability of such estimates. To illustrate our point and make the best international comparison we can in this context, we must restrict ourselves to income tax (whereas the figures Mr Boucher quoted above refer to all taxes) and go back to 1986-87, where compliance cost studies in the United Kingdom, Canada and Australia appear to offer roughly comparable data. We then get table 7.1.

Table 7.1 Comparison of Operating Costs of Personal Income Tax and Capital Gains Tax (including Social Security Contributions in the UK and Canada)

Percentages of Tax Revenue

	UK 1986-87	Canada 1986	Australia 1986-87
Administrative cost	1.53	1.00	1.13
Compliance costs:			
– to individuals	2.21	2.53	7.9
– to employers (PAYE)	1.02	3.57	1.26[a]
– other private costs[b]	0.17	0.03	not calculated
Total Operating Costs	**4.93**	**7.13**	**10.29**

Notes: [a] The Australian figure relates to 1989-90, because no estimate for PAYE was included in the 1986-87 study. It is derived from Pope *et al*, 1993.
[b] Mainly costs to banks and other financial institutions.

Sources: Sandford *et al*, 1989, p. 109; Vaillancourt, 1989; and Pope *et al*, 1990 and 1993.

On the basis of these figures it would appear that the United Kingdom, with the highest administrative cost:revenue ratio, had the lowest ratio of operating costs:revenue – indeed, the United Kingdom total operating cost:revenue ratio was less than half that of Australia. However, before we jump to any conclusions about relative efficiencies we need to examine a number of factors which may account for the differences.

Methodology. The Canadian study used a polling organisation for carrying out the survey, the Australian and United Kingdom studies both used large-scale mail surveys to obtain their data. However, there were important differences between the United Kingdom and Australian studies. Because of co-operation from the Inland Revenue, the United Kingdom study of personal taxpayers was able to draw on a sample directly taken from the income tax-paying population; whereas in the Australian study, the sample was drawn from a less representative population. Also, Pope's Australian study was under-funded, so no reminders were sent out and the response rate achieved was only 16.3 per cent, compared with 43 per cent for the United Kingdom study. These and other features have led to criticism of the conclusions of Pope's study, especially by the ATO, on the grounds that they are unreliable and exaggerate compliance costs. Subsequently a study by Evans *et al* (1997) which was not subject to the same methodological limitations as the Pope study, has come out with a figure of 5.3 per cent for the compliance costs of individuals, as compared with Pope's 7.9 per cent, but still one which is very much higher than the comparable United Kingdom or Canadian figures.

Definitions. The figures of administrative costs are official figures (though, as we have seen, they may not necessarily be on the same base). The United Kingdom and Canadian figures include social security contributions, which Australia does not levy. It might be argued, therefore, that it would be more appropriate to compare Australia and the United Kingdom after excluding the United Kingdom national insurance (NI) contributions. In 1986-87, the UK income tax and CGT brought in £39.6 billion of revenue and NI contributions £25.7 billion. The marginal cost of collecting NI contributions along with income tax was very low, so if we leave out NI contributions, the operating costs rise considerably as a ratio of revenue receipts. The administrative costs attributed to income tax alone increase to 2.29 per cent, the compliance costs of individuals to 3.63 per cent and other relevant private costs to 0.23 per cent. Employers were unable to separate out the costs of collecting PAYE from those of collecting NI contributions. But even if we assumed (quite incorrectly) that all the employers' costs were attributable to PAYE and none to collecting NI contributions, the costs to employers would then be 1.68 per cent and total operating costs 7.83 per cent of tax revenue. This figure is still well below Pope's estimate for Australia. However, there are strong arguments for including NI contributions. They are a form of income tax and, if they did not exist, as in Australia, income tax would undoubtedly be at much higher rates, raising substantially more revenue at little or no extra administrative or compliance costs. Including them puts Australia and the United Kingdom on a more nearly equivalent basis in respect of tax rates and revenue. For the year 1986, income tax and NI contributions together amounted to 45 per cent of total taxation in the United Kingdom, representing 17 per cent of GDP; in the same year income tax in Australia amounted to 47 per cent of total taxation or 14 per cent of GDP (OECD, 1992, tables 10, 11, 14 and 15).

Special Factors. Of course, there are many special factors distorting this comparison. For example, Vaillancourt attributes the much higher costs to employers in the Canadian system to 'the high costs associated with the unemployment insurance and public pension system'. The year 1986-87 in Australia was the first full year of major tax reform, including the new CGT which may well have raised compliance costs exceptionally. In the United Kingdom in 1986 husband and wife were still treated as a single tax unit, whereas in Australia and Canada the individual was the tax unit, which distorts comparison with the other two countries.

Administrative Methods.   We have just mentioned one administrative difference between Australia and the United Kingdom, ie the difference in tax unit. However, probably the biggest reason for the difference in both administrative and compliance costs between Australia and the United Kingdom was the markedly different systems of administration. Things have moved on since 1986-87 and the United Kingdom has since adopted a system of self-assessment for about one-third of personal taxpayers, but, at the time of these estimates, this change to a partial self-assessment system to income tax had not taken place. Moreover there was (and largely still is) a structure by which around 90 per cent of United Kingdom taxpayers paid tax at the same marginal rate (known as the 'basic rate'). Tax was deducted at source at the basic rate from a very wide range of types of income. Various tax allowances or reliefs were also dealt with at source. (Thus, for example, the relief on mortgage interest which applied in 1986-87 took the form of the taxpayer paying the building society or bank the interest net of tax relief, with the government paying the balance direct to the financial institution.) Moreover, the PAYE system was cumulative so that, in principle, at the end of the tax year, exactly the right amount had been deducted from employment incomes. No payments had to be made on account. As a consequence of these features about two-thirds of United Kingdom personal taxpayers did not have to fill in an annual tax return. The number of taxpayers employing tax advisers or agents was estimated at just over 10 per cent in 1986-87.

Australia, on the other hand, had a system of self-assessment, though it fell short of full self-assessment for individuals. The multiple rates of income tax lent themselves less well to deduction at source. Payments on account were required and all taxpayers had to complete a tax return annually. Around 70 per cent of individual taxpayers employed tax advisers or agents. Given these basic facts it would be very surprising if the compliance costs of the United Kingdom income tax system had not been significantly less than those of Australia.

The purpose of this analysis is not to argue that the United Kingdom system is superior to the Australian, even if, as is likely, the operating costs of the United Kingdom tax system are substantially lower than those of Australia. It could be argued that the lower operating costs are bought at too high a price in terms of lack of flexibility of the rate structure or of the scope for deductible items; or that self-assessment for taxpayers is a requisite of a healthy democracy where people are more aware of their obligation to the state. The point being made is simply that international comparisons of administrative cost:tax revenue ratios have little meaning if considered in isolation from compliance costs. And even when administrative and compliance costs are considered together, there are a range of factors affecting either or both of them which need to be taken into account before one can pontificate about the relative efficiencies of the tax systems.

Indeed, the relationship between administrative and compliance costs is a complicated one. There are various ways in which the tax collecting function (using that term in its widest sense) can be carried out; and they involve different mixes of administrative costs, costs to individual taxpayers, costs to employers, and costs to businesses, especially financial institutions. Often a reduction (or increase) in administrative costs will also reduce (or increase) compliance costs. But a government can reduce administrative costs by putting more obligations on individual taxpayers (for example, by self-assessment) or on employers (PAYE) or on financial institutions (deduction at source or/and information reporting). Conversely, an increase in administrative costs on taxpayer services can reduce compliance costs for the taxpayer. That being so, it is pretty meaningless to make comparisons of administrative costs only, without seeing what has happened to the various elements of compliance costs.

Thus our prime concern should be with total operating costs, the total costs required to run the tax system. Subject to other political objectives, it is this cost, with a given revenue requirement and a given level of tax effectiveness, that administrators should seek to minimise. While that should be the main concern, the distribution of these costs between the public and private sectors remains important. There is a strong case for arguing that, if there is any choice, with any given level of operating cost, the bias should be in favour of higher administrative costs and lower compliance costs rather than *vice versa*. Administrative costs are met from taxation and can be assumed to be distributed across the population in accordance with some criterion of equity held by the government. Compliance costs, on the other hand, are more haphazard in their distribution and often regressive. They generate more resentment than administrative costs ('It is bad enough to have to pay taxes, but to have to incur costs for the privilege of doing so is to add insult to injury'.) They also generate more psychic or psychological costs – costs of stress and anxiety. It could even be that heavy compliance costs reduce voluntary compliance and thus have a detrimental effect on tax revenue and hence cost:revenue ratios.

Before we leave the subject of tax compliance costs it is useful to classify them further, which has an important bearing on some forms of international comparisons; to take a look at an international comparison of VAT, which particularly reveals the significance of different methodologies in comparing tax compliance costs; and then briefly review the growth of research in the field and the various reactions of governments to the growth of compliance costs.

Classifying Tax Compliance Costs

The figures of tax compliance costs in table 7.1 above are what are variously called 'total', 'gross' or (to use the term of Evans *et al*, 1997) 'social' compliance costs. They are the costs to the economy as a whole. The costs to taxpayers, often referred to as net compliance costs, may be less because of any, or all, of the following offsets.

(1) There is a cash flow benefit (the value of which depends on the current level of interest rates.) This offset arises where the taxpayer, individual or business, has the use of tax for a period between the date of the economic transaction which gives rise to the liability and the date the tax is remitted to the authorities. This, of course, is the counterpart of the 'tax free loans', discussed at the beginning of the chapter. Its value represents a transfer payment. It is a real benefit to the individual or business, but a cost to the Exchequer.

(2) Some compliance costs can be deducted against tax. Deductibility reduces the cost to the taxpayer but at the expense of the government's revenue.

(3) There are managerial benefits associated with tax compliance. For example, the stricter and more comprehensive accounting which VAT entails for many small businesses generates data which can be used to manage the business more effectively, reducing costs arising, for example, from bad debts, and also reducing accountants' bills for making up the annual accounts. (See, for example, Sandford *et al*, 1981, pp. 90-96; Sandford and Hasseldine, 1992, pp. 76-78). Such benefits represent a more efficient use of resources in the economy as a whole and thus are not solely an offset to the taxpayer's costs; but they are very difficult to measure satisfactorily and, in most tax compliance cost studies, no attempt is made to do so.

In international comparisons of net compliance costs, ie the costs to taxpayers after allowing for the benefits, differences in administrative rules may make considerable differences to the outcome. For example, countries differ according to the length of the collection period and grace period they allow for VAT, and according to the frequency with which employers have to remit PAYE receipts, thus affecting the level of cash flow benefits. Also in relation to tax deductibility, countries differ in their generosity. Thus, for example, Australia allows tax deductibility to personal taxpayers for all tax agents' fees, whereas personal taxpayers are not allowed to deduct such fees in the United Kingdom unless they can be presented as the costs to a business. There is no allowance in either country for the costs of doing the tax compliance work oneself, which may partly account for the very high proportion of Australian income tax payers who use tax agents. (There is, indeed, a case for arguing that the revenue lost by tax deductibility should be added to administrative costs in making international comparisons.)

Other useful distinctions are between temporary compliance costs (start up and learning costs for a new tax or a major change in an old tax) and regular, recurring or continuous costs (when the system has been running for some time without major change). Also important are the psychic or psychological costs of compliance – the stress, anxiety and hassle which may be involved in dealing with tax affairs. Whilst widely recognised, little attempt has so far been made to evaluate psychic costs. The distinction between temporary and regular costs can also be applied to administrative costs (and some tax officers also maintain that they too can suffer from psychic costs!).

Comparing the VAT Compliance Costs of Small Businesses

Table 7.2, which compares the VAT compliance costs of small businesses in three countries is taken from Cnossen, 1994. He has very conveniently taken studies from the United Kingdom (Sandford *et al*, 1986-87), New Zealand (Sandford and Hasseldine, 1990-91) and Canada (Plamondon, 1993), converted the studies to common US dollars at the 1991 exchange rates and extrapolated as required to give figures for comparable size groups. It should be noted that the basis differs from that of administrative costs above. The relationship is of compliance cost to turnover, not revenue.

Table 7.2 VAT Compliance Costs of Small Businesses in the United Kingdom, New Zealand and Canada

Compliance Costs as a Percentage of Taxable Turnover

Size of Business Taxable Turnover $US	United Kingdom (1986-87)	New Zealand (1990-91)	Canada (1992)
Under 50,000	1.49	2.06	not available
50,000-100,000	0.70	0.91	0.39
100,000-200,000	0.50	0.67	0.36
200,000-500,000	0.44	0.47	0.15
500,000-1m.	0.34	0.28	0.09
1m.-10m.	0.07	0.04	0.06

Sources: see text.

The first point to make is that these figures only show compliance costs, not administrative costs as well, and we have argued strongly that we need to look at both. In fact, in New Zealand in 1992, no separate calculation of VAT administrative costs was made; but, even more to the point, we are analysing compliance costs by size of business and no country provides administrative costs broken down in this way.

The second point to note is that all three studies (in common with all other studies on VAT compliance costs) show VAT compliance costs diminishing markedly with size. In other words, VAT compliance costs fall disproportionately on small firms. Indeed, the figures in the table, which relate to total or gross compliance costs, probably underestimate this effect. Whilst small businesses may get more managerial benefits from VAT than larger firms, this benefit is probably more than offset by the greater value (proportionately) of the cash flow benefit to large firms and of the scope for deducting the costs of VAT work against income or profits tax; the sole proprietor, who does VAT accounts himself or herself (or whose spouse or partner does them) is not able to claim a deduction for the time so spent.

However, of more interest to us is the difference between countries. Before we try to explain the differences in the findings we need to examine the different methodologies employed. The United Kingdom and New Zealand studies follow the same methodology. In both cases the extracts in the table are the findings of a part of a study, undertaken with the support of the revenue authorities, which provided a representative sample of the VAT population. The surveys were conducted by mail questionnaires, supplemented by some interviews, by telephone or in person, primarily to query unusual responses. The methodology of the Plamondon study in Canada was completely different. It did not include large businesses; and the findings are the outcome of 200 interviews carried out across Canada by a number of accountants in private practice who interviewed a random sample of their own clients. As a result of this method, the Plamondon sample obtained close to 100 per cent response, against 24 per cent and 31 per cent for the United Kingdom and New Zealand studies, respectively. But the Canadian study under-represents the smallest firms which were the majority of small businesses and also under-represents the largest category in table 7.2. Presumably the under-representation of these categories arose because the smallest business proprietors employed accountants on a casual rather than a regular basis and in the largest firms the VAT work was undertaken by in-house staff.

Apart from the smallest and largest size in the table, the Canadian figures come out at around half the United Kingdom and New Zealand figures, or even less.

Reasons for the Compliance Cost Differences

Three main possibilities would appear to account for the differences, apart from any question of the different efficiencies of the tax structure or tax administration.

(1) *Differences arising from methodology and definitions.* The explanation on which Plamondon places great emphasis is that the previous research failed to segregate and measure incremental VAT compliance costs – the costs that are distinct from the core accounting function and would be saved if a VAT did not exist – and that consequently there was a considerable over-statement of VAT compliance costs. This is certainly a plausible hypothesis and he is correct in stating that, despite careful wording aimed at excluding costs which would be incurred anyway, even if VAT was abolished, 'there is no evidence that previous research was successful in segregating VAT compliance costs from the core accounting function'.

There is, however, another and equally plausible hypothesis, that the accountant/interviewers' view of what is a core accounting function is rather different from the taxpayers' view; VAT obliged many business taxpayers to keep more meticulous and extensive accounts than they otherwise would have done. Accountants would consider this additional work part of core accounting; many taxpayers would consider it compliance costs – costs which they would not have incurred, but for the tax. To take a very simple example from income tax. Suppose that there are two professors, A and B, in a country with no income tax. Each engages in consultancy work. Professor A keeps detailed accounts of dates, hours of work, charging rate, invoice records, receipts and the like and prepares an annual account of consultancy earnings and expenses. Professor B, on the other hand, keeps no formal accounts but just enough notes to ensure that he is paid for what he does. Then income tax is introduced. The compliance costs for Professor A are minimal. To comply with the new tax Professor B now has to keep formal accounts. But for the tax he would not be keeping them. To Professor B the costs of the formal accounting are a compliance cost; but an accountant would regard them as core accounting costs.

That this situation arises with VAT is clear. The Plamondon study never defines core accounting costs, but would presumably include all costs necessary for the efficient running of the business. That being so, no managerial benefits can result from VAT – and none are mentioned in the Plamondon study. But in both the United Kingdom and the New Zealand studies a significant proportion of small businesses recognised managerial benefits resulting from compliance with VAT – that, as a result of the tax, their purchase and sales records were better kept and they saved money in various ways as a result. To take the New Zealand figures: 47 per cent of respondents agreed that purchase records were better kept since GST (VAT) came in; 40 per cent agreed that their sales records were better kept and 40 per cent also held that they saved money by doing more of their own accounts. Other benefits – discounts claimed more frequently, reduced losses from bad debts and better stock control – were claimed by between 7 and 13 per cent of respondents. All these benefits were heavily concentrated amongst the smaller firms; for example 90 per cent of the respondents who considered that they saved money by doing more of their own accounts were from businesses with a turnover of under one million NZ dollars (in 1990-91). The benefits found in the United Kingdom study were similar in kind to those in New Zealand, but somewhat less.

In short, a significant part of the differences between the estimated compliance costs for Canada on the one hand and the United Kingdom and New Zealand on the other, lie in the field of methodology and definitions. This is not entirely surprising. The objectives of the studies were different. The United Kingdom and New Zealand studies were primarily concerned to obtain a picture of the total and distribution of compliance costs – for which a large and representative sample of taxpayers was required. The Canadian study never sought overall representativeness but sought to discover from detailed investigation of relatively few cases, where the shoe most pinched. Each method was the most appropriate for its purpose.

(2) *Existing taxes and the marginal cost of compliance.* All the studies sought to measure the marginal costs of VAT compliance – which might be defined as what would be saved if the tax were abolished. In the United Kingdom and New Zealand VAT replaced a wholesale sales tax. In both cases the number of registered traders increased enormously as compared to the previously existing situation. (In the United Kingdom the number of businesses responsible for collecting a sales tax rose from 70,000 to one and a quarter million.) Most of these had never before been sales tax collectors. There was no continuing sales tax to which a large proportion of the new registrants had to add a VAT. In Canada the GST replaced a manufacturers' sales tax. But a large proportion of the GST registrants were already used to collecting sales tax and, for retail sales, many had

only to add GST on top of an existing tax. Only one Canadian province, Alberta, did not already levy, and continue to levy, a retail sales tax. Of Plamondon's sample of 200, 94 (47 per cent) were registered to collect and remit provincial sales tax. For such traders, the marginal compliance cost of adding a VAT (or the saving if it were abolished) would almost certainly be much less than complying with a VAT if no other sales tax was involved.

Credence is given to this explanation of the difference between the studies of compliance costs of Canada as against the United Kingdom and New Zealand by the fact that under VAT tax is levied on inputs (or purchases) which is not the case with RST; and in the breakdown of incremental costs in the Canadian study, the item 'Identify and total GST on purchases' is by far the biggest component. It represents three times the cost of charging GST on sales and approximately 40 per cent of total gross compliance costs (Plamondon, 1993, p. 50). This strongly suggests that where RST is not applicable, incremental costs are much higher.[1]

(3) *The use of computers.* The Canadian study recorded that 40 per cent of the sample used computers in their GST accounting routines (p. 45) and that these businesses had compliance costs that were 20-40 per cent lower than similar businesses using manual accounting systems (p. 79). Because of the different composition of the population sampled, no precise comparisons can be made, but, it is clear that the number of United Kingdom and New Zealand VAT payers using computers was much lower; perhaps half as many in New Zealand in the comparable categories (p. 69) and less still in the United Kingdom (Sandford *et al*, 1986-87, p. 125). The other significant difference is that in neither of these two countries was there a clear cost advantage from the use of computers.

There may be several explanations of these differences. Whilst North America is undoubtedly ahead of both New Zealand and the United Kingdom in the introduction of computers, the differing dates of the studies, particularly the six years between the United Kingdom and the Canadian studies, may account for a considerable part of the difference in a period in which computers have been making rapid advances. The time difference may also help to account for the lack of clear advantage of computer users in the United Kingdom and New Zealand; the introduction of computers would have been more recent in these countries, with

---

[1]Unfortunately the breakdown of the data in the published Plamondon study does not enable us to compare the GST compliance costs of businesses with, and those without, the requirement to comply with the provincial sales tax.

consequent teething problems for the users and the software available at the time of their introduction may have been less suitable than in the later year of the Canadian study.

However that may be, the more widespread and more effective use of computers in Canada must be a factor reducing the compliance costs of the Canadian tax compared to that of New Zealand and the United Kingdom.

Turning now to a comparison of the New Zealand and United Kingdom figures, the most marked difference lies at the bottom end of the scale. Because compliance cost as a percentage of turnover are negatively correlated with size, the overwhelming reason for the difference will be the much lower registration level for the New Zealand tax (about one-third of the United Kingdom threshold of 1986-87) and its wider coverage and the pressure put on small operators in New Zealand to register voluntarily (Sandford and Hasseldine, 1992, pp 120-21).

Conclusions on International Comparisons of Administrative and Compliance Costs

In the light of the international comparisons of administrative costs and of compliance costs illustrated in this chapter, it might seem that such comparisons are likely to mislead rather than reveal the truth and that they are useless. Such a conclusion would be wrong. But it is important that international comparisons of administrative and compliance costs should be regarded as tools to raise questions rather than providing immediate answers.

Significant differences between countries in administrative cost: revenue ratios of tax systems or of individual taxes are no automatic guide to the relative efficiency of the tax administrations; they are simply a starting point on a quest to discover the reasons for the differences which may or may not have to do with administrative efficiency. The causes of the differences will only be unravelled by a knowledge of the definitions used, a detailed study of the taxes being investigated, the composition of the taxpayer population, the macroeconomic backgrounds, together with some idea of relative tax effectiveness (the size of the tax gap) and some reliable measures of compliance costs.

Where compliance costs are being compared it is vital that the data be analysed by size and, where appropriate, by economic sector. The appropriate measure of size will not normally be tax revenue, but rather income or wealth for personal taxpayers, and for businesses a measure such as turnover or employment – though these measures are themselves often imperfect. The starting point for comparing compliance costs is a consideration of the definitions employed and the robustness of the methodologies used. Beyond that, comparisons may be affected by tax structures, related taxes, the accounting methods used by taxpayers and the requirements of the tax administration (such as frequency of filing). Where possible administrative costs should also be considered along with compliance costs.

This list of relevant factors is not intended to be exhaustive, but to give some idea of the care needed and knowledge required if international comparisons of administrative and compliance costs are to be useful. It may well be that, for at least some time to come, policy-makers will get most value from very detailed comparisons of the administrative and compliance costs of small bits of the tax system, such as particular features of a particular tax.

Growth of Interest in Compliance Costs

Governments have always had an interest in administrative costs. They are a part of government expenditure for which finance has to be found. That said, many countries fail to produce estimates of the overall costs of tax collection (especially where different government levels or agencies are involved) and few allocate costs to different taxes and to different administrative functions (Sandford, 1989). There is a need for more revenue departments to collect more information on administrative costs and to analyse it in such a way as to improve management (see chapter 8).

Adam Smith recognised the importance of compliance costs in the *Wealth of Nations*, 1776. Of his four famous 'canons' of taxation, usually summarised as equity, certainty, convenience and economy, two were wholly concerned with tax compliance costs and one partly so. After Smith, however, the subject was largely neglected and no serious attempt to measure tax compliance costs was undertaken until the 1930s (Haig, 1935). Thereafter studies of compliance costs generally were small scale or lacking in rigour until the 1970s (for an account of the earlier studies see Sandford *et al*, 1989, chapter 2 and appendix A and Vaillancourt, 1987); the period since then has seen an increasing number of high quality studies, often with direct or indirect government support and finance. The International Fiscal Association made administrative and compliance costs of taxation a main subject for their 1989 conference and the ensuing cahiers listed studies of varying size and rigour, in nine countries, Argentina, Belgium, Canada, Germany, Netherlands, Sweden, Switzerland, United Kingdom and United States. A 1995 publication (Sandford, 1995) added three more countries to the list, Australia, Spain and New Zealand, whilst outlining further important studies that had also been undertaken in the Netherlands, Canada and the United States. The number of important studies continues to grow, notably large-scale studies in Australia (Evans *et al*, 1996 and 1997), Canada (Plamondon, 1997) and the United Kingdom (Centre for Fiscal Studies, 1998) as well as smaller studies in Singapore (Ariff *et al*, 1994 and 1995) and Malaysia (Loh *et al*, 1997). Other studies extending the scope of tax compliance costs to particular features, such as appeals tribunals (Copp, 1998) and the compliance costs of particular tax legislation including psychic costs, are in progress (Woellner *et al*, 1998). The number of studies continues to grow.

The earlier research preceded government interest, but, from the 1980s, research and government action have often gone hand in hand. The recent major studies have mainly been government financed. Moreover, some governments have officially recognised the importance of compliance costs for tax policy-making and taken measures to try to minimise compliance costs, subject, necessarily, to other objectives. Thus, United Kingdom governments have incorporated this objective in a Taxpayers' Charter and, as part of a general de-regulation exercise, since 1985 have required the tax departments to produce assessments of the costs of all new legislation affecting business, formerly referred to as compliance cost assessments, but subsequently renamed regulatory impact assessments (for further details, see T*he Better Regulation Guide and Regulatory Impact Assessment*, 1998). In New Zealand the Inland Revenue Department issued a *Compliance Cost Reduction Strategic Plan* in 1994 and established a specific unit to implement it. The Australian Taxation Office, in response to recommendations of the Joint Committee of Public Accounts, is committed to producing Tax Impact Statements on tax changes and has commissioned the recent Australian studies mentioned to help it implement this undertaking. All three of these countries are also engaged on major exercises to simplify tax legislation with a view to reducing compliance costs. In the Netherlands governments have required qualitative assessments of compliance costs since 1985 and have more recently adopted targets for reducing compliance costs; whilst in the United States the Internal Revenue Service has commissioned a series of studies on reducing the paperwork burden of tax compliance and is committed to reducing the burden of paperwork by 7 per cent and the expense of tax compliance by 3 per cent by fiscal 2001. Doubtless there are other examples of government action. It is also notable that the OECD has undertaken a study of compliance costs amongst its members.

Why this recent government interest and concern? Partly, it springs from the research findings: that tax compliance costs are 'large' – a multiple of administrative costs in respect of the main central government taxes – taking up a significant volume of resources, possibly reducing international competitiveness and, in so far as compliance costs are tax deductible, costing government revenue. It is also clear that tax compliance costs have undesirable distributional effects, falling with particular severity on small businesses. Especially amongst the proprietors of small businesses, compliance costs generate resentment which may spill over into anti-social behaviour in the form of reduced compliance.

Whilst these features indicate the importance of compliance costs, they have been given impetus in recent years by the widespread introduction of VAT – a transaction-based tax which, in many countries, requires many businesses to collect taxes on their products for the first time; by the spread of the 'enterprise culture' which favoured small firms, which are those particularly hit by compliance costs; by the increasing complication of tax systems and the increasing number of citizens with more complicated affairs; and by the increased emphasis in many OECD countries in securing voluntary compliance. Above all, the computer revolution has played a part; large-scale research on compliance costs can be undertaken with far more ease and the results of this research are far more reliable than hitherto, so that many governments have taken the findings seriously.

The response of governments has, however, been patchy, as is revealed by a recent survey of OECD countries (Evans and Walpole, 1999) to which twenty countries, plus the EU representative, responded. The authors sought to discover the use and effectiveness of tax impact statements, otherwise known as compliance cost assessments or regulatory impact assessments. The authors categorised countries according to a series of criteria such as whether such statements were mandatory for tax changes, the extent of their coverage, whether quantitative as well as qualitative, whether formal guidelines and pro formas were available, if the impact statement was public, and so on. On the basis of such criteria a table was drawn up according to the level of country involvement. Four countries, in fact the ones we have already mentioned, Australia, New Zealand, the United Kingdom and the United

States, together with the European Union, occupy the category of Extensive Use of Tax Impact Statements; nine countries comprised the 'partial use' category; seven were categorised as minimal use. (It might also be hazarded that the five non-respondents – after repeated attempts to contact them – would have fallen into this lowest category as nothing is known of any attempted compliance cost studies in these countries.) The authors acknowledge that there is inevitably a degree of arbitrariness about their classification and some borderline cases; the Netherlands and France, in the 'partial use' category, were particularly close to the upper borderline.

The obvious question is why some countries are so much ahead of the others in taking tax compliance costs seriously. There is no wholly satisfactory answer, but it cannot be coincidence that, in three of the four in the top category, major studies of tax compliance costs were undertaken by independent researchers before government had shown much interest: Pope *et al* in Australia (1990, 1993, 1995); Slemrod and Sorum (1984) in the United States; Sandford (1973) and Sandford *et al* (1981) in the United Kingdom. A major study in New Zealand preceded the setting up of the compliance cost reduction unit there, but the study, whilst carried out by an independent research organisation (the Institute of Policy Studies at Victoria University, Wellington) was, in fact, instigated and financed by the New Zealand Treasury. In all four countries subsequent studies have been undertaken at the behest of the revenue or finance departments. Also it will be no accident that the Netherlands, which is at the top of the list for partial use of tax impact statements, benefited from a major study by Allers (1994). However, this is not a complete answer. One of the early and best pioneering studies took place in Canada (Brydon, 1961), which country also benefited from the work of Vaillancourt (1986) and which subsequently commissioned work from Plamondon (1993 and 1997) and also had the benefit of work by Erard (1997), but failed to make significant use of tax impact statements.

However, recognition of the importance of tax compliance costs is relatively new for all countries and that recognition is rapidly becoming more widespread.

CHAPTER 8

MINIMISING THE TAX GAP

Introduction

In this chapter we look at policies to minimise the tax gap – the gap between what revenue authorities would collect if everyone paid the tax legally due and what is actually collected. Putting the same point in another way, we look at policies to reduce tax evasion. Attempts to measure the underground, black or informal economy, from which the size of the tax gap can be estimated, have been made for many countries, but according to the methods used the results vary widely. The best estimates of the tax gap have been in the United States, through the use of the Taxpayer Compliance Measurement Program (see below p. 147); but even here, as Long and Burnham remind us, 'The problem is that "tax gap" figures, whether those developed by the IRS or by others, are not hard numbers but 'guestimates'. By definition, a tax gap estimate attempts to calculate the billions of dollars of taxable income that is not reported by all Americans – including such groups as moonlighting plumbers and street vendors. By their very nature, many of these kinds of transactions are almost impossible to identify, let alone quantify. This means that the tax gap numbers necessarily are quite inaccurate, even speculative.' (Long and Burnham, 1990).

Where reliable data is so lacking it seems pointless to try to make direct international comparisons. Instead we explore administrative, economic and social/psychological approaches to the problem of tax compliance with a view to framing policies which offer prospects of success in reducing tax evasion. In the process the chapter does provide clues towards answering the vital question: 'Why is tax evasion a more serious problem in some countries than in others?'

Meaning and Analysis of Tax Evasion

Tax evasion is the failure, by an individual or organisation to pay tax legally due, or alternatively to claim a refund to which they are not legally entitled. Tax evasion takes one or both of two main forms.

(1) An understating of taxable income, profits or sales and excise tax receipts (of which the extreme form is a failure to declare any such income or receipts by not making a tax return or not registering for a particular tax when legally required to do so).

(2) An overstating of tax exemptions, allowances, reliefs, credits (of which the extreme form is to claim credits in excess of tax liability).

A survey (Hasseldine, 1993) of a range of studies of admitted evaders consistently shows more cases of undeclared income than of falsely claimed deductions, perhaps because sins of omission are more easily committed (perhaps through carelessness) and may be judged less harshly than sins of commission.

Understating income or overstating deductions are the main but not the only forms of tax evasion. For example, delaying payment, especially in times of inflation, is a form of evasion. Tax evasion embraces both deliberate acts and unintentional evasion arising from ignorance of the law or forgetfulness. Tax evasion ranges from minor omissions to major fraud. In analysing tax evasion we can use the same diagram as in the previous chapter (figure 7.1); for convenience we reproduce it below as figure 8.1. The qualifications listed on p. 124-5, of course, still apply.

Figure 8.1 Relationship beween Total Tax Revenue and Administrative Cost

Policy on tax evasion can be thought of as having two broad aspects, to some extent interconnected, but which, for convenience, can be analysed separately.

(1) How many resources should a government put into tax administration? Additional resources (eg more inspectors and more frequent audits) bring a move to the right on the diagram; this increases revenue, reducing the tax gap, but at a diminishing rate.

(2) How can the position of the curve be raised i.e. how can we increase revenue (reduce the tax gap) for any given level of administrative cost?

How Many Resources in Tax Administration?
(Moving Along the Curve)

The natural response of economists, thinking of the theory of the firm, is to suggest that resources should continue to be employed in tax administration up to the point at which marginal cost (MC) equals marginal revenue (MR); ie more resources should be put into tax administration as long as the incremental addition to tax revenue exceeds the incremental addition to administrative cost.

This raises two issues – the conceptual and the practical. Let us start with the practical, in particular, what should count as revenue, what should count as marginal costs and how do we measure them?

Practical Problems

What should count as marginal revenue? Clearly the extra tax directly collected in the year of investigation as a result of additional enforcement activities should count as revenue; but should an allowance be made for the present value of the future tax revenue expected from the continuance of this additional revenue in future years (on the assumption that convicted tax evaders will behave themselves in the future)? Again, should we include in marginal revenue additional tax arising from the deterrent effect that the knowledge of additional enforcement activities may generate; and even include the present value of the tax revenue generated by a continuation of the deterrent effect beyond the year of investigation? Should fines collected as a result of enforcement activities count as marginal revenue?

What should count as marginal cost? Increasing enforcement activities may not only increase administrative costs (the costs to the revenue authorities); they may also put up tax compliance costs. An increase in enforcement activities may frighten honest taxpayers, who may now feel that they need to be increasingly meticulous about their accounts, or perhaps incur the expense of employing an accountant to make sure that they are doing everything correctly. In other words, ideally, (as we argued in the previous chapter) the cost to take into account is not just the cost to the revenue authorities, but the cost to the economy, marginal social cost or marginal operating cost (ie administrative cost to the revenue authorities plus compliance cost to the taxpayers).

How do we measure them? Clearly, some of these items are very difficult if not impossible to measure: such as the present value of revenue from the deterrent effects; determining marginal administrative cost where resources are jointly supplied; or measuring the marginal compliance costs resulting from additional enforcement activity.

Conceptual Problems

The conceptual problems are even more fundamental. There are reasons for querying whether the MC=MR principle is appropriate. The tax revenue, which is the outcome of the application of real resources to tax administration, represents a transfer of income. Resources applied to tax administration do not generate new goods or services. Thus the analogy of the firm is misleading. The rule of equality between MC and MR does not tell us what total resources should be applied to tax administration. The realisation that tax revenue is a transfer suggests that the level of resources applied to tax administration should be less than that at which MC=MR; but how much less? Moreover, there is a contrary argument: that tax administrative resources should be increased beyond the point where MC=MR. The gap between the total revenue curve and the MPR line represents the extent of tax evasion. It can be argued that tax evaders should be pursued as criminals – they steal from the rest of the community. No-one argues that police expenditure on catching criminals should be related to the loot that can be recovered from them. (In that case plain murderers would not be pursued at all!) Additional expenditure on tax administration, so the argument goes, is therefore justified in order to bring criminals to justice even when the incremental cost is greater than the increment of revenue gained.

Practical Applications

Where does all this lead us in practice? The total resources to be allocated to a revenue department is a decision for a government which may, indeed should, take account of the considerations we have outlined as well as other economic and political considerations. Whilst a revenue department may properly urge the case for an increase in budget because of the additional revenue that it could generate, the more practical decision for a revenue department is, given its total budget, how to allocate its resources. Here the marginal principle is helpful.

There are some expenditures of a revenue department, in the shape of HQ staff and overheads which, whilst essential, cannot directly be related to revenue yield. There are others, notably customer services, which add to costs in the short term but, in the long run, may reduce administrative costs (because, with the benefit of guidance, more taxpayers get their returns right in the future) and even increase revenue (because taxpayers come to view the tax office in a more favourable light and comply more willingly). But for branches of the tax administration concerned with enforcement, such as audit and investigation, the marginal principle is important.

It can be argued that resources in these activities should be so allocated that the ratio between administrative costs and revenue is the same, at the margin, for all taxes. If this is not so, then additional revenue can be raised from the same total resources by transferring resources from where the cost:yield ratio is high to where the cost:yield ratio is low and continuing so to do until the ratios equalise. (It should be noted that we are talking about marginal cost and marginal revenue. The average cost of collection of Tax A may be higher than that of Tax B, but it may still pay (ie generate more income) to transfer resources from B to A.) Indeed the same principles apply within a tax to different income levels, socio-economic groups and types and sizes of business and other characteristics of tax filers. Thus, to over-simplify, if income tax applied only to taxi drivers and publicans and the cost:yield ratio is lower for taxi drivers than publicans, enforcement activities should be increased for taxi drivers and reduced for publicans until the ratio is the same for both.

In practice many revenue departments attempt something like this by what is sometimes referred to as 'risk analysis' – concentrating resources in areas where the risk of revenue loss is greatest. In so doing they usually simplify the issue by ignoring the indirect revenue increases which may come from increased enforcement and concentrating on the direct revenue gain; and without taking effects on compliance costs into the calculation save, perhaps, not pursuing enforcement in too aggressive a manner. Further, in order to maintain the perception of the fairness of the tax system, tax authorities may choose to maintain at least minimum activity in some areas, even though the yield:cost ratios are low. (For a discussion of this issue, see Keith Report, 1993, volume 2, chapter 27, paragraph 5.1.)

The most famous and thorough example of risk analysis work by a revenue department is the discriminant function analysis until 1988 undertaken by the Internal Revenue Service of the United States, leading to the Discriminant Index Function (DIF) (Graetz *et al*, 1989, p.317). About every three years the Internal Revenue Service conducted the Taxpayer Compliance Measurement Program (TCMP) which was a series of special audits, which covered some 50,000 taxpayers randomly selected except for some heavier weighting of high income taxpayers. The audits were exceptionally comprehensive and the prime object was to identify the characteristics of those taxpayers who, if audited, would generate above average revenue. The details of the analysis were kept secret. Filers were given a DIF score according to their characteristics. The higher the DIF score the more likely that an audit of the return would yield additional revenue above a threshold amount. The prime purpose of the DIF score was to select returns for routine audits (which are less comprehensive that the TCMP audit). In calculating the revenue yield, the uncollected tax plus fines from would-be evaders were taken into account. No allowance was made for deterrent effects or future yield. (For further details see Roth, Scholz and Witte, 1989, pp.65-69.)

In 1996, Kenneth Clarke, the then United Kingdom Chancellor of the Exchequer, inaugurated what he described as a 'Spend to Save' initiative to which he allocated £800m. Most of this projected expenditure was to combat benefit fraud, but £187m for Inland Revenue was expected to bring in about ten times as much over three years (with 1,000 extra tax inspectors and another 1,000 transferred from other duties as processing work was computerised). Additional money for Customs and Excise was expected to yield a similar or higher ratio. (*Financial Times*, Nov 27, 1996). After the first full year of operation, the Report of the Board of Inland Revenue recorded that the results of the series of initiatives under the 'Spend to Save' programme were 'very encouraging', yielding revenue in excess of the forecast (Board of Inland Revenue, 1998, p.21).

Referring back to our diagram, in so far as more resources are put into tax administration using the same methods, then evasion diminishes as we move to the right along the curve. In so far as a revenue department adopts more effective methods than hitherto within a given budget (such as better targeting in its audit programme) then the effect is to raise the position of the curve. To other ways of raising the curve we now turn.

Increasing Revenue for the Same Administrative Cost
(Raising the Position of the Curve)

Methods of raising the curve, ie reducing evasion from (broadly the same) administrative cost, can be considered under three heads, which might be thought of respectively as the administrative, the economic and the socio/psychological approach:

(1) minimising evasion opportunities;
(2) reducing the net advantages of tax evasion;
(3) reducing the willingness to evade, ie fostering voluntary compliance.

Minimising Evasion Opportunities (The Administrative Approach)

In his writings on tax evasion, Wallschutzky (for example, Wallschutzky, 1993) rightly stresses the importance of minimising opportunities for evasion. This may be achieved in a number of ways, of which the following are among the most important.

(1) An administrative structure whereby tax is deducted at source wherever possible, whether it be PAYE for employees, dividends and interest of businesses or interest of banks and other financial institutions. If direct deduction at source is not possible the next most effective method is a system of third party reporting, eg by financial institutions, which can provide information to cross-check the taxpayer's own statements. Least satisfactory is sole reliance on the word of the taxpayer.

It was William Pitt the Younger who first introduced income tax into the United Kingdom in 1798, during the Revolutionary War with France. The tax was abolished in 1802 with the Treaty of Amiens, but re-introduced in 1803 by Addington at the Exchequer, when hostilities started in the Napoleonic War. If Pitt takes the credit for introducing the tax Addington must receive equal plaudits for putting it on a sound administrative footing. He introduced taxation at source where possible. The effect: almost the same yield as Pitt's Act from half the rates (Sabine, p.30, 1966).

There is much to be said in favour of the United Kingdom income tax by which the vast majority of taxpayers pay the same marginal rate of tax. As a result, deduction at source is easier and more accurate and, because of this feature and a cumulative PAYE system, for most taxpayers the correct amount of tax is deducted without the need for them to complete a tax return – thus minimising compliance costs for the ordinary taxpayer.

However, it is important to have only a short time lag between the collection of tax by the third party (eg the employer) and its payment to the revenue authorities and to enforce payment by the due date. Delayed payment amounts to evasion and the extent of evasion may be considerable if the inflation rate is high. Unfortunately, deduction at source is not an administrative method that can be applied to self employment earnings. Not surprisingly, compliance rates for income classes not subject to withholding are much lower than for employee income.

(2) Opportunities for tax evasion can be reduced by a simplified tax structure which minimises the number of exemptions, reliefs, concessions and rebates, all of which can be a source of false claims. This statement applies equally to sales taxes as to income and capital taxes. The form of tax may also be important – thus a VAT is generally considered to be less evasion prone than an RST because of its self-policing properties, the audit trail and the fact that only a proportion of the revenue is collected at the vulnerable retail stage (see above, chapter 5). On the other hand if the VAT contains extensive zero rating it opens the way to false claims. Even the existence of multiple rates can encourage evasion by claims that sales relate to lower-taxed goods rather than higher-taxed. A simple tax system is not only important for reducing the scope for false returns, but also for reducing unintentional evasion. Long and Burnham report that 'According to the IRS' own findings, most of the tax returns with errors are the product of complexity and ambiguity in tax requirements, not tax fraud.' (Long and Burnham, 1990).

(3) A further vital component in minimising the opportunities for evasion is an honest tax administration. Corrupt officials invite evasion. A key factor here is again a simple tax structure which minimises tax officer discretion. (For a more detailed consideration of corruption relating to taxation, see, for example, Bowles, 1998.)

(4) Some countries, such as Australia, have found it useful to give all taxpayers a unique tax identification number which has to be used, for example, in the opening of a bank account. If no number is forthcoming, tax is deducted from the interest at the top marginal rate.

(5) In an increasingly global market place it is important to develop links with other tax administrations and exchange information; also to adopt measures of control of the activities of companies operating in more than

one jurisdiction, eg controlled foreign company (CFC) regimes – though these are aimed more at avoidance than evasion.

Reducing the Net Advantages of Evasion (The Economic Approach)

A second way to raise the curve is to reduce the net advantages of evading by increasing the risk:gain ratio. This method is based on the traditional economic approach following Allingham and Sandmo (1972). The taxpayer is viewed as an amoral (if not immoral) rational being concerned to maximise his/her expected utility. Four elements are involved – the level of income, the tax rate on the relevant band of income, the probability of being caught and the penalty if caught. The risk of being caught is increased by more audit or more effective audit activity (which we have already discussed) – making evasion less attractive; a higher penalty structure has the same effect. It is generally taken that the higher the income the more the gain from evasion and the lower the tax rate the less the gain; but there are some complicated interconnections.

It is usually maintained that the higher a person's income the less their aversion to risk. If the effect of reducing the rate of tax is to increase net of tax income, this reduces risk aversion and acts in the opposite way to the effect of the tax reduction, leaving the net outcome unclear. On the other hand if the tax rate reduction is compensated for by an increased tax take elsewhere, either by broadening the tax base or by raising other taxes, there will be no income effect and the lower tax rate can be expected, unequivocally, to reduce evasion from the tax which has been reduced.

However, there is a further problem of interconnections. Often the tax penalty is a fixed multiple of the tax unpaid, eg twice the unpaid tax plus the tax due. If so, then the penalty falls with the tax rate. So the tendency for evasion to fall with a lower tax rate is reduced or offset. However, it is obviously open to a government, if lowering tax rates, to raise the multiple or to impose some additional fine.

There are also some interrelationships regarding the effect of higher penalties on the level of evasion. Higher penalties will be a deterrent to engaging in evasion. But, as Bowles points out (Bowles, 1998) the higher the penalty for evasion, the larger the bribe it is worthwhile for an evader to offer to the tax officer who has found him out; thus high penalties may increase corruption.

Three further comments need to be made about this approach to reducing tax evasion. First, the deterrent effects of increased audits or higher penalties only applies if would-be evaders are aware of these changes. (In fact it is the perception that their chances of being caught have increased that will deter, even if the perception does not accord with reality.) It is vital, therefore, that publicity be given to an anti-evasion programme, increased penalties highlighted and convictions made public (by number if not by name) to generate the perception of increased risk and reduced gain.

A second consideration is that too much emphasis on convictions and punishments may be counter-productive. A heavy-handed policy may set up attitudes which militate against voluntary compliance. On the one hand convicted evaders (and others who have witnessed their punishment) may feel that they have been treated with excessive harshness and may develop an anti-tax department attitude of 'we'll get even'. Whilst such convicted evaders may be more careful in the future, they may then take every opportunity to evade in circumstances where they are most unlikely to be discovered. (One of the limitations of the Allingham and Sandmo analysis is that it assumes that all evasion carries the same probability of detection. In practice this is not so. Some evasions are almost guaranteed to succeed; others are more risky.) The second unfortunate effect of a heavy handed policy is that, as we have mentioned above, even entirely honest taxpayers feel threatened. As a result, their compliance costs may rise, either because they become over-meticulous with their tax record-keeping or/and because they decide to shelter behind an accountant and hence incur professional fees. This, in itself, is an unfortunate use of resources, but, also, as we shall argue in the next section, high compliance costs generate resentment and militate against voluntary compliance. In addition, in so far as compliance costs are tax deductible, they actually reduce tax revenue.

Thirdly, this approach assumes that penalties are actually imposed and collected. Long and Burnham point out that, in the United States, many people appeal tax assessments successfully and they assert that when deliberate cheats are audited by the IRS, rarely does the agency require more than the payment of the taxes it claims plus accrued interest. They conclude 'Even when audited the calculating tax cheat seldom is worse off than if he or she had reported the correct amount in the first place. Some deterrent!' (Long and Burnham, 1990).

This economic analysis is interesting and subsequent work has increased its sophistication; it is useful in focusing on some of the instruments which can be adjusted to combat evasion, but it is far from being the whole story.

Reducing Willingness to Evade (The Socio-Psychological Approach)

The third category focuses on attitudes and motivations to behaviour. Reducing willingness to evade means fostering a positive attitude towards tax paying and the tax department. As some recent researchers, Coleman and Freeman, argue, it is a matter of researching into why people wish to evade taxes and then doing something about it (Coleman and Freeman, 1996). They particularly look at what they call 'cultural background' influences, which formed early attitudes, such as family values, civics, peer groups, aspirational group attitudes and personal experiences.

In what follows some of the more important issues that emerge from research in this field are put forward. Much of the research is reviewed in Roth, Scholz and Witte, 1989, and Roth and Scholz, 1989, but not all of the propositions can be regarded as having been conclusively validated by research findings. Some must be regarded as more in the nature of plausible hypotheses. Unfortunately, too, none of the proposed measures for promoting voluntary compliance is likely to have speedy results.

In what follows we group the considerations under three heads, starting with the broadest and most abstract and narrowing to the personal experience of the individual.

(1) Commitment to obey the law. The overall weight of evidence from various kinds of research suggests the importance for tax compliance of commitment to obey the law. 'Commitment to obey the law refers to the individual's perceived moral obligation to obey, based on internalised beliefs and attitudes' (Roth, Scholz and Witte, p.118, 1989). Clearly, then, any way of maintaining and increasing that general commitment will maintain or increase tax compliance; important in this regard are features such as demonstration of the fairness of elections; the impartiality of the law; the independence of the courts; the availability of a cheap, speedy and accessible appeal system; and a strong civic sense. There is some evidence that even conscience appeals to taxpayers can increase compliance (Hasseldine, 2000).

(2) Conviction of the integrity of government and the efficiency and equity of government expenditure and taxation. Unfavourable to tax compliance are a series of negative perceptions of government: that government is corrupt; that it is wasteful in its expenditure (eg by extravagant buildings); that in its expenditure it favours certain ethnic groups or economic classes over others; that taxation lacks horizontal and

vertical equity; that reliable information is hard to get and there is a lack of transparency.

There is a link between avoidance and evasion. If the poor see the rich avoiding taxes on a large scale, the poor, who lack avoidance opportunities and perceive the tax system as inequitable, are more likely to engage in evasion.

The relationship between tax and expenditure, sometimes referred to as the exchange relationship, is important. The stronger are the feelings of inequity about the way taxes are disbursed the less compliant taxpayers are likely to be; they will resent seeing their hard-earned money go to be wasted in extravagant or inefficiently run schemes, line the pockets of corrupt politicians and civil servants, or favour some group to which they do not belong. Conversely a government which is democratic, is generally perceived to be clean, where breaches of conduct are severely punished and which provides detailed and reliable information about just how the taxpayers' money is spent, is more likely to generate a favourable attitude to paying taxes.

There is much circumstantial evidence that complexity in a tax system and, in particular, high tax compliance costs, have negative effects on tax compliance. Thus, the small businessman, who faces disproportionately high compliance costs for his own income tax, sales tax and the tax he has to collect from his employees, may well revolt against paying his due amount. He may feel that it is bad enough to have to pay tax in the first place, but it is adding insult to injury to have to incur high compliance costs on his personal tax, and in acting as the unpaid tax collector for the government. In these circumstances the small business taxpayer may decide that he will cheat on his tax return at least to the extent of recovering the compliance costs which the government imposes on him.

There is some limited evidence in the United States that complicated tax forms discourage some less educated taxpayers from filing. Further, some very detailed aspects of the tax code (for example, in the United Kingdom in the field of fringe benefits) are not adhered to by all taxpayers from ignorance or from the feeling that it is just not worth the hassle. The answer, therefore, is to seek to minimise tax compliance costs. Governments should publicly express their intention so to minimise them (subject to other objectives), automatically take them into consideration in all tax policy discussions and, like the United Kingdom, New Zealand and Australia, require the revenue departments to produce assessments of the compliance costs of changes in the tax law.

There is also a case, under strictly controlled circumstances, for compensating taxpayers who have incurred exceptional compliance costs.

For example, suppose a taxpayer has been the subject of an in-depth investigation as a result of which he has emerged blameless; there is a strong case in equity, for compensating him for the exceptional compliance costs that investigation has imposed on him. The case for compensation is particularly strong if this has happened twice within a short period.

(3) Relationship to the tax office. The relationship between the taxpayer and the tax office is an important element in achieving compliance. A helpful customer services unit; a special small business unit which is aware of the needs and stresses of the small business sector; above all, an attitude on the part of the tax office by which taxpayers are seen as clients, to be helped; as people innocent until proved guilty. Bad personal experience of a tax office militates against compliance whilst a good experience has the reverse effect.

A particularly important aspect is an appropriate complaints system. In June 1993 the United Kingdom Government set up a Citizen's Charter Complaints Task Force, which listed seven principles which should characterise a complaints system: it should

- be easily accessible and well publicised;
- be simple to understand and use;
- allow speedy handling with established time limits for action and keep people informed of progress;
- ensure a full and fair investigation;
- respect people's desire for confidentiality;
- address all points at issue and provide an effective response and appropriate redress;
- provide information to management so that services can be improved.

However efficient, there are bound to be some mistakes in a large organisation and how well complaints are dealt with is very important in generating a favourable atmosphere amongst taxpayers.

An interesting and successful experiment in the United Kingdom has been the appointment of an Adjudicator, since 1993, initially for Inland Revenue with subsequent extension to Customs and Excise and the Contributions Agency. The Adjudicator doesn't deal with technical issues of tax and tax liability (for which there is a separate appeals system) but with complaints against the administration of the revenue departments (Filkin, 1998).

These three approaches, the administrative, the economic and the socio/psychological should not be seen as separate or competitive, but rather as complementary. (For an interesting attempt to fuse the economic and socio-psychological approach, see Cullis and Lewis, 1997.)

Summary of Most Important Policy Measures for Tackling Evasion

The most important policy measures for reducing the tax gap may be summarised as follows:

- fostering a commitment to obey the law;
- taxing at source wherever possible and, where not possible, using third party reporting;
- operating a simple tax system with minimum tax expenditures (in other words with a tax base which is measurable, observable and verifiable);
- employing an efficient system of auditing to maximise revenue from given resources subject to giving some coverage to each class of taxpayer;
- undertaking regular reviews of the penalty structure – particularly important in times of inflation – with appropriate publicity for increased penalties;
- engaging in public spending which is perceived as non-wasteful and equitable;
- levying taxes which are perceived as equitable;
- running an honest and customer-friendly tax administration;
- developing effective links with other tax administrations.

The more successful a country in implementing these policy measures and balancing the 'carrot and stick', the smaller the tax gap is likely to be.

CHAPTER 9

TAX POLICY-MAKING AND TAX REFORM

Introduction

This chapter explores the interconnected themes of tax policy-making and tax reform. The process of tax policy-making consists of a series of stages which are necessarily common to all democratic countries, although the stages themselves 'blur, overlap and intermingle' (Parsons, 1995, p.17). But countries differ in the emphasis on each stage and the process within each stage may differ markedly between countries (and to some extent also, between different periods or taxes in the same country). The chapter explores these differences in recent tax history, centring on what, for convenience, we can call the world-wide tax reform of the 'eighties.

The chapter begins with a generalised account of this tax reform movement. Then aspects of the tax policy-making process are set out and differences between countries explored by a more detailed analysis of tax reform in six countries. The six countries examined in detail are Australia, Canada, Ireland, New Zealand, the United Kingdom and the United States. It may be regarded as a disadvantage that they are all English-speaking countries. Clearly this has been a practical advantage for the author/researcher whose native tongue is English, but the selection can be defended on more robust grounds. By and large the English-speaking countries were the leaders in the tax reform movement of the 1980s. Moreover these six countries offer a wide diversity of experience on which to draw. They cover three continents – Europe, America and Australasia. Three are unitary states (Ireland, New Zealand and the United Kingdom) and three federal (Australia, Canada and the United States) and within each group differences of constitution and political practice are marked. Whilst there are major common threads in their tax reform programmes, they differ in significant ways, for example, in their tax background and history, in the emphasis placed on the objectives of reform, in the ease or difficulty of legislating for tax reform, in the structure and relationship between relevant government departments, in

156

the range of tax reform and in the degree of success which it achieved. Altogether they comprise a rich ore from which to quarry.

We then assess the success of tax reform using three criteria: (1) how far the reform met the reformers' declared objectives; (2) how far the reform has stood the test of time; and (3) whether the reform had significant side effects.

The chapter concludes with some reflections on the policy-making process.

World-wide Tax Reform of the 'Eighties[1]

The Meaning of 'Tax Reform'

We need to start by defining terms. Dictionaries give essentially two meanings of 'reform'. One is to 'improve', 'make better', 'remove imperfections'. The other is, literally, to 're-form', to 'restructure', to 'change'. When politicians claim to be reforming taxation they use the term in both senses – a restructuring which is also an improvement. But whether a particular change in the tax structure is an improvement or not is very much a matter of personal value judgment. History abounds in examples of tax changes made by one government in the name of tax reform which are then reversed by a succeeding government also claiming the mantle of tax reform. And whilst this is most frequent when a new government comes to office of a different ideological persuasion from its predecessor, it can also happen with successive governments of the same political persuasion, witness the introduction and replacement of the community charge by successive Conservative governments in the United Kingdom, as described in chapter 3.

In this chapter we seek to avoid value judgments as far as possible by using 'reform' in its second sense of restructuring or change without necessarily implying that the change is for the better. Clearly not any and every change can be dignified by the designation 'reform'. To justify that title it needs to be a non-trivial change and to have as its objective something more than simply adding a little to government revenue or returning something to the taxpayer. Within that rubric, 'tax reform' could embrace the introduction of a substantial new tax, the abolition of a tax, major changes in tax rates, a change in the tax mix, significant changes in tax administration such as the introduction of a system of self-assessment, a change in the tax unit or the indexation of the tax system.

[1] For a full account of the world-wide tax reform movement of the 'eighties, see Sandford, 1993.

The Tax Reform Movement of the 'Eighties

By the 'tax reform of the 'eighties', we mean the world-wide tax reform movement, with common characteristics, causes and philosophy, centred on the decade of the 1980s. For some countries it began before the 1980s, as in the United Kingdom with Sir Geoffrey Howe's Budget of 1979. For others it continued well beyond the 1980s. In Canada, the introduction of its GST took place on January 1, 1991; the Swedish 'tax reform of the century' did not begin until 1990; and the tax changes in Australia, including a GST, legislated for in 1999, could be regarded as unfinished business from the Australian Government's tax reforms of the mid '80s. But the designation of 'tax reform of the 'eighties' can be justified because the philosophy and the motive power came essentially from that decade.

The tax reform of the 'eighties was remarkable for its world-wide nature. Every continent was affected and developing countries as well as advanced countries – though we shall concentrate on the latter. Such a world-wide tax movement was without precedent except for the financial exigencies of two World Wars.

No less remarkable than the geographical extent were its common characteristics. The universal feature of tax reform in advanced countries was a reduction in the rates of personal income tax, the dominant element being the slashing of top marginal rates. Table 9.1 shows, for a selection of OECD countries, the top rates of central government personal income tax rates in 1976, before reform, in 1986, a mid year of reform and in 1992, when reform for most countries was complete. The table needs to be interpreted with care (as discussed in chapter 4 p. 51) because of the existence of local/state income taxes, especially in the Scandinavian countries and in federal countries, and because the table makes no allowance for the differing thresholds at which top rates applied or for any other income-related taxes, like social security contributions. Nonetheless the overall message is clear; top rates were almost everywhere massively reduced.

The lower rates of income tax were also reduced, if less dramatically, and along with the reduction in rates came a reduction in the number of steps in the income tax, typically reduced to two or three.

The loss of revenue from income tax reductions was at least partly made good by a widening of the income tax base. Many tax expenditures were eliminated or reduced; the taxation of expenses and fringe benefits was tightened up in many countries and in Australia and New Zealand a tax, payable by employers, was introduced on the fringe benefits of employees. As part of this base broadening, taxes on capital gains were introduced, as in Australia, or tightened up and levied at, or more nearly at, marginal income tax rates, as, for example, in the United States and the United Kingdom.

Table 9.1 Top Rates of Central Government Personal Income Tax for 1976, 1986 and January 1992 for Selected OECD Countries

Country	Top rates per cent			Percentage points reduction
	1976	**1986**	**1992**	**1992** *minus* **1976**
Australia	65	57	48	17
Austria	62	62	50	12
Canada[a]	43	34	29	14
Finland[a]	51	51	39	12
France	60	65	57	3
Germany	56	56	53	3
Ireland	77	58	52[d]	25
Italy	72	62	50	22
Japan[a]	75	70	50	25
Netherlands[b]	72	72	60	12
New Zealand	60	57	33	27
Norway[a]	48	40	13	35
Sweden[a]	57	50	20	37
United Kingdom[c]	83	60	40	43
United States	70	50	31	39
Unweighted average	**63.4**	**56.3**	**41.7**	**21.7**

Notes: [a] Countries with income tax at lower levels of government, typical rates for 1992 being flat: Canada 17, Finland 16, Norway 28, Sweden 31; progressive: Japan 5 to 14, United States 2 to 14.
[b] 1976 and 1986 figures refer to personal income tax only; 1992 includes social security contributions now levied on same base as income tax.
[c] In 1976 only, an additional 15 percentage points for investment income above a threshold.
[d] Reduced to 48 per cent in the 1992 Budget.

Source: OECD various.

Another feature of the reform was a reduction in company income tax rates (typically falling from around 40 or 50 per cent to the mid-30s) and again, as with personal income tax, accompanied by a reduction in reliefs, concessions and allowances. One feature in some, but not all reforming countries, was a move towards an imputation system of corporate income tax.

A number of countries saw changes in the tax mix, with indirect taxation increasing to offset the decline in revenue from personal income tax. This usually took the form of higher rates of VAT, where that already existed, as in the United Kingdom, or the introduction of a VAT, as in New Zealand. In Canada and the United States the tax mix change took the form of revenue from corporate income tax replacing that from personal income tax; even though, in both these countries, corporate income tax rates were reduced, the gain in revenue from the reduction of tax expenditures more than offset the fall from lower rates.

Other features, common but not universal, were the general tightening up of tax administration, the introduction of new measures to combat evasion in the most vulnerable economic sectors, actions to limit tax avoidance and, in a few countries, the introduction or extension of indexation of tax thresholds and allowances against the effects of inflation.

To sum up: the typical characteristics of the tax reform movement of the 1980s were reductions in personal and corporate income tax rates allied to base broadening, with a change in the tax mix usually taking the form of an increase in indirect taxation to replace revenue from lower direct taxes.

Causes of Reform

The obvious question is: 'Why did reform come when it did and take the form it did?' Whilst taxes can never be popular with those who have to pay them, the late 1970s and early 1980s witnessed a large and growing discontent with the tax system. Avoidance was rife in some countries, perhaps especially in the United States and Australia, to the point where it was in danger of undermining tax morality and voluntary compliance. There was also evidence that evasion was increasing. In Ireland in 1980 employees downed pens to march through Dublin and other cities to protest at the unfair burden of taxation which fell on them as compared with farmers and the self-employed – a view with echoes in many other countries. In some countries, notably Australia and New Zealand, whilst the top rates of tax were not amongst the highest, they cut in at relatively low incomes, eg the 60 per cent rate in Australia applied at only 1.5 times average earnings, which compares with 18 times 30 years earlier (Commonwealth Government, 1985).

Moreover, taxes were failing to achieve the social and economic objectives expected of them. As table 9.1 suggests, the 1960s and 1970s were characterised by very high marginal tax rates, intended to reduce inequalities of income. But they were failing to achieve this objective, not least because of the increasing avoidance and evasion. The rates were also high because of the wide range of tax expenditures, many intended as incentives to stimulate investment of various kinds. Yet the evidence suggested that such incentives rarely achieved their purpose, were very expensive in terms of lost revenue and introduced new distortions into the economy, in addition to the distortions and disincentives generated by the high marginal tax rates themselves (see, for example, Holland, 1991). Furthermore, a series of econometric studies in the early 1980s (Browning, 1978; Ballard *et al*, 1982; Stuart, 1984; Ballard *et al*, 1985) suggested that the costs of these distortions were much higher than had previously been recognised.

The high tax rates were partly a product of increased government spending, which resulted in an overall increase in the tax burden. Amongst the 24 member countries of the OECD in 1984, taxation, as a percentage of GDP at market prices, was on average 10 percentage points above its 1965 level – an increase as a percentage of GDP of nearly 40 per cent.

The inflation of the 1970s added to the dissatisfaction with the high tax levels by generating additional inequities. Acting on unindexed tax systems inflation hit hardest those dependent on allowances, pushed people into higher tax brackets when their real income had not risen, discouraged saving and undermined the living standards of pensioners on fixed money incomes.

Whilst these various influences helped to generate tax reform, it was assisted by international agencies and international example. Countries joining the EEC were required to introduce VAT. The IMF and World Bank advocated tax reform. The OECD, whilst not an advisory organisation, served to publicise, at meetings and conferences, the reforms of its members. More broadly, in an increasingly global marketplace, countries could not be indifferent to the tax levels of their competitors; and the need to take note of another's tax reductions was particularly acute for those countries with similar language and close proximity to much larger economies; as with Canada *vis-à-vis* the United States, and Ireland *vis-à-vis* the United Kingdom.

Above all, however, the tax reform movement of the 1980s can only be properly understood as part of a broader change in economic philosophy and economic policy. The 1980s witnessed disillusionment with the capability of the state as an agent of economic policy and a revival of belief in the efficacy of markets – a change of attitude no less true of Labour governments in Australia and New Zealand than of Thatcher's Britain and Reagan's United States. The tax reform movement of the 'eighties was essentially part of a world-wide movement to curtail the economic role of the state – to push back the boundaries of state intervention in the economy and to revert to the market. Thus the characteristics of this wider movement were privatisation, de-regulation, freeing exchange rates, promoting competition and, in the remaining public sector increasing managerial efficiency – and tax reform.

This change in philosophy accounts for the characteristic features of the tax reform of the 'eighties. Equity (in the sense of horizontal equity – the equal treatment of equals) and simplicity (simplifying the tax system) usually figure in the official objectives of tax reform, but it is efficiency, in the sense of the efficient allocation of resources, that almost invariably has pride of place. The 'tax reform of the 'eighties' was primarily aimed at minimising tax distortions, removing or reducing tax hindrances to the free working of markets, both markets for products and markets for labour and capital. The phrase which became current in the economic world was 'the level playing field'. Taxation, especially where rates were high and reliefs widespread, created bumps in the playing field. Tax reform aimed to remove or reduce these bumps.

This emphasis on efficiency, or tax neutrality, contrasts markedly with reform attempts in the 'sixties and 'seventies; then the emphasis had been on equity in the sense of vertical equity, interpreted as highly progressive taxation to reduce inequalities in income and wealth.

The Process of Tax Policy-Making

In the literature on the policy-making process it is common practice to distinguish a number of stages, such as **conception** covering the origins, background and objectives of the proposed policy; **formulation** – the process of turning the policy ideas into workable form; **preparation** – the work of the departments, consultation and measures to promote acceptability; **legislation** – the parliamentary stage; **implementation** – the means by which the legislation is brought into effect and finally **monitoring** and **modification**.

In practice the stages are nothing like as discrete as this outline suggests. Moreover, on its way through the policy-making machine tax proposals will be subject to influences affecting more than one stage, most notably the pressure from lobbies and the media. Partly for these reasons, but more especially because we are comparing countries in relation to policies which were sometimes spread over a number of years, we have discarded a sequentially phased or staged approach. To provide a firm basis for understanding we start by comparing the significant constitutional features and differences of the six countries we are examining in detail. We then look at objectives and background influences, at significant features of the preparation and implementation process and then at the politicians who were responsible for advancing or hindering the reform process and the relations between them. Amendment and modification is considered in the context of an assessment of the success of tax reform.

Content of Tax Reform

Before tackling this analysis we need to summarise the reforms of the six countries between 1979 and 1992 (table 9.2). The order in which they appear in the table approximates to the chronological order of their core tax reform.

The content of the tax reforms follows very much the general characteristics outlined in the earlier pages of this chapter - reduction in personal income tax rates (especially top rates) allied to base broadening; a similar pattern for corporate income tax; capital gains tax (introduced for the first time in Australia) allied more closely to personal income tax, with the exception of New Zealand, where a reform was prepared but then dropped; and a general tightening up on fringe benefits with administrative measures to combat evasion and avoidance. On indexation there are differences between the countries: only the United Kingdom and the United States went in for full indexation of the thresholds, brackets and allowances of personal income tax, whilst Canada, after being the first of the six countries to introduce indexation (1974) ultimately settled for indexation in excess of 3 per cent inflation in any one year. There was no indexation of income tax in Australia, Ireland and New Zealand, although Australia had flirted with it in earlier years (Sandford, 1993, p. 88). Australia and Ireland did, however, include cost base indexation in their CGTs and Ireland indexed its Capital Acquisitions Tax.

Table 9.2 Summary of Tax Reforms, 1979-92

	Personal Income Tax (PIT)	Corporate Income Tax (CIT)	Capital Gains Tax (CGT)	Indirect Taxes	Benefits in Kind	Administrative Measures	Indexation	Death and Gift Taxes	Comments
United Kingdom	Top rate cut in 2 stages from 83% to 40%. Basic rate cut in stages from 30% to 25%. Investment income surcharge abolished. Base broadening. No. of brackets cut to 2	'84 Rates cut in stages from 52% to 35% (lower for small companies.) Base broadening	'88 Rates aligned with PIT but separate tax free allowance	'79: 15% rates replaced dual rate (8% and 12.5%). '92: rate increased to 17.5%	Increases on company cars	Tightening of administration following 'Keith' Committee	Extended to CGT and Death duties. (From '77 had applied to PIT threshold, brackets and main allowances)	Gradual reduction to single rate of 40%. Limited tax on gifts. More reliefs	Community Charge (poll tax) replaced local rate (see chap 3). New tax expenditures added intended to promote enterprise and saving
New Zealand	Rate cuts in stages. By '88, 2 rates 24% and 33%. Base broadening	'88: Full dividend imputation Rate cut to 28% (33% non-resident companies). Base broadening	CGT proposed but never implemented	GST on wide base replaced WST. Initial rate 10%; raised to 10.5% in '88	'85: new fringe benefit tax on employers	Various anti-avoidance measures	None	No change	At introduction of GST, a new family benefit. '88: Roger Douglas proposed single rate PIT; repudiated by Prime Minister Lange.
Australia	'85-87: top rate cut 60% to 49%. Other rates small reductions. Base broadening	'87: Full dividend imputation. Rate from 46% to 39%. Base broadening	Rationalisation of WST	'86: New fringe benefit tax on employers	'86: new fringe benefit tax on employers	Various anti-evasion measures. From '86 implementation of self-assessment for PIT	None in PIT but cost base indexation for CGT	No death or gift taxes (abolished, '77)	Detail relates to federal government; states did not levy these taxes. Proposals for RST to replace WST discarded at Tax Summit

Table 9.2 Summary of Tax Reforms, 1979–92 (continued)

	Personal Income Tax (PIT)	Corporate Income Tax (CIT)	Capital Gains Tax (CGT)	Indirect Taxes	Benefits in Kind	Administrative Measures	Indexation	Death and Gift Taxes	Comments
United States	'81: top rate cut from 70% to 50%. '86: 2 rates, 15% and 28% (previously 14 rates). Minimum tax strengthened. Base broadening	'86: top rate cut 46% to 34%. Minimum tax strengthened. Base broadening	'86: capital gains taxed at full (new) IT rates	No change	Limits on tax deductibility of business meals	'82: tightening up on tax administration	'85: indexation of PIT personal exemption, standard deductions and brackets implemented	'81: big reductions and concessions	Detail relates to federal government; states generally levy income tax and RST. *From '86*: PIT rates nominally 2; because of phasing out of personal exemption and 15% rate, effective rates 15, 28, 33, 28%
Canada	'85: minimum PIT introduced. '87: rate cuts; top rate 34% to 28%. Tax credits replaced major exemptions and deductions. Brackets from 10 to 3	'87: standard rate cut 36% to 28%. Base broadening	'87: larger proportion of gains to count as income. Lifetime exemption limited	'91: GST at 7% replaced MST. GST zero rated 'basic groceries'. New tax credit	'87: deduction for entertainment expenses limited	New general anti-avoidance rule	For PIT inflation over 3%	No death or gift taxes (abolished '71)	Detail relates to federal government; provinces generally levy income tax and RST
Ireland	Gradual rate reduction. Top rates cut from 60% to 48%. Brackets from 3 to 2. Limited base broadening	Standard rate cut 50% to 40%. Base broadening	*From '92*, single rate of 40% replaced tapering (60% maximum)	Number of VAT rates reduced. VAT standard rate cut 25% to 21%. VAT base broadening	Various measures to tighten up	Measures to combat evasion and avoidance. Extension of self-assessment	None for PIT. Indexation of capital acquisition tax (death and gifts) and CGT	Top rate cut 50% to 40%. Rationalisation	The changes were incremental over a period of 7 governments, 6 general elections and 9 finance ministers (including non-consecutive repeats). Particular progress '87–'88 and '89–'92

Changes in death and gift taxes, referred to in the final column, were
not a general feature of the tax reform of the 'eighties, but are of some
interest in the context of the overall effects of tax reforms in these
countries, which we discuss below. Before the period started Australia and
Canada had already abolished their death and gift taxes and New Zealand
was to follow suit with its estate duty, but not its gift tax, in 1993 (see
above chapter 6). The United States and the United Kingdom both cut
back significantly on the severity of their death and gift taxes over the
reform period.

Constitutional Features

The constitution is the framework within which the tax policies are
effected and it influences those policies in highly significant ways. Table
9.3 summarises important constitutional features of the six countries.
Three are unitary and three federal. All but one country, the United States,
follow the 'Westminster' pattern, by which the government is drawn from
members of the legislature and the chief executive, the prime minister, is
normally the leader of the majority party. By contrast, under the
'Washington' system of separation of powers, the executive, consisting of
an elected president and a cabinet chosen by the president, is completely
separate from the legislature; any member of the legislature who joins the
cabinet has to resign his or her seat.

Under federal constitutions the upper house or senate is intended to
represent the states as such, with each state usually having equal
representation irrespective of its population; whilst in Australia and the
United States the Senate is elected, in Canada all senators are appointed,
nominally by the Governor-General as the Queen's representative, but on
the nomination of the Prime Minister; however, the appointments must be
on a regional basis.

New Zealand is the only unicameral country of the six, but in the other
two non-federal countries, the United Kingdom and Ireland, the upper
house has virtually no powers over taxing bills. In the federal countries the
position varies. Apart from the requirement that taxing bills must be
introduced in the lower house, the two chambers of the United States
Congress have equal powers; any disagreements between them must be
resolved by a conference committee. In Australia the House of
Representatives originates money bills which require the approval of the
Senate; the Senate cannot amend a taxing bill, but it can send it back to the
lower house for amendment and, by implication, can effectively reject

such a bill. In a case of deadlock there is provision for a double dissolution with the possibility of a joint sitting of the two houses if the general election fails to provide a solution. No such provision was called into play during the tax reform period. The Canadian House of Commons originates money bills but they require the approval of the Senate. As senators serve for a period of 15 years, at any one time the party composition of the Senate may be different from that of the federal government. To break a deadlock, the constitution gives the prime minister the right to appoint eight extra senators. In 1990 Prime Minister Mulroney invoked this power, never before used, to secure the passage of the bill providing for the GST.

In all cases except the United States, where election dates are fixed, there is a maximum term specified for the lower house and elections are frequently called before the term is completed. The partial exception is New Zealand, where, although a general election may be called before the three year term is up, there is a convention that parliament should run for the full term and, save for very good reason, a prime minister calling an early election might suffer for it at the polls. For the United Kingdom, Canada and Ireland the maximum term is five years; for Australia and New Zealand, three years. This shorter period is hardly enough to enable a new government to introduce, from scratch, a tax as complicated as a VAT and have it bedded down before the ensuing election. The New Zealand Government of 1984 managed this, but work on a possible VAT had been undertaken by the Treasury during the previous administration. In Australia this constraint on tax reform had a significant effect. As we saw in chapter 5 (p. 89), the restriction imposed by the three year period was, according to former Prime Minister Bob Hawke, the main reason the Government preferred a retail sales tax to a VAT – which the Commissioner of Taxation had said would take one year longer to introduce. This, in turn, resulted in the lack of business support for the proposal for a broad-based consumption tax at the Tax Summit (see below p. 180) and helped to undermine the 1985 tax reform.

For lower house elections four countries use the voting system of single member constituencies with single non-transferable vote, colloquially known as 'first past the post', which favours the large parties and makes for strong government. In Australia, whilst single member constituencies are the rule there are two divergencies from the practice of the other four: voting is compulsory and there is preferential voting, so that, where no candidate has an absolute majority, the second preferences of the candidate with least votes are divided amongst the other candidates, a procedure continued until one candidate has an absolute majority.

Table 9.3 Constitutional Features, 1979-92

	Type	Legislature		Parliamentary Terms		Election/Selection Procedures		Comments
		Houses	Financial Powers	Lower House	Upper House	Lower House	Upper House	
United Kingdom	Unitary Westminster	Bicameral: House of Commons House of Lords	House of Commons only	5 years maximum	Not relevant	Single member constituencies with non-transferable vote	Not relevant	Usually strong single party government
New Zealand	Unitary Westminster	Unicameral: House of Representatives	House of Representatives	3 years maximum	Not applicable	Single member constituencies with non-transferable vote	Not applicable	Strong single party government in this period
Australia	Federal Westminster	Bicameral: House of Representatives Senate	House of Representatives originates money bills; Senate can request amendments	3 years maximum	Senators elected for 6 years, half retiring at any one time	Single member constituencies with compulsory preferential voting	Equal representatives of states; transferable vote; constituency the whole state	Often government does not control the Senate
United States	Federal Washington	Bicameral: House of Representatives Senate	Equal powers except House originates taxing bills	Fixed date 2 years	Senators elected for 6 years, one-third retiring at each election	Single member constituencies with non-transferable vote	Equal representatives of states; 2 senators per state	Loose party ties. President (usually) proposes but Congress disposes
Canada	Federal Westminster	Bicameral: House of Commons Senate	Taxing bills originate in Commons but require assent of Senate	5 years maximum	Senators appointed for life or until age 75	Single member constituencies with non-transferable vote	All senators appointed under prime minister's patronage on regional basis	Provision for PM to appoint 8 additional senators to break a deadlock
Ireland	Unitary Westminster	Bicameral: Dail Senate	Essentially Dail only	5 years maximum	Not relevant	Multi-member constituencies with single transferable vote	Not relevant	PR system means generally coalition governments and frequent elections

The exception to single member constituencies is the Irish electoral system of proportional representation in the form of multi-member constituencies with single transferable vote – a system which resulted in minority or coalition governments for all except the first two years of the period 1979-1992. Such governments are more prey to pressure groups of various kinds than governments with a clear majority and are less inclined to risk embarking on a potentially controversial programme of tax reform. Reforms that are attempted are likely to be modest in extent and incremental in method. Moreover, minority and coalition governments make for instability. The thirteen years 1979-1992 witnessed six general elections in Ireland and an even larger number of finance ministers. Such instability must reduce the prospect of a sustained programme of tax reform with a consistent set of objectives. Nonetheless there are counter influences. The nature of the electoral system and the nature of Irish political parties (based on historical differences to partition rather than on ideological or class lines) promote 'centrist' policies, so that any reform enacted by one government is less likely to be overturned by the next government. Furthermore, by a strange turn of fate, Fianna Fail's inability to govern on its own in 1989 gave its junior partner in the Coalition, the Progressive Democrats, who were pledged to promote tax reforms, the chance to make reform a condition of support. Again, the instability of Irish governments should not be over-emphasised; a Fine Gael-Labour Coalition was continuously in office from December 1982 to March 1987, a period in which the five other countries achieved major reforms; the Irish government had a blue-print for reform provided by the Commission on Taxation (set up by its predecessor) but did nothing; what was lacking was the political will.

Turning to the process of election of the relevant upper chambers; United States senators are elected for six years (one-third retiring every two years) whilst members of the House of Representatives are elected for only two years; this means that the party composition of the upper house is often different from that of the lower; and a president, elected every four years, can find one or both houses dominated by the party of a different persuasion to his own. Given the looseness of party ties, however, a contrary party dominating one of the legislative chambers is not necessarily a fatal bar to a president's proposals any more than party consonance between president and legislature is a guarantee of success.

The electoral system for the upper house is also of tax policy significance for Australia. The Australian Senate is elected on a transferable vote system with the whole state constituting the constituency; currently 12 members are elected for each of the six states, with two each for the Northern Territory and the Australian Capital Territory. The result of this form of proportional representation is that the Senate gives more opportunity for independents and small parties which, allied to the six year period of service of senators, means that the government frequently lacks a majority in the Senate. To get its legislation through, it may have to make concessions. Thus, to ensure the passage of its 1985 tax reform bill, the Labor Government had to make a series of changes, mainly affecting capital gains tax, to satisfy the Democrats, who held the balance of power in the Senate. More recently, in 1999, the Liberal/National Government was forced to modify its GST proposals, by agreeing to zero rate some products, in order to secure Democrat support in the Senate.

Objectives and Background Influences

Under the Westminster system a taxing bill is normally introduced by the finance minister[1] (called the Chancellor of the Exchequer in the United Kingdom and the Treasurer in Australia). The third column of table 9.4 represents a summary of the stated objectives of the finance ministers (we assume the declared objectives were the real objectives).

The degree of independence of the finance ministers differs between countries. At one extreme is the United Kingdom, where the Chancellor of the Exchequer holds a very powerful position. The prime minister apart, he does not have to discuss tax reform proposals with cabinet colleagues or obtain cabinet approval. Since 1987 it has been customary to hold a cabinet discussion on economic policy each July and to have a budget strategy discussion in Cabinet in January or February each year, but these are general discussions which do not inhibit a Chancellor's freedom of action. As Nigel Lawson writes: 'From my own experience as Chancellor, I can confirm that these concessions in no way derogated in practice from the sovereignty of the Chancellor of the day over the Budget, subject only to the need to carry the Prime Minister with him' (Lawson, 1992, p. 96). The actual contents of a budget are only revealed to the cabinet a few hours before they are presented to parliament.

---

[1] 'Finance minister' is here used as a convenient generic term - but in Australia, in addition to the Treasurer, there is another minister called the 'Minister of Finance', primarily responsible for expenditure control.

Table 9.4 Objectives and Background Influences, 1979-1992

	Reform Initiator	Stated Objectives	Official Tax Reports (Pre-reform)	Intellectual Background	Historical and Economic Influences	Specific External Influences
United Kingdom	Finance Minister (Chancellor of the Exchequer)	To improve the performance of the economy	No major reports since Royal Commission on Profits and Income, 1955	Institute for Fiscal Studies, responsible for Meade Report, 1978	Discontent with very high PIT and effects of high inflation on tax system	None on early reforms; some on 1988 changes: PIT rates, CGT
New Zealand	Finance Minister	Efficiency/neutrality horizontal equity certainty and simplicity	Ross Committee 1967; McCaw Task Force, 1982 – signposted later reforms	Institute of Policy Studies, Victoria University, Wellington, gave prominence to tax issues	Economic crises in 1984; used to promote radical tax reform	Only general influences
Australia	Finance Minister (Treasurer)	Fairness, efficiency/ neutrality, simplicity	Asprey Committee, 1975; recommended simplifying PIT; partial imputation for CIT; and VAT	Report of Social Science Research Council (Downing), 1964; Economic Planning Advisory Council	Excessive tax avoidance and evasion; Labor wary of tax reform pledges	Main influence on 1988/9 reduction in corporate tax rates
United States	President/Secretary of Treasury	Fairness, simplicity and economic growth	Treasury Report: *Blue Prints of Basic Tax Reform*, 1977	Brookings Institution; American Enterprise Institute; Hoover Institute; Congressional activity	Effects of inflation on federal income tax; concern at avoidance and evasion	None
Canada	Finance Minister	Vertical and horizontal equity, competitiveness, simplicity, consistency, reliability	Carter Commission, 1966-7. Powerful long term influence	Almost continual discussion since Carter; Canadian Tax Foundation	Debate dominated by Carter proposals; history of opposition to radical reform; concern at avoidance	US reform '86 speeded up Canadian reform
Ireland	Finance Minister	Growth, neutrality, equity, improvements in tax collection	Commission on Taxation, 1982-85	Tax forum lacking; occasional discussions at National Economic and Social Council; Foundation for Fiscal Studies, 1986	Severe economic crisis inhibited tax reform	Influenced by UK and EC especially on VAT rates

In all the other Westminster type constitutions the cabinet is much more involved. The opposite extremes to the United Kingdom are represented by Ireland, with its coalition governments where cabinet members of coalition parties must go along with the proposals; and New Zealand, where Roger Douglas (now Sir Roger) as Finance Minister, having tested out his ideas with his Associate Finance Ministers, would then take them to the Prime Minister and Deputy Prime Minister, then to an eight member Cabinet Policy Committee (which included the three Finance Ministers), then to cabinet and finally to the party caucus. (However, as the House of Representatives consisted of only 97 members, if the cabinet of some 20 members and the half a dozen ministers outside the cabinet were all of one mind, they would usually constitute a majority, or near majority, of the caucus.)

In the United States taxing powers reside in Congress. Tax proposals of the president are prepared under the responsibility of the Secretary of Treasury with the particular assistance of the Assistant Secretary (Tax Policy). Tax proposals are considered first in the Ways and Means Committee of the House of Representatives and then ratified (or sent back) by the whole house which usually operates under rules restricting amendments. In relation to Tax Reform Act 1986 (TRA 86) the restrictions which helped to keep reform on course were revenue neutrality – the proposer of any amendment which involved a reduction of revenue had to say where the revenue would be made good – and distributional neutrality. When passed by the house a tax bill goes to the Senate which refers it to the Finance Committee. Public hearings take place at the committee stages of both houses, where special interests can formally present their views. After approval in both houses the bill goes to the president, who has ten days in which to decide to sign it or exercise his veto – a veto which can be overridden by a two-thirds majority in Congress. The whole process may take many months; TRA 86 took seventeen months going through Congress. At the end of the day a tax bill may bear little resemblance to the president's proposals. Thus, although the president may propose, it is Congress which disposes.

Whilst there is much common ground in the stated objectives of tax reform in the six countries, the emphasis varies. In the United Kingdom the emphasis was almost wholly on efficiency in the sense of the efficient use of resources in the economy as a whole: to quote Chancellor Nigel Lawson, 'My main objective in reforming taxes had been to improve the performance of the economy; and that is the over-riding test by which the reforms stand to be judged' (Lawson, 1988, p. 4). He mentioned two other objectives, simplicity and a fair deal for married women, but says nothing of horizontal or vertical equity. Efficiency, dressed up in various forms of words, figures prominently in the objectives of all the countries. With the exception of Canada, equity as an objective refers only to horizontal equity – the equal treatment of those similarly placed; in the United States vertical equity is mentioned but only as a constraint, ie that proposals must be distributionally neutral. Following on from the emphasis of the Carter Commission, equity does have pride of place in the Canadian list of objectives and it refers to vertical as well as horizontal equity, but 'competitiveness', another word for efficiency, also figures prominently. Most countries put forward simplicity as an objective.

An interesting features of the background to tax reform is the number of instances in which official committees of earlier years – in New Zealand, Australia, the United States and Canada – have reported on the tax system. At the time of publication these reports seem to have made little impact, but they often set the path which reform was to take. In the United Kingdom, whilst there was no similar official report, a report under the auspices of the Institute for Fiscal Studies, with Nobel prize-winner James Meade as its chairman, on *The Structure and Reform of Direct Taxation*, 1978, stimulated discussion; although its main proposal, for a direct expenditure tax, was expressly repudiated by the Conservative Government, the report undoubtedly highlighted many of the deficiencies of the tax system, especially the gross distortions in the treatment of savings and investment. In Ireland a Commission on Taxation was set up at the beginning of the tax reform period, following the tax demonstrations referred to above (p. 160). It produced a series of reports, 1982-85, which were completely ignored by the Fine Gael-Labour Coalition, 1982-87, but undoubtedly influenced later reforms even though, like the Meade Committee, its main recommendations were never accepted. All these tax reports helped to promote an intellectual forum in which taxation was discussed and analysed. Such a forum was already well developed in the United States and Canada and growing in the other countries.

In looking at the general causes of the tax reform movement we stressed the significance of the economic environment, especially the overall growth in tax as a percentage of GDP and the iniquitous effects of inflation. These influences affected all six countries, but perhaps especially the United Kingdom, New Zealand and Ireland. The United Kingdom inflation had peaked at nearly 24 per cent in 1974 and the top rate of PIT had been increased to an absurd 98 per cent marginal rate on investment income (83 per cent on earned income with a 15 per cent surcharge above a certain level of investment income). There is little doubt that the tax situation helped to bring about the change of government in 1979 which ushered in the period of tax reform. In both New Zealand and Ireland the economic situation assumed crisis proportions. The Labour Government elected in 1984 in New Zealand inherited an over-protected and highly regulated economy, a government revenue deficit of nearly 9 per cent, a growing balance of payments deficit and a foreign exchange crisis, to meet which the new government devalued the currency by 20 per cent. Ireland faced deficits which were even higher; between 1978 and 1986 the government deficit only fractionally fell below double figures and the balance of payments deficit was in double figures from 1979 to 1982 inclusive, with high and rising unemployment from 1980 to a peak of 18.2 per cent in 1986. The two countries reacted very differently. Finance Minister Roger Douglas of New Zealand took advantage of the crisis conditions to promote radical tax reform as part of a policy of deregulation. The Irish Government took the view that tax reform was a luxury that could not be afforded in the extreme economic circumstances.

A potent influence in the United States, Canada and Australia was the level of tax avoidance. 'The United States tax system has become a swamp of unfairness, complexity and inefficiency' wrote Aaron and Galper (1986 p.1). Discontent with the tax system and the federal income tax in particular had been growing over the previous decade or so, accentuated by the effects of inflation. Expense account living and tax sheltering had taken on the proportions of a national scandal. Many instances were given prominence in the media of millionaires and large corporations that managed to pay hardly any income tax or none at all. (Birnbaum and Murray, 1988, pp.11-12). In Canada, likewise, there was public concern, not to say anger, that the rich, by taking advantage of tax shelters and other avoidance opportunities, were succeeding in paying little or no tax. In response to this public outcry, in the lead up to the 1984 General Election, both major parties pledged, if elected, to introduce a minimum personal income tax; it fell to the Progressive Conservatives to do so. The position in Australia was hardly any better. In 1974 a case in the High Court had gone against the Commissioner of Taxation and from then the situation on tax avoidance had gone from bad to worse until it became a national scandal with avoidance merging into evasion. It took much anti-avoidance legislation and changes in the composition of the High Court to restore the situation to something approaching order; even then, as late as 1985, Treasurer Paul Keating could refer to 'An avalanche of avoidance, evasion and minimisation' (Keating, 1985).

Apart from economic aspects, other features of recent history influenced tax reform in some countries, most notably Australia and possibly Ireland. Australia had something of a history of aborted tax reform; there was also a widespread belief in the Labor Party that they had lost the election in 1980 because the shadow spokesman on finance had talked of introducing a capital gains tax. In the 1984 election the Leader of the Liberal Party was campaigning on the issue of 'No wealth taxes, no estate duties and no capital gains tax'. Bob Hawke the Leader of the Labor Party, wished to combat the suggestions that a Labor Government would introduce these taxes, but also favoured tax reform and wished to keep all options open. His solution was to pledge that a Labor Government would hold a Tax Summit and seek reform by consensus. As we consider below, this commitment had a considerable impact on the process and outcome of tax reform in Australia. In Ireland the Fine Gael-Labour Coalition Government of 1973-77 had carried through a reform of capital taxes, which included the introduction of an annual wealth tax. This tax provoked a storm of opposition and when, following the 1977 election, Fianna Fail replaced Fine Gael, the wealth tax was repealed. This somewhat unhappy experience of tax reform, as well as its pre-occupation with the economic crisis, may have disposed the Fine Gael-Labour Government of 1982-87 to keep clear of such a contentious area.

How far were these tax reforming countries influenced by external factors? All were influenced by the changes in philosophy which we have described and most showed an awareness of the need to keep corporate income tax rates low to maintain competitiveness in a global economy. Of the more specific influences, Nigel Lawson, in his tax changes in 1988, referred to lower personal income tax rates in the United States, Canada, Australia and New Zealand and also acknowledged that he had been reinforced in his desire to equalise rates of capital gains tax and income tax (and thus check income tax avoiders from dressing up income as capital gain) by the example of the United States TRA 86.

With the possible exception of Ireland, Canada was the country most influenced by external factors, in particular, what was happening in the United States. It is significant that the objective, designated 'efficiency' or 'promoting economic growth' in the tax reforms of other countries was described as 'competitiveness' in the Canadian White Paper of 1987, which stated 'It is important that our tax system not place Canadians at a competitive disadvantage in domestic or international markets. We must recognise the competitive reality of tax systems in other countries' (p.4). The prime effect of the United States reforms in Canada was to speed up reforms already in train and to convert what had been an incremental approach into a 'package' approach. As summed up by Dodge and Sargent (1988, p.5): 'The U.S. example raised the profile of comprehensive tax reform as an issue in public discussion in Canada and gave encouragement to the approach of lowering rates and broadening bases, which was the Government's general intention'.

The most potent specific influence on Irish tax reform was probably the EC. Once the Community had decreed a minimum standard rate of VAT of 15 per cent with reduced rates of 5 per cent, Ireland moved in the direction of reducing the number of its rates and lowering the standard rate from 25 to 21 per cent (which was a much more sustainable position by comparison with the United Kingdom 17.5 per cent). Its widening of the VAT base was also in line with EC promptings. The abolition of minor excises and modifications to the rates of the principal excises were a further outcome of EC requirements and competitive pressures.

Preparation and Implementation

Significant differences amongst the six countries are to be found in some aspects of the preparation and implementation of reform. There are differences in the departmental responsibilities for tax policy and the allied issue of the legislative drafting. In four of the countries, New Zealand, Australia, Canada and the United States, the Treasury, or Department of Finance, had primary responsibility for tax policy-making, with input from the revenue departments only on administrative issues. In the United Kingdom and Ireland responsibility for policy was shared and more diffuse. It is perhaps significant that those countries where the finance departments had clear primacy all produced 'packages' of reform, whereas the other two followed the incremental route.

In the United Kingdom, New Zealand and Australia, tax legislation is prepared by parliamentary draftsmen outside the departments but acting on their instructions. In Ireland drafting is undertaken within the Revenue Commissioners, whilst in the United States it is a more or less continuous process as the bill struggles through Congress. Professor Brian Arnold (1990) has stressed the importance of closely integrating policy-making and drafting. He has been particularly critical of the Australian system, where tax policy is primarily the responsibility of the Treasury, the Legislative Services Group of the ATO prepares the instructions for legislation and the Office of Parliamentary Council drafts the legislation.

Table 9.5 Aspects of Preparation and Implementation of Tax Reform, 1979-1992

	Policy Department (s)	Use of Tax Experts	Legislative Drafting	Incremental or Package	Consultation and Discussion
United Kingdom	Treasury Inland Revenue Customs and Excise	Limited	Parliamentary draftsmen	Incremental	Minimal
New Zealand	Primarily Treasury	Team assembled for reform. Much use of private sector	Parliamentary draftsmen	Package	Very extensive on first package
Australia	Primarily Treasury	Team assembled for reform. Some use of private sector	Parliamentary draftsmen	Package	Tax Summit, 1985
United States	Treasury	Large Treasury team. Interchanges with private sector	Continuous	Package	Treasury I and II Continuous media comment
Canada	Primarily Department of Finance	Large team in Finance Department. Interchanges with private sector	Finance Department	At first incremental, from '87, package	Extensive
Ireland	Department of Finance, Revenue Commissioners	Limited	Revenue Commissioners	Incremental	Minimal

This separation, Arnold maintains, is harmful to tax formulation. He holds up Canada, where the policy makers in the Finance Department do the drafting, as a model for the Westminster systems, and concludes 'The drafting of tax legislation cannot be done effectively and efficiently without both policy and technical expertise' (Arnold, 1990, p.382). It is, perhaps, not wholly coincidental that the United Kingdom, New Zealand and Australia have all embarked on major programmes for re-writing their tax legislation; and, in the United Kingdom, for the first time, parliamentary drafters are closely involved, on a day to day basis, in this re-writing process (Howe, 1998, p. 105).

Allied to the departmental process is the degree of concentrated expertise – economic, legal, accounting – which can be brought to bear on policy-making. The United States Treasury and the Canadian Finance Department have large teams of experts. On a smaller scale, New Zealand and Australia assembled expert teams to prepare reform. New Zealand is particularly notable for its extensive use of private sector expertise. In the United Kingdom and Ireland the resources drawn upon in the relevant departments were relatively small – a situation not unrelated to the incremental approach adopted.

The alternative merits and drawbacks of the package approach and the incremental approach need to be explored, but first the terms must be clarified. Tax reform by the incremental approach consists of a series of small steps, which, in principle, should be directed towards a pre-determined goal. The package approach comprises a series of essentially inter-related measures affecting more than one tax, and possibly social expenditure items, which are conceived and presented together, but not necessarily all implemented at the same time. The distinction is clear enough at the extremes, but often a matter of judgment at the margins. Broadly speaking we can say that New Zealand and Australia followed the package approach. Canada began with incremental change but the White Paper of 1987 presented a more comprehensive package. In the United States tax policy-making has normally been incremental, but the Tax Reform Act of 1986 was a package. Ireland and the United Kingdom (despite some major stages on the way, such as Sir Geoffrey Howe's first budget and the reform of corporation tax in 1984) have followed the incremental route.

From the administration's viewpoint, incrementalism has much to commend it. It goes with the grain of the tax departments for whom the 'Big Bang' involves a leap into the unknown. Incremental change can be more easily managed by the revenue departments called on to implement reform and enables better control to be kept over the revenue inflow. For the politician it means less, or even no commitment to the future – or easier withdrawal if circumstances change or the tax measures become unpopular. On the other hand, incrementalism has disadvantages. Reform takes longer. Partly for that reason and partly because it is often not accompanied by a clear statement of objectives it may lack purpose and continuity. Pressure groups have to be fought one by one and they have time to anticipate the next moves and prepare for them. Further, where tax expenditures are removed one at a time, the gain each time, spread over the whole body of taxpayers, is minimal and barely appreciated, so there are no approving cries from the gainers to offset the loud squeals of the losers. Additionally, there is likely to be insufficient scope from the revenue gain to provide compensation where that may be needed; and attempts to provide a small amount of compensation for a lot of people carry disproportionate administrative cost.

The package approach requires exceptional administrative measures and is more of a political risk; but, carefully constructed, it remedies the defects of the incremental approach. It can be accomplished more quickly, effecting an earlier improvement of the existing system. Because the package offers the opportunity for big changes, the gains are large enough to be appreciated and everyone is a gainer in some respects if a loser in others. A substantial package provides the scope for new welfare payments should they be needed to compensate the less well off. A package virtually requires a government to publish a statement which specifies the measures it proposes and its objectives. Moreover, if the package attacks all the vested interests without exception, they can be more readily defeated than if the attempt is made to fight them one by one; the recognisable benefit to the general body of taxpayers provides a counter-weight to the special pleaders and may generate a public interest lobby in favour of reform. The most successful reform in the 1980s was that of Roger Douglas in New Zealand, who presented a package by which a GST (VAT) with a wide base replaced a wholesale sales tax; a massive reduction in income tax was made possible partly through the GST and partly by the removal of tax expenditures; a fringe benefit tax on employers was brought in; and a new welfare provision compensated poor families for the extra costs under the GST. These measures were presented as a package and implemented over a two year period.

Another difference between countries was the extent of discussion and consultation on the major policies. In the United Kingdom and Ireland the discussion was fairly minimal. The presentation of a major package necessarily generated more discussion in the other countries; in the United States, views could be formally presented to the House Ways and Means Committee and the Senate Finance Committee and throughout the seventeen months which TRA 86 took through Congress the media reporting was continuous. The most interesting cases are those of New Zealand and Australia. In New Zealand the election of the Labour Government in 1984 was followed, shortly afterwards, by an 'Economic Summit' representing every sector of the community, with the aim to promote unity and understanding of New Zealand's economic problem; here tax reform received a general airing. Later in 1984, the tax proposals were taken to the regional and national conferences of the Labour Party and widely presented by ministers in the country as a whole. On the GST a private sector advisory panel was set up to receive submissions on draft legislation and further discussion took place in a Select Committee of the House of Representatives to which the GST draft bill was referred. All this was accompanied by a major public education campaign about the tax reform and the GST in particular.

We have already mentioned the circumstances leading to the Australian Tax Summit (p. 175). After the re-election of the Hawke Labor Government in December 1984, the Tax Summit was duly held in July 1985, preceded, one month before, by a Draft White Paper (of nearly 300 pages) setting out the major criteria for tax reform, outlining the deficiencies of the Australian tax system and offering three options for reform. Option C was the Government's preferred option. It consisted of lowering the rates and broadening the base of income tax, introducing a tax on real capital gains and on fringe benefits and replacing the wholesale sales tax with a broad-based consumption tax (a retail sales tax) with measures to compensate the lower income groups. At the Summit, significant opposition emerged to Option C and Prime Minister Hawke was responsible for dropping the idea of the broad-based consumption tax. The Government proceeded to implement the remainder of the proposals.

Most commentators at the time regarded the Summit as a dismal failure. Groenewegen (1985) offers a somewhat different view. He stresses that the Summit did achieve a high degree of consensus on a number of important issues and that it cannot be judged in isolation. It has to be seen in the context of the history of failed tax reform attempts, of the Labor Party's need to combat the wilder allegations of the Opposition and of the short electoral cycle which limited discussion time. A fair judgment on the Summit is that, as a way of securing agreement to the Government's preferred package it was a high risk strategy which partly failed; but it was a politically rational strategy.

Public discussion and consultation help to give a reform its legitimacy and increase the chances that it will be sustained thereafter. But important questions are raised by a comparison of the consultation and discussion processes in New Zealand and in Australia; in particular, how much of a package should be discussed and what should be the forum of discussion? In New Zealand the Government gave a clear lead; it said what it proposed to do with discussion being concerned with full explanation and possible modification of the detail. In Australia the Summit only set out options with a Government preference; there was no decisive lead. As to the forum, the Summit, with set-piece contributions from different interests left no scope for probing or negotiation. The New Zealand Select Committee procedure enabled statements to be probed and challenged.

One other lesson on discussion and consultation emerges from the Canadian experience: how long should it be allowed to continue? In Canada the announcement that the Mulroney Government had 'for some months' been examining the possibility of replacing the manufacturers' sales tax by a GST (VAT) was made in the budget of February 1986; but the sales tax legislation did not finally pass into law until the end of 1990 for implementation on 1 January 1991. There were good reasons for this delay (which we partly consider below) but they undoubtedly worked against this component of the Canadian tax reform which was only passed after the Government had made concessions on the standard rate and on zero rating and after a minor constitutional crisis. Douglas Hartle, who headed the research team for the Carter Commission, has argued that the time between announcement and implementation has an important bearing on the success of reform:

'I would take from this post-Carter experience the following general rule: the longer the period of time between announcement by the party in power that a particular tax structure is under consideration and the final decision on its disposition the greater the influence of entrenched interests. Virtually by definition, closely-knit, well-informed and well financed organised special (narrow) interest groups have the resources to maintain a protracted struggle to keep their tax advantages; public interest groups are usually not closely-knit, are poorly informed in relative terms, and are financially weak' (Hartle, 1988, p.413).

The Lobbies

As our previous discussion has made clear and the quotation from Hartle emphasises, issues of incremental or package approach, and of consultation and discussion, raise the question of the role of pressure groups in tax policy-making. All countries are affected by pressure group activity. Sometimes their submissions are valuable in bringing to the notice of governments details in danger of being overlooked. But, especially where the objective of tax reform is tax neutrality, they are usually concerned to obtain a tax concession or defend an existing concession.

The United States is pre-eminent in the strength and influence of the lobbies. Its constitution, with its separation of powers and the formal opportunities for presenting views to the relevant House and Senate Committees, favours pressure groups; moreover these factors have been accentuated in recent years by the loosening of party ties and the dependence of representatives and senators for election and re-election on campaign funds raised in their constituencies. Hedrick Smith writes of the 'sky-rocketing growth of corporate political action committees (PACs) to raise money and make contributions to election campaigns of candidates friendly to corporate interests' (Smith, 1988). In 1974 there were 89 corporate PACs; in 1984 there were 1,682; by 1991 there were 4,172 PACs. By 1990 more than half the members of Congress got at least 50 per cent of their campaign funds from PACs. Members of Congress inevitably look favourably on requests from constituents – individual or corporate – who have helped them. As Steinmo puts it: 'It is not that they are bribed, but they become very susceptible to and agreeable towards constituency requests which can be justified on equity or general interest grounds' (Steinmo, 1993). The strength of the lobbies can be gained by the title of the book by Birnbaum and Murray (1988) brilliantly chronicling the saga of TRA 86: *Showdown at Gucci Gulch: Lawmakers, Lobbyists and the Unlikely Triumph of Tax Reform*. Witte, the author of the most authoritative study of the United States federal income tax could write in 1985, 'There is nothing, absolutely nothing in the history or politics of the income tax that indicates that any of these [contemporary tax reform] schemes has the slightest hope of being enacted in the forms proposed' (Witte, 1985). Witte's view was that tax reform would not take place without constitutional reform. The near euphoria with which the successful passage of TRA 86 was greeted in the United States owed much to the fact that it was so unexpected; for Henry Aaron it was 'The Impossible Dream Comes True' (Aaron, 1987).

The power of vested interests to influence tax reform was not confined to the United States. Nigel Lawson, the United Kingdom Chancellor 1983-89, records that, after the extension of the VAT base in his first budget, more moves to broaden the VAT base were anticipated and campaigns took place against the possible standard rating of books and newspapers. But, as Lawson put it, 'The campaigns against VAT extension were as nothing compared to the barrage that emanated from the beneficiaries of occupational pensions and the industry that catered for them'. Following the abolition of tax relief on new life insurance premiums in the 1984 budget it was guessed that the tax free treatment of lump sum payments might come next. 'There followed the most astonishing lobbying campaign of my entire political career, devoted both to the preservation of the lump sum relief and to pension fund privileges in general.' His conclusion was that 'reform would be most likely to be achieved by a well-directed side offensive with no prior warning' (Lawson, 1992, pp. 367-69). Thus, the lack of consultation on Lawson's United Kingdom reforms was deliberate – as a way of dealing with, or circumventing, the lobbies. This approach contrasts starkly with that of Roger Douglas in New Zealand, who sought to face down the vested-interest groups *en masse* by seeking widespread public support for a comprehensive package (Douglas, 1987, pp. 195-96).

The lobbying the Canadian Government faced had an additional twist to it: opposition from the provinces, mainly because the proposal for a VAT (to replace the manufacturers' sales tax) was a threat to their monopoly of general sales taxation at the retail level (operated by all the provinces except Alberta). The result of this opposition was that at first the federal Government sought to devise a form of VAT on an accounts basis (referred to as a Business Transfer Tax) which would not so obviously offend the susceptibilities of the provinces; when this attempt was abandoned the Government sought to establish a national VAT in co-operation with the provinces; when this, in turn, was getting nowhere, the federal Government decided to go it alone. The outcome was that, although the first announcement of the possible change was made in February 1986, the GST did not become law until December 1990 – and then on a narrower base and at a lower rate than the Government had intended. As Hartle writes, 'Provincial governments are, in effect, the most powerful of all lobby groups' (Hartle, 1985, p. 50). Cultural, religious, linguistic and economic differences make for strong rivalries between the federal and provincial governments; federal and provincial governments may be dominated by different political parties; a provincial government is likely to become the mouthpiece for its economic interests in any dispute with the federal government; rivalries between federal and provincial civil servants may accentuate differences between their governments; added to which the provincial governments are well-endowed with resources and with extensive media access and can strengthen their bargaining power on one issue by refusing co-operation on another unrelated matter.

It may be asked why the other federal countries, the United States and Australia, did not run into similar problems. With the United States the answer may partly have been that the Senate, directly representing the states, was a part of the tax policy-making process in a way that the Canadian Senate was not; but, more importantly, the tax changes proposed in the United States did not impinge on the states in the same way as in Canada; had the President proposed a federal VAT the response might well have been different. As for Australia, none of the tax changes proposed directly impinged on the (effectively very limited) tax powers of the states. But federal tax policy could be affected by the federal nature of the constitution. In Australia state elections generally take place at different times from federal elections and, on occasion, federal governments appear to have altered policies in order to accommodate the views of a state government facing an imminent election (eg in 1987, the Commonwealth Labor Government is widely believed to have reversed its policy on 'negative gearing' under pressure from the Labor Government in New South Wales).

Politicians, Political Will and Personal Relationships

One feature to stand out prominently from this consideration of tax policy-making in six countries in the 1980s is the importance that individuals play in the process. Tax reform requires a champion, or, in the case of the United States, several champions, who are prepared to put their reputation on the line. Such champions must have conviction about the reforms they are espousing, whether intellectual conviction of the outstanding value of the policy, or some less noble belief, as with some of the United States players, that tax reform will significantly advance their career or, at least, save it from disaster.

In the Westminster system the key figure to champion reform is the finance minister. In the reforms of the '80s, where reform has included removing tax advantages, the finance minister has needed to be energetic, resilient and tough to take on the pressure groups. Roger Douglas of New Zealand, Paul Keating in Australia, Michael Wilson in Canada and, to a less extent, Sir Geoffrey Howe and Nigel Lawson in the United Kingdom, were such champions. With the possible exception of Ray MacSharry, whose relevant tenure as finance minister was restricted to 20 months, Ireland never produced a finance minister with the political will, conviction and toughness to tackle tax reform in this period. The nearest to a champion of tax reform amongst the Irish politicians was Desmond O'Malley, as leader of the Progressive Democrats; but the PDs were back seat drivers who ran out of a vehicle when Fianna Fail no longer needed them.

The United States system of separation of powers required more than one champion and, apart from President Reagan himself, included Secretary Don Regan, Chairman of the House Ways and Means Committee, Dan Rostenkowski, Robert Packwood, Chairman of the Senate Finance Committee and Senator Bill Bradley.

In different degrees, according to their various constitutional practices, the finance ministers in the Westminster systems needed the support of colleagues; but, in every case, the support, active or tacit, of the prime minister was vital; where that support was in place, tax reform flourished; where that support lapsed or was withdrawn, reform faltered. In the United Kingdom Margaret Thatcher generally was in agreement with the policies of her Chancellors, but she lacked conviction about the objectives and she hamstrung her Chancellors in various ways; to quote Lawson, 'The majority of the tax reforms I had hoped to introduce [in the 1985 Budget] were controversial changes that I had to abandon, for the most part because Margaret was not prepared to swallow them. They included extending the coverage of VAT to newspapers and children's clothes, confining mortgage interest relief to the basic rate, introducing a tax on consumer credit and taxing pension lump sums' (Lawson, 1992, p.362).

In New Zealand, Roger Douglas' first big package had the consistent support of Prime Minister David Lange; but the relationship between the two started to turn sour just before the 1987 General Election when proposals by Douglas for changing the social services in a market-oriented way were not to Lange's liking; and the breach probably became irrevocable with Douglas' flat tax proposal. Originally receiving Cabinet approval and published, the suspicion developed that the proposals had been hurried and the figures did not add up; whilst Douglas was abroad, Lange unilaterally announced the postponement of the proposals, which was but a prelude to their withdrawal. A single rate of income tax had long been an objective of Douglas. Once he was forced to abandon it his departure from the Government was only a matter of time and, indeed, marked the beginning of the end of Lange's career as Prime Minister and the break-up of the Labour Government.

In Australia the relationship between Paul Keating as Treasurer and Bob Hawke as Prime Minister was one of mutual dependence rather than mutual affection. In general Hawke was prepared to allow Keating his head, but it was Hawke who was responsible for the Summit strategy. At the Summit, Hawke's actions were decisive. Keating was fighting hard for Option C, including the broad-based consumption tax; but it was scuttled by Hawke. Following the opposition to it, on the Wednesday night of the Summit, Hawke made a deal with the trade unions to drop the consumption tax. Keating was not a party to the deal; it was presented to him as a *fait accompli*. This decision accorded with Hawke's view of the need for consensus, but it undercut the basis of his Treasurer's reform. Keating felt betrayed; he never again took up the cudgels for a broad-based consumption tax and relations between the two men deteriorated.

In Canada, the courage and tough-mindedness of Finance Minister Michael Wilson helped to ensure that the GST reached the statute book, even if he had to make some concessions on the way; but it would never have got there but for the staunch support of the Prime Minister in a Cabinet split on the issue.

The role of the chief executive is no less crucial with the United States reforms. It was President Reagan who initiated the process of reform by instructing the Treasury to prepare a report. He saw that 'Treasury I' was refashioned to improve its chances of success. He spoke up in favour of it on the campaign trail and on television. When it was in danger of foundering in the House of Representatives because of the opposition of disgruntled Republicans, he took the bold step of going to the House himself to urge Republican representatives to keep the reform process going – a move which, if unsuccessful, would have seriously damaged his presidency. Without his intervention at a crucial moment it is widely believed that the bill would have failed (Birnbaum and Murray, 1988, pp. 153-75).

How Successful was Tax Reform?

We can measure the success of the tax reform in the '80s in these six countries on the basis of three criteria: (1) how far the tax reforms met the declared objectives of the proponents at the time; (2) how far the reforms have been sustained; (3) whether there were any anticipated or unanticipated side effects of reform, for good or ill, which affect our assessment.

How far the Reforms met the Reformers' own Objectives

An extended assessment of the success of tax reform in the six countries by reference to the objectives the reformers set themselves has appeared in Sandford, 1993, on a detailed, country by country, basis. Here we offer some broad generalisations.

The objective common to the reforms in all these countries, and the philosophy under-pinning the world-wide tax reform of the '80s, was efficiency, in the sense of tax neutrality, reducing tax distortions. On the basis of this criterion all countries achieved considerable progress – by reducing income tax rates, eliminating or reducing tax expenditures and in most cases, taxing capital gains and fringe benefits more heavily. But the degree of success varied and in every case there were important limitations. To mention some of the main ones. In the United Kingdom, partly because of Mrs Thatcher's interventions, neither Sir Geoffrey Howe nor Nigel Lawson was able to go as far as he wished in getting rid of tax concessions in income tax and VAT. Moreover, there was ambivalence; both Howe and Lawson, whilst reducing some tax expenditures introduced new ones, designed as incentives, eg a Business Expansion Scheme, and tax reliefs for employee-shareholding and profit-related pay. Thus they got rid of some tax breaks to create others likely to be as distorting and open to tax avoidance as the old. New Zealand's reform scores the highest marks for efficiency, but the capital gains tax was aborted and Roger Douglas would regard the demise of his plans for a single rate income tax as a major setback. In Australia the biggest failing of the 1985-86 tax reform was the ditching of the broad-based consumption tax, without which the scope for reducing income tax was much less. The United States' tax reform was in some respects more limited than in most other countries in that reform did not embrace the structure of the corporate income tax, the taxation of fringe benefits or a federal sales tax. Income tax rates were dramatically reduced and many tax expenditures cut. Even so, many more tax expenditures were left untouched. Neubig and Joulfaian of the Treasury staff estimated that tax reform reduced $77 billion of tax expenditures directly by base broadening and another $116 billion indirectly because of their reduced value as a result of lower rates (at 1988 levels of activity); post reform $315 billion of tax expenditures remained. John Witte estimated that TRA 86 repealed 14 tax expenditures (a figure roughly equal to the total repealed from 1913 to 1985) compared with the 38 which would have been repealed in the original Treasury I proposals. (Both estimates in

Steuerle, 1991, pp. 139-41.) The Canadian reform left income tax rates higher than in the other countries, in part because the intended GST rate had to be lowered and unintended concessions introduced into it. In Ireland the story on tax expenditures was similar to the United States. The OECD reported that 'In 1981-82 total income tax allowances and reliefs amounted to 62.4 per cent of the tax base and by 1985-86 this had risen to 77 per cent. Subsequent reforms have only reduced this proportion to 68 per cent' (OECD, 1991, p. 71). The OECD quotes the National Economic and Social Council: 'Given the modest scale and ambiguity of these changes in the tax base it is not surprising to find that the income tax base continues to be severely diminished by a wide range of allowances, reliefs and exemptions' (NESC, 1990, p. 71).

Horizontal equity was an objective of most countries and the outcome was much as with efficiency – progress but also limitations; any 'levelling of the playing field' by eliminating tax expenditures met both objectives. Additionally, capital gains taxes, heavier taxation of fringe benefits and the measures to combat evasion and avoidance, promoted horizontal equity.

Four countries expressly aimed at simplicity – or simplification. None can be said unequivocally to have achieved it. Certain aspects of tax reform did simplify, such as fewer personal income tax rates, the removal of some tax expenditures and, in the United States, the higher personal exemption which cut the number of filers by several million. However, overall these simplifications were nullified, or, even dwarfed, by new complications. In the United States, for example, there were new complex distinctions between passive and active income; many taxpayers, individual and corporate, needed to calculate their income tax liability under both regular income tax and the expanded alternative minimum tax; and wealthy taxpayers faced the complication of the rules for withdrawal of the standard deduction and the 15 per cent rate. In New Zealand and Canada, complication was increased by a new GST, collected at every stage of production and distribution – a situation made far worse in Canada by the failure to agree a national tax with the provinces, so that many retailers had both GST and RST to face. Australia had a new capital gains tax, complicated by 'grandfathering' provisions and in both Australia and New Zealand, employers had to battle with a new fringe benefit tax. It is a telling comment on the outcome of simplification that, in New Zealand, in 1989, David Caygill, Roger Douglas's successor at the Ministry of Finance, set up a Tax Simplification Consultative Committee; and in Australia, a tax simplification review of income tax and sales tax was set up in 1990. Subsequently, in both countries, increased government interest was shown in reducing tax compliance costs and, in both, major programmes were set up for re-writing the tax law.

How far have the Reforms been Sustained?

There is little to be gained by a tax reform which is speedily abandoned by a successor government. It is now 10 to 15 years since the tax reforms were enacted; how have they stood the test of time?

On the fundamental question of the rates of personal and corporate income tax the remarkable feature is the way the reforms have stayed in place. At the end of the '90s four of the countries had the same top rate of personal income tax as at the time of reform. Canada's was fractionally higher and the biggest increase was in the United States where the top marginal rate had risen from 28 to 39.6 per cent. Similarly with corporate income tax, where the changes since reform had been small and generally in a downward direction. There is nothing sacrosanct about a particular set of tax rates (although, in the United Kingdom, both Conservative and Labour Parties appear to believe that any increase in nominal rates of income tax would be electorally disastrous). The fundamental change is seen in the contrast between the rates of the '60s and '70s, when the top marginal rates of personal income tax of the six countries ranged from 60 per cent to 83 per cent[1] (with an additional 15 percentage points on investment income in the United Kingdom) and the position at the end of the '90s, when the variation was between 33 and 47 per cent. The one possible change to this picture is in New Zealand. Following the General Election of November 1999, a new coalition government of Labour and the left wing Alliance Party has come to office with plans to increase the top rates of personal income tax and assist poor families; but given a top rate of tax of only 33 per cent, there is scope for a considerable increase without taking it anywhere near the pre-reform level. The lesson seems to have been learnt that very high marginal rates of tax are both distorting and self-defeating.

In two countries, Canada and Australia, important victories have been won for the principles of the reform. In Canada, as we have seen, the opposition to the GST was fierce and this antipathy to the tax was one reason the Progressive Conservatives suffered a crushing defeat in the following General Election. The incoming Liberal Government had

[1]This statement includes the provincial income taxes in Canada, which generally piggy-back on the federal rate.

promised to review the tax, and its continuation was very much in doubt. The outcome of an extensive review by the House of Commons Standing Committee on Finance, which considered a range of alternatives, was the recommendation that the GST be retained in the form of a Harmonised Sales Tax (HST) with the provinces. In 1997 the Government was able to announce the agreement for an HST with Nova Scotia, New Brunswick and Newfoundland and Labrador, by which, in effect the provincial retail sales taxes were replaced by a higher GST with revenue shared between the federal government and the provinces. However, the most populous and wealthy provinces have not yet (end 1999) come into line. In Australia one of the main objectives of the 1985 reform, which eluded Treasurer Paul Keating at the Tax Summit, has been legislated for by the Liberal-Country Coalition. A broad-based consumption tax in the form of a VAT (called a GST) has been passed by Parliament to come into effect July 1, 2000. Because of the concessions the Government was obliged to make to secure its passage through the Senate it is not as broad-based as the Government intended; but (as we argued in chapter 5) a VAT is a superior form of tax to the wholesale tax it supersedes.

One area of widespread falling away from the principles of the tax reform has been capital gains tax. Under TRA 86 capital gains in the United States were treated as ordinary income for tax purposes. However, when in 1991, the top rate of federal income tax was raised from 28 per cent, the CGT rate remained at that (maximum) level. Following the 1997 budget the CGT rate was cut to 20 per cent for assets held for at least 18 months (subsequently reduced to 12 months) with provision for a further reduction to 18 per cent for assets purchased in the year 2000 or later and held for at least 5 years. Lower rates applied to taxpayers in the lowest tax bracket. Capital gains tax in Ireland, first introduced in 1975, underwent a series of changes until, in 1992-93, a single rate of 40 per cent was adopted, with cost base indexation. More recently indexation has been withdrawn and the rate cut to 20 per cent. In the United Kingdom Nigel Lawson raised the CGT to income tax rates (maximum 40 per cent) in 1988, though with a separate and substantial threshold. From 1998 Gordon Brown, Chancellor in the Labour Government elected in 1997, has withdrawn indexation of the cost base and introduced a taper relief: the rate for non-business assets held for more than 3 years is reduced by 5 per cent for each year the asset has been held, with a maximum reduction of 40 per cent (cutting the rate to 24 per cent); relief for business assets is greater, partly in compensation for the phasing out of retirement relief. In Australia, likewise, the Government has (1999) frozen indexation of the cost base and effectively dropped the rate to 24.25 per cent (by excluding 50 per cent of the gain from the charge to tax for individuals). In conditions of low inflation it is probably a sensible simplification to remove the cost base indexation, which, in any case, had given preferential treatment to capital gains as compared with investment income. But the rate reductions all have the effect of departing from the principle of keeping capital gains tax rates at, or closely related to, income tax rates, both for efficiency reasons, to stop the dressing-up of income as capital gain and limit investment distortion, and for reasons of horizontal equity.

On another major feature of reform, tax expenditures, the removal or curtailment of which was a major way of broadening the personal and corporate tax bases and 'levelling the playing field', the overall outcome since reform is unclear. Some measures have increased tax neutrality whilst others have reduced it. Perhaps, on balance, in the early and mid-nineties the direction of change was to promote the objectives of reform. To mention some of the most notable: in the United Kingdom, relief on the mortgage interest of home owners has been gradually whittled away, the Business Expansion Scheme ended and the scheme of profit related pay phased out. In Australia the concessions to R and D have been reduced whilst the FBT rate has been grossed up to the top rate of income tax and made tax deductible, which meant there was no tax advantage from fringe benefits. Latterly the balance may have gone the other way. In the United Kingdom, Gordon Brown, as well as tax exemption for new schemes to promote savings (replacing schemes of the Conservative administrations) has proposed a new share ownership scheme and has handed out a plethora of small tax reliefs. As *The Economist* wrote of the 1999 Budget: 'The budget included a lorry-load of preferences, allowances and credits for every good thing Mr Brown could think of: a lower rate of corporation tax for the smallest businesses, assorted tax breaks for research and development, for entrepreneurial 'risk-takers', for employees buying shares in their companies, and on and on' (*The Economist*, March 13-19, 1999, p. 17). As for the United States, John Witte has written of 'the inability of the system to resist change' (Witte, 1985) and inevitably, as Congressmen continually seek 'lollipops' for their constituents, tax expenditures creep back. However, the maintenance of income tax rates at or around the tax reform levels is likely to impose some constraints on the cost if not the number of tax expenditures. (Indeed, there must be at least a strong suspicion that, in the United Kingdom at any rate, the cutting back of some major tax expenditures has been undertaken in recent years less on grounds of principle than as a means of gaining revenue without appearing to put up rates.)

Side Effects of Reform

Whilst there were a number of not unimportant side effects in various countries, the most important and widely applicable, and that on which we concentrate, is how far the tax reform of the '80s generated or accentuated income inequalities. An increase in inequality is not a necessary consequence of tax reform aimed at increased efficiency and horizontal equity. Demolishing tax shelters, introducing or increasing capital gains taxes, extending fringe benefit taxes, tightening up on tax administration, are all ways by which the rich may pay as much at lower tax rates as they previously paid at higher rates, especially where these were largely avoided. Moreover, tax measures which might harm the poor can be made the subject of compensation. Thus, in seeking to answer whether inequality increased as a result of tax reform, we need to look not only at taxation but also at public expenditure: in New Zealand, as part of the reform package, a new public expenditure measure was introduced to offset the effect of VAT on poor families and in Canada a new income tax credit was introduced for the same purpose. However, we must also look not only at the immediate but also at the longer term effects. Thus, in New Zealand when VAT was introduced at 10 per cent in 1986, the new welfare benefit may have been enough to offset its effect on poor families; but when the VAT rate was raised to 12.5 per cent in 1988, there was no compensating increase in welfare payment. Similarly, for the United States, Jane Gravelle has suggested that, whilst there may be uncertainty about the short term, the longer term effects of TRA 86 were regressive (Gravelle, 1992).

Another problem is potentially perverse statistical effects. For example, in Australia, with the introduction of a CGT as part of income tax, capital gains appear in the income statistics for the first time. Thus, even after tax, the beneficiaries of capital gains appear to be better off. A similar situation may arise with the taxation of fringe benefits which had previously escaped tax.

A further major complication is that, in the '80s and '90s market changes were accentuating inequalities in most advanced countries. Disentangling the effects of market changes from discretionary tax measures is difficult, as is the effect on income distribution of different stages in the trade cycle, especially when the effective incidence of corporate income taxes is uncertain. Moreover the question is not only whether the tax changes themselves increased inequality directly, but also whether the market-caused increase in inequality was no longer offset to the extent it would have been under the pre-reform regime.

The answer to the difficult question of whether the tax reforms increased inequality would appear to be that, in the United Kingdom, United States and New Zealand, the effect of the tax reform of the '80s was to increase inequality (Hills, 1995). Canada was the only country which sought an 'improvement' in vertical equity from tax reform and it seems likely that, overall, the reforms may even have slightly reduced inequality in that country: much of the opposition to the GST stemmed from groups concerned at the increasing inequality of wealth and income in Canada, (Brooks, 1992, pp. 168-69) and this opposition may well have influenced the Canadian Government to increase its compensation measures. In Australia and Ireland, the overall effect is more difficult to determine, although with unindexed income taxes, there were undoubtedly periods in both countries when discretionary increases in thresholds and brackets failed to match increases in prices and those on lower and medium level incomes lost out more than those at the top (who had no higher brackets to be pushed into).

In considering the effect of tax reform on inequality, it is worth bearing in mind the changes in death and gift taxes – in particular the big reduction in top rates of death duty in the United Kingdom and in the United States and the abolition of estate duty in New Zealand in 1993. In Ireland, also, Capital Acquisitions Tax has been reduced. Such changes accentuate both future capital inequalities and future income inequalities.

Whether the accentuation of inequalities of income and wealth is regarded as good or bad is a matter of value judgment. Some people have felt that the regime pre-tax reform had unduly compressed differentials by incomes policies of various kinds. For others the increase in inequalities is a serious blemish on the tax reform of the '80s to set against the gains in efficiency.

Reflections on Tax Reform and Tax Policy-making

Generalising about tax reform and tax policy-making from a sample of six, from one period of tax reform, is a hazardous and unreliable business; even so it may be worthwhile to seek to gather some threads together and suggest what, in the light of this very limited experience, are the keys to success in tax reform.

Success in tax reform rests very much on individuals. In the Westminster system this almost invariably means a finance minister with clear objectives and with energy, conviction and the toughness to take on the lobbies. In the United States system a number of such players are needed. In both systems the support of the chief executive, whether prime minister or president, is essential.

Success in major tax reform is more likely to follow from a carefully crafted package than from an incremental approach. A package remedies defects more quickly; almost of necessity requires a statement of objectives which makes it easier to keep on course; offers substantial recognisable gains to taxpayers as well as losses; provides revenue scope for necessary or desirable measures of compensation; and, by attacking all vested interests together, enables reformers to stand on principle and present the lobby groups as the enemies of the public interest. But it carries dangers for its proponents and it takes courage to embark on it.

A package requires careful implementation: gains and losses must be seen to be interdependent; the government should give a clear lead; consultation and discussion should be extensive but conducted without undue delay; the forum of discussion must be appropriate, with the opportunity for views, both for and against, to be publicly presented and probed.

Other measures which can aid success in tax reform are the assembly of a policy-making team of high quality tax specialists from various disciplines; the close integration of policy-making and legal drafting; the use of private sector expertise in preparing and implementing a major package; and imaginative programmes of education and guidance for public, taxpayers and tax practitioners.

Whilst these elements in the process are largely within the control of the policy-makers, they operate in an environment much of which is outside their control. The most significant of these environmental features is the constitution, with the constraints it imposes – constraints likely to be most marked in a federal state. External constraints imposed by a powerful neighbour, an international grouping or international competition, can also be crucial. Tax history or the macro-economic situation may sometimes be perceived as setting limits to action.

Some constraints are not necessarily a disadvantage – indeed there may well be an optimum level of constraints. Of the six countries, the United Kingdom is the least hampered by constitutional constraints, but it is far from emerging top of the success list for tax reform, added to which it had the biggest failure – the community charge[1] (see chapter 3). Had there been more checks and balances in the United Kingdom system, for example, the constitutional requirement that all new taxes had to be considered by a Select Committee of Parliament taking evidence in public, it is likely that this tax catastrophe would have been averted. Where constraints exist it is the art of the politician to treat them as conditions rather than limitations and, where possible, turn them to advantage – as Michael Wilson did in using the United States reform as a reason for pressing on more rapidly with reform in Canada or as did Roger Douglas, in presenting the economic crisis in New Zealand in 1994 as a reason for radical tax reform.

The constraints faced by the leading actors in tax reform make it clear that tax reform cannot be wholly a matter of economic rationality; the main actors are all politicians – and will generally be politicians first and economists second. Kenneth Clarke, Chancellor of the Exchequer in the United Kingdom, 1993-97, was fond of saying that 'Good economics is good politics'; but this is not invariably seen to be so. Our statement of the keys to success in tax reform is something of an economic ideal. Our story of tax reform in the six countries and its aftermath reveals many instances when economic rationality gave way to perceived political rationality. Thus Hawke ditched the broad-based consumption tax at the Summit, Lange aborted Douglas's flat tax proposal and Margaret Thatcher curbed her Chancellor's proposals for widening the income tax and the VAT base, all in the interests of political rationality – because they deemed the moves would be electorally unpopular. (Perhaps, in retrospect, in view of the heavy defeat of their party at the polls, Brian Mulroney and Michael Wilson in Canada regret that they did not drop the GST.) Moreover, governments may find it expedient to cave in to pressure groups, especially those that contribute heavily to party funding.

Similarly, since tax reform, governments have introduced new tax expenditures for no better reason than that they feel they ought to be seen to be doing something – sending signals that they have a concern for a particular problem even if what they propose will have little impact on it and considerable cost in complicating the system. We have to accept that in the last resort pragmatism is likely to prevail over economic principle, perceived political rationality over economic rationality.

[1] In this chapter we have not hitherto mentioned the community charge because it was outside the mainstream of tax reform. As a local government tax it was not the responsibility of the Chancellor of the Exchequer nor did it go through the revenue departments. But the point about the lack of checks applies equally to mainstream taxes.

Perhaps the art of statesmanship in tax policy-making is to convince the population, or at least a majority, of the rightness of the tax reform proposals so that good economics does become good politics, as Roger Douglas succeeded in doing with his first tax reform package in New Zealand, 1984-86, or as Ronald Reagan and his reforming allies in Congress managed, against all the odds, to achieve with TRA 86. This is no easy task. It may well require, as one interviewee said in explaining the success of the United States tax reform in 1986, some 'sheer dumb luck'.

REFERENCES

Books and Articles

Aaron, H.J., 'The Impossible Dream Comes True', in ed. J.A. Pechman, *Tax Reform and the U.S. Economy*, The Brookings Institution, Washington, DC, 1987.

Aaron, H.J. and H. Galper, *Assessing Tax Reform*, The Brookings Institution, Washington, DC, 1986.

Allers, M.A., *Administrative and Compliance Costs of Taxation and Public Transfers in the Netherlands*, Wolters-Noordhoff, Groningen, 1994. (A summary appears in ed. C.T. Sandford, 1995, pp. 173-95).

Allingham, M.G. and A. Sandmo, 'Income Tax Evasion: A Theoretical Analysis', *Journal of Public Economics*, Vol. 1, pp. 323-38, 1972.

Ariff, M., A. Loh and A. Talib, *Compliance Costs of Corporate Income Taxation in Singapore*, 1994, mimeo, Department of Finance and Banking, National University of Singapore, 1995.

Arnold, B.J. 'The Process of Tax Policy Formation in Australia, Canada and New Zealand', *Australian Tax Forum*, Vol. 7, No. 4, 1990.

Ballard, C.L., J. B. Shoven, and J. Whalley, 'The Welfare Costs of Distortions in the United States Tax System: A General Equilibrium Approach', *Working Paper No. 1043*, National Bureau of Economic Research, 1982.

Ballard, C.L., J.B. Shoven and J. Whalley, 'General Equilibium Computation of the Marginal Welfare Costs of Taxes in the United States', *American Economic Review*, Vol. 75, No.1, 1985, pp. 128-38.

Bird, R.M., 'A New Look at Indirect Taxation in Developing Countries', *World Development*, Vol. 15, No. 9, 1987.

Birnbaum, J. H. and A.S. Murray, *Showdown at Gucci Gulch: Lawmakers, Lobbyists and the Unlikely Triumph of Tax Reform*, Vintage Books, Random House, New York, 1988.

Blumenthal, M. and J. Slemrod, 'Recent Tax Compliance Research in the United States' in ed. C.T. Sandford *Tax Compliance Costs, Measurement and Policy*, Fiscal Publications, Bath, 1995.

Boadway, R., N. Bruce and C. Beach, *Taxation and Savings in Canada*, Economic Council of Canada, Ottawa, 1988.

Bowles, R., 'Minimising Corruption in Tax Affairs', in ed. C.T. Sandford, *Further Key Issues in Tax Reform*, Fiscal Publications, Bath, 1998.

Brooks, W.N., *The Canadian Goods and Services Tax: History, Policy and Politics*, Australian Tax Research Foundation, Sydney, 1992.

Browning, E.K., 'The Burden of Taxation', *Journal of Political Economy*, Vol. 86, No.4, 1978, pp. 649-71.

Bryden, M.H., *The Cost of Tax Compliance*, Canadian Tax Foundation Paper No. 25, Toronto, 1961.

Casenegra de Jantscher, M., 'Administering the VAT' in eds. M. Gillis, C.S. Shoup and G. Sicat, *Value Added Taxation in Developing Countries*, World Bank, Washington, DC, 1990.

Cnossen, S., *Excise Systems: A Global Study of Selective Taxation of Goods and Services*, John Hopkins University Press, Baltimore, 1977.

Cnossen, S., 'Administrative and Compliance Costs of the VAT', *Tax Notes International*, 1649, June 20, 1994.

Cnossen, S., 'The Role of Corporation Tax in OECD Member Countries', in eds. J.G. Head and R Krever, *Company Tax Systems*, Australian Tax Research Foundation, Sydney, 1997.

Cnossen, S., 'Global Trends and Issues in Value Added Taxation', *International Tax and Public Finance*, Vol. 5, No. 3, 1998.

Coleman, C. and L. Freeman, 'Taxpayer Attitudes to Voluntary Compliance', paper in series *Current Issues in Tax Administration*, ATAX, University of New South Wales, 1996.

Copp, A., 'Compliance Costs and Value Added Tax' in ed. C. Evans and A Greenbaum, *Tax Administration: Facing the Challenge of the Future*, Prospect, St. Leonards, NSW, 1998.

Cullis, J.G. and A. Lewis, 'Why People Pay Taxes: From a Conventional Economic Model to a Model of Social Convention', *Journal of Economic Psychology*, Vol. 18, pp. 305-21, 1997.

Diaz, C. and M.L. Delgado, 'The Compliance Costs of Personal Income Tax in Spain', *Tax Compliance Costs, Measurement and Policy*, Fiscal Publications, Bath, 1995.

Dilnot, A., 'The Income Tax Rate Structure' in ed. C.T. Sandford, *Key Issues in Tax Reform*, Fiscal Publications, Bath, 1993.

Dilnot, A., 'The Taxation of Savings', in ed. C.T. Sandford, *Further Key Issues in Tax Reform*, Fiscal Publications, Bath, 1998.

Dodge, D.A. and J.H. Sargent, 'Canada' in ed. J.A. Pechman, *World Tax Reform: A Progress Report*, The Brookings Institution, Washington, DC, 1988.

Douglas, R., *Tax Reform Strategy in New Zealand*, lecture to Foundation for Fiscal Studies, Ireland, 16 Oct. 1989.

Douglas, R. and L. Callen, *Towards Prosperity*, David Bateman, Auckland, 1987.

Downing, R.I., H.W. Arndt, A.H. Boxer and R.L. Mathews, *Taxation in Australia: Agenda for Reform*, Melbourne University Press, 1964.

Due, J.F., 'The Enactment of a Value-added Tax in Switzerland', *Canadian Tax Journal*, Vol. 42, No. 5, 1994.

Erard, B., *The Income Tax Compliance Burden on Canadian Big Business*, Working Paper 97/2, Technical Committee on Business Taxation, Department of Finance, Ottawa, April 1997.

Evans, C., K. Ritchie, B. Tran-Nam, M. Walpole, *A Report into the Incremental Costs of Taxpayer Compliance*, ATAX, University of New South Wales, Sydney, 1997.

Evans, C., K. Ritchie, B. Tran-Nam and M. Walpole, *Taxpayer Costs of Compliance*, Australian Taxation Office, AGPS, Canberra, 1997.

Evans, C. and C.T. Sandford, 'Capital Gains Tax – The Unprincipled Tax?', *British Tax Review*, No. 5, 1999.

Evans, C. and M. Walpole, *Compliance Cost Control, a Review of Tax Impact Statements in the OECD*, Australian Tax Research Foundation, Research Study No. 7, 1999.

Filkin, E., 'Dealing with Complaints – The Adjudicator: A United Kingdom Experiment', in ed. C.T. Sandford, *Further Key Issues in Tax Reform*, Fiscal Publications, Bath, 1997.

Financial Times, 'Spend to Save', November 27, 1996.

Fisher, I., *The Nature of Capital & Income*, Macmillan, New York, 1906.

Gibson, J., *The Politics and Economics of the Poll Tax: Mrs Thatcher's Downfall*, EMAS, Warley (West Midlands), 1990.

Graetz, J.M., J.A. Dublin and L.L. Wilde, chapter on 'United States' in IFA Cahiers de droit fiscal international, *Administrative and Compliance Costs of Taxation*, Kluwer, The Netherlands, 1989.

Gravelle, J.G., 'Equity Effects of the Tax Reform Act of 1986', *Journal of Economic Perspectives*, Vol. 6, No.1, Winter 1992.

Groenewegen, P.D., 'The National Taxation Summit: Success or Failure?' *Economic Papers*, Vol. 4, No. 3, September 1985, pp. 1-17.

Haig, R.M., *The Federal Income Tax*, Columbia University Press, New York, 1921.

Haig, R.M., 'The Cost to Business Concerns of Compliance with Tax Laws', *Management Review*, 1935, pp. 232-333.

Hartle, D.G., *Political Economy of Tax Reform: Six Case Studies*, Discussion Paper No. 270, Economic Council of Canada, Ottawa, 1985.

Hartle, D.G., 'Some Analytical, Political and Normative Lessons from Carter' in ed. W.N. Brooks, *The Quest for Tax Reform: The Royal Commission on Taxation Twenty Years Later*, Carswell, Toronto, 1988.

Hasseldine, J., 'How Do Revenue Audits Affect Taxpayer Compliance?', *Bulletin*, IBFD, July/August 1993.

Hasseldine, J., 'Using Persuasive Communication to Increase Tax Compliance: What Experimental Research Has (and Has Not) Told Us', forthcoming, *Australian Tax Forum*, 2000.

Hawke, B., *The Hawke Memoirs*, Heinemann, London, 1994.

Head, J.G., 'Company Tax Structure and Company Tax Incidence', *International Tax and Public Finance*, Vol. 4, Number 1, 1997.

Hills, J., *Joseph Rowntree Foundation Inquiry into Income and Wealth*, Vol. 2, Joseph Rowntree Foundation, York, 1995.

Holland, D., 'Corporate Tax Incentives: Lessons from the Canadian Experience' in *The Role of Tax Reform in Central and Eastern European Economies*, OECD, Paris, 1991.

Howe, G., 'Tax Law Simplification in the United Kingdom' in ed. C.T. Sandford, *Further Key Issues in Tax Reform*, Fiscal Publications, Bath, 1998.

Kaldor, N., *An Expenditure Tax*, Allen & Unwin, London, 1955.

Kaldor, N., *Indian Tax Reform*, Ministry of Finance, Government of India, New Delhi, 1956.

Kay, J.A. and M.A. King, *The British Tax System*, OUP, Oxford, 1st ed. 1978 (and subsequent editions).

Lawson, N. *Tax Reform, The Government's Record*, Conservative Political Centre, London, 1988.

Lawson, N. *The View from No. 11, Memoirs of a Tory Radical*, Bantam Press, London, 1992.

Little, Arthur D., Corporation, *Development of Methodology for Estimating Taxpayer Paperwork Burden, Final Report to Department of Treasury*, IRS, Washington, DC, 1988.

Lodin, S.O., *Progressive Expenditure Tax – An Alternative*, Liber Forag, Stockholm, 1978.

Loh, A., M. Ariff, Z. Ismail, M. Shamsher and M. Ali, 'Compliance Costs of Corporate Income Taxation in Malaysia, 1995', *Pacific Accounting Review* (New Zealand) Vol. 9, No. 1, 1997.

Long, S.B. and D. Burnham, 'Solving the Nation's Budget Deficit with a Bigger, Tougher IRS: What are the Realities?', *Special Report, Tax Notes*, August 6, 1990.

Malmer, H., 'The Swedish Tax Reform and Tax Compliance Costs in Sweden', in ed. C.T. Sandford, *Tax Compliance Costs, Measurement and Policy*, Fiscal Publications, Bath, 1995.

O'Hagan, J. and A. Reilly, 'The Taxation of Alcoholic Beverages' in ed. C.T. Sandford, *More Key Issues in Tax Reform*, Fiscal Publications, Bath, 1995.

O'Hagan, J., 'The Taxation of Tobacco', in ed. C.T. Sandford, *Further Key Issues in Tax Reform*, Fiscal Publications, Bath, 1998.

Owens, J.P., 'Tax Expenditures and Direct Expenditures as Instruments of Social Policy', in ed. S. Cnossen, *Comparative Tax Studies, Essays in Honor of Richard Goode*, North Holland, Amsterdam, 1983.

Parsons, W., *Public Policy – An Introduction to the Theory and Practice of Policy Analysis*, Edward Elgar, Cheltenham, 1995.

Pechman, J.A., *Federal Tax Policy*, The Brookings Institution, Washington, DC, 5th ed., 1987.

Pigou, A.C., *The Economics of Welfare*, London, Macmillan, 1920.

Plamondon and Associates Inc., *GST Compliance Costs for Small Business in Canada*, A Study for the Department of Finance and Tax Policy, Ottawa, 1993.

Pope, J., R. Fayle and M. Duncanson, *The Compliance Costs of Personal Income Taxation in Australia, 1986-87*, Australian Tax Foundation, Sydney, 1990.

Pope, J., R. Fayle and D. Chen, *The Compliance Costs of Employment-Related Taxes in Australia*, Australian Tax Foundation, Sydney, 1993.

Pope, J., 'The Compliance Costs of Major Taxes in Australia', *Tax Compliance Costs, Measurement and Policy*, Fiscal Publications, Bath, 1995.

Public Policy Forum/Plamondon & Associates, *Cutting the Costs of Tax Collection Down to Size*, Revenue Canada, Ottawa, 1997.

Roth, J.A., J.T. Scholz and A.D. Witte, *Tax Payer Compliance, Vol I An Agenda for Research* and Roth, J.A. and J.T. Scholz, *Tax Payer Compliance, Vol. 2, Social Science Perspectives*, University of Pennsylvania Press, Philadelphia, 1989. (These volumes provide a comprehensive review of research in the field, providing many further references.)

Sabine, B.E.V., *A History of Income Tax*, George, Allen & Unwin, London, 1966.

Sandford, C.T., *Hidden Costs of Taxation*, IFS, London 1973.

Sandford, C.T., *Taxing Wealth in New Zealand*, Victoria University Press for the Institute of Policy Studies, Wellington, New Zealand, 1987.

Sandford, C.T., 'Carter Twenty Years On', *British Tax Review*, 1987, No.4, pp. 148-65.

Sandford, C.T., 'General Report', in *Cahiers de droit fiscal international, Administrative and Compliance Costs of Taxation*, IFA, Rotterdam, 1989.

Sandford, C.T., *Economics of Public Finance*, 4th ed., Pergamon Press, Oxford, 1992.

Sandford, C.T. (ed.), *Tax Compliance Costs: Measurement and Policy*, Fiscal Publications, Bath, 1995.

Sandford, C.T., *Successful Tax Reform, Lessons from an Analysis of Tax Reform in Six Countries*, Fiscal Publications, Bath, 1995.

Sandford, C.T., 'Taxing Wealth', in ed. C.T. Sandford, *More Key Issues in Tax Reform*, Fiscal Publications, Bath, 1995.

Sandford, C.T., J.R.M. Willis and D.J. Ironside, *An Annual Wealth Tax*, London, 1975.

Sandford, C.T., M. Godwin, P. Hardwick and I. Butterworth, *Costs and Benefits of VAT*, Heinemann Educational Books, London, 1981.

Sandford, C.T. and O. Morrissey, *The Irish Wealth Tax – A Case Study in Economics and Politics*, Economic and Social Research Institute, Dublin, 1985.

Sandford, C.T., M. Godwin and P. Hardwick, *Administrative and Compliance Costs of Taxation*, Fiscal Publications, Bath, 1989.

Sandford, C.T. and J. Hasseldine, *The Compliance Costs of Business Taxes in New Zealand*, Institute of Policy Studies, Victoria University of Wellington, Wellington, 1992.

Simons, H.C., *Personal Income Taxation*, University of Chicago Press, Chicago, 1938.

Slemrod, J. and N. Sorum, 'The Compliance Cost of the US Individual Income Tax System', *National Tax Journal*, Vol. 37, Dec. 1984, pp. 461-74.

Slemrod, J. and M. Blumenthal, 'The Income Tax Compliance Cost of Big Business', *Public Finance Quarterly*, Vol. 24, No. 4, Oct. 1996, pp. 411-38.

Smith, A., (1776), *Inquiry into the Nature and Causes of the Wealth of Nations*, Book 5, Chapter 2, Part 2, 'Of Taxes', Everyman Edition, pp. 307-9, 1977.

Smith, H. *The Power Game*, Random House, New York, 1988.

Smith, S., 'Green Taxes – the Scope for Environmentally-friendly Taxes', in ed. C.T. Sandford, *Key Issues in Tax Reform*, Fiscal Publications, Bath, 1993.

Smith, S., 'The Carbon Tax: A Tax Whose Time has Come?' in ed. C. T. Sandford, *Further Key Issues in Tax Reform*, Fiscal Publications, Bath, 1998.

Stark, G., 'Taxing Families', in ed. C.T. Sandford, *More Key Issues in Tax Reform*, Fiscal Publications, Bath, 1995.

Steinmo, S., *Taxation and Democracy*, Yale University Press, New Haven, 1993.

Steuerle, C.E., *The Tax Decade*, Urban Institute Press, Washington, DC, 1991.

Strumpel, B., 'The Disguised Tax Burden', *National Tax Journal*, Vol. 19, No. 1, 1966, pp. 70-77.

Stuart, C., 'Welfare Costs per Dollar of Additional Tax Revenue in the United States', *American Economic Review*, Vol. 74, No. 3, 1984, pp. 352-62.

Surrey, Stanley S., *Pathways to Tax Reform*, Harvard University Press, 1973.

Tait, A.A., *Value Added Tax – International Practice and Problems*, IMF, Washington, DC, 1988.

The Economist, 'A Taxing Time for Squirrels', Leader Article, 20-27 Jan., 1995.

The Economist, 'Toil and Muddle', Leader Article, March 13-19, 1999.

Vaillancourt, F., *The Administrative and Compliance Costs of Personal Income Taxes and Payroll Taxes, Canada, 1986*, Canadian Tax Foundation, Toronto, 1989.

Wallich, H.C., 'Taxation of Capital Gains in the Light of Recent Economic Developments', *National Tax Journal*, June, 1965.

Wallschutzky, I., 'Minimising Evasion and Avoidance', in ed. C.T. Sandford, *Key Issues in Tax Reform*, Fiscal Publications, Bath, 1993.

Willis, J.R.M., and P. Hardwick, *Tax Expenditures in the United Kingdom*, IFS/Heinemann Educational Books, London, 1978.

Witte, J.F., *The Politics and Development of the Federal Income Tax*, University of Wisconsin Press, Madison, 1985.

Woellner, R., C. Coleman, S. Gaylard, M. McKercher, M. Walpole and J. Zetler, 'Once More into the Breach ... A Study of Comparative Compliance Costs under the 1936 and 1997 Acts: Progress Report', in ed C. Evans and A. Greenbaum, *Tax Administration: Facing the Challenges of the Future*, Prospect, St. Leonards, NSW, 1998.

Reports and Official Publications

Australia

Fightback! The Liberal and National Parties'Plan to Rebuild and Reward Australia, November 1991.
Reform of the Australian Taxation System, Draft White Paper, AGPS, Canberra, 1985.
Reform of the Australian Taxation System, Statement by the Treasurer, the Hon. Paul Keating, AGPS, Canberra, September 1985.
Taxation Review Committee (Asprey), Full Report, Canberra, AGPS, 1975.
Towards a World Class Tax Administration: Submission to the Committee of Public Accounts, T.P.W. Boucher, AGPS, Canberra, 1992.

Canada

Report of the Royal Commission on Taxation (Carter), Queen's Printer, Ottawa, 1967.
White Paper on Tax Reform, Department of Finance, Canada, 1987.

Ireland

A Strategy for the Nineties, National Economic and Social Council, Report No. 89, Dublin, 1990.
Reports of the Commission on Taxation, Stationery Office, Dublin, Five Reports over period July 1982-October 1985.

New Zealand

GST the Key to Lower Income Tax, Government Printer, Wellington, March 1985.
Report of the Committee on Taxation in New Zealand (Ross), Government Printer, Wellington, 1967.
Task Force on Tax Reform, (McCaw), Government Printer, Wellington, 1982.

United Kingdom

Board of Inland Revenue, *Annual Report for the year ending 31 March, 1998*, HMSO, 1998.

Centre for Fiscal Studies, University of Bath, *The Tax Compliance Costs for Employers of PAYE and National Insurance in 1995-96*, Inland Revenue, London, 1998.

Report of the Committee on Enforcement Powers of the Revenue Departments, (Keith) Vol. 2, Cmnd. 8822, HMSO, 1983.

Confederation of British Industry, *Tax: Time for Change*, Report of a Working Group, CBI, 1985.

Department of the Environment, *Local Government Review: A New Tax for Local Government*, Consultation Paper, London, 1991.

Local Government Finance, Green Paper, Cmnd. 6813, London, HMSO, 1977.

Local Government Finance, Report of the Committee of Enquiry (Layfield), Cmnd. 6453, London, HMSO, 1976.

Paying for Local Government, Green Paper, Cmnd. 9714, London, HMSO, 1986.

Report of the Royal Commission on the Taxation of Profits and Income, (Cohen), HMSO, London, 1955.

Report of a Committee on the Structure and Reform of Direct Taxation (Meade), IFS/George Allen and Unwin, London, 1978.

The Better Regulation Guide and Regulatory Impact Assessment, Cabinet Office (OPS), London, 1998.

United States

Blue Prints of Basic Tax Reform, Department of the Treasury, GPO, Washington, DC, 1977.

Tax Reform for Fairness, Simplicity and Economic Growth (Treasury I), Department of the Treasury, GPO, Washington, DC, 1984.

The President's Tax Proposals to the Congress for Fairness, Growth and Simplicity (Treasury II), GPO, Washington, DC, 1985.

International

IBDF, *European Tax Handbook*, International Bureau of Fiscal Documentation, Amsterdam, 1999.

IMF, *Government Finance Statistics Yearbook*, IMF, annual publication.

International Fiscal Association, *Cahiers de droit fiscal international, Administrative and Compliance Costs of Taxation*, IFA, Rotterdam, 1989.

KPMG, *Director's Toolkit*, (CD), KPMG International Tax and Legal Centre, Amsterdam, 1999.

OECD, *The Taxation of Net Wealth, Capital Transfers and Capital Gains of Individuals*, Paris, 1979.

OECD, *Taxes on Immovable Property*, Paris, 1983.

OECD, *Taxation of Net Wealth, Capital Transfers and Capital Gains of Individuals*, Paris, 1988.

OECD, *Taxing Consumption*, Paris, 1988.

OECD, *Ireland*, Paris, 1991.

OECD, *Tax Expenditures – Recent Experiences*, Paris, 1996.

OECD, *Environmental Taxes in OECD Countries*, Paris, 1996.

OECD, *Revenue Statistics 1965-1998*, Paris, 1999.

INDEX

Aaron, H.J. 174, 197
Accessions tax 43, 100
Addington, Lord 148
Adjudicator 154, 199
Administrative costs – see Costs
Advanced (developed, industrial)
  countries 1, 2, 7, 11, 16-19, 36-
  37, 42, 52, 54, 64, 73, 80, 91,
  94, 103, 158, 192
Agents (tax) – see Tax
Alcoholic drinks
  – government monopoly of 3, 67
  – taxes 69, 70, 201
Allers, M.A. 141, 197
Allingham, M.G. 150-51, 197
Allowances – see Tax
American Enterprise Institute 171
Annual wealth tax (AWT) 1-3, 18,
  38, 41, 54, 94-95, 98-113, 175,
  202, 206
Ariff, M. 139, 197
Arnold, B.J. 176, 178, 197
Asia 7-9, 13, 15-16
Asprey Committee 171, 204
Australia 1, 9, 17, 18, 21, 43, 48,
  50, 65, 70, 74, 76, 149, 156,
  197-99, 201, 204
– administrative and compliance
costs 118-21, 126-29, 131,
  139-41, 153
– CGT 115, 170
– GST (VAT) 77-78, 87-89, 167
– state and local taxes 23-27
– tax reform and tax policy
making 158-64, 166, 168-71,
  173-77, 180-81, 184, 186-93
– wealth transfer taxes 98-104,
  106

Audit - see Tax
Australian Tax Office (ATO) 118,
  120, 127, 176
Austria 1, 17-18, 24-25, 27, 48,
  50, 65, 74, 76, 78, 90, 99, 102,
  104, 106, 159
Avoidance – see Tax

Ballard, C.L. 79, 161, 197
Beach, C. 37, 198
Belgium 1, 17-18, 24-25, 27, 46,
  48, 65, 74, 76, 78, 90, 99, 102,
  104, 106, 139
Bird, R. viii, 15, 197
Birnbaum, J.H. 174, 182, 186,
  197
Boadway, R. 37, 198
Boucher, T. 119-20, 126
Bowles, R. 149-50, 198
Bradley, B. 185
Brookings Institution 171
Browning, E.K. 79, 161, 197
Brown, G. 61, 190-91
Bruce, N. 37, 193
Burnham, J.H. 142, 149, 151. 201

Callan, L. 88, 199
Canada (Canadian) vii, 1, 8, 17-
  19, 21, 37, 42-43, 48, 52, 65,
  70, 74, 76-78, 89, 156
– administrative and compliance
costs 117, 126-28, 132-33, 135-
  37, 139, 141
– CGT 105, 115, 121, 165
– GST (VAT) 77, 181, 183, 188,
  190
– MST 77, 80-82, 181

207